EMILY LLOYD

WISH I WAS THERE

I WAS THE GOLDEN GIRL OF BRITISH CINEMA...
THEN MY LIFE FELL TO PIECES. THIS IS MY STORY.

JOHN BLAKE

Published by John Blake Publishing Ltd,
3 Bramber Court, 2 Bramber Road,
London W14 9PB, England

www.johnblakepublishing.co.uk

www.facebook.com/Johnblakepub facebook
twitter.com/johnblakepub twitter

First published in hardback in 2013
This edition published in 2014

ISBN: 978 1 78219 753 9

British Library Cataloguing-in-Publication Data:

A catalogue record for this book is available from the British Library.

Design by www.envydesign.co.uk

Printed and bound in Great Britain by CPI Group (UK) Ltd, Croydon, CR0 4YY

1 3 5 7 9 10 8 6 4 2

© Text copyright Emily Lloyd and Douglas Wight 2014

The right of Emily Lloyd and Douglas Wight to be identified as the authors
of this work have been asserted by them in accordance with the Copyright,
Designs and Patents Act 1988.

Papers used by John Blake Publishing are natural, recyclable products made
from wood grown in sustainable forests. The manufacturing processes
conform to the environmental regulations of the country of origin.

Every attempt has been made to contact the relevant copyright-holders, but
some were unobtainable. We would be grateful if the appropriate people
could contact us.

For my most favourite girls – Sheila and Charlotte

★★★★★

Midway upon the journey of our life
I found myself within a forest dark,
For the straightforward pathway had been lost.

Inferno, Divine Comedy – Dante

ACKNOWLEDGEMENTS

Mummy and Charlotte, thank you for your exceptional love and unerring support.

To Randolph IV (my dog), thank you for your irrepressible smile and contagious charisma.

Thanks Dad for your name, love and thespian influence.

To Dougie, thank you for listening and for capturing my voice – but can I have it back now please?

To Roz and Bobby, for all your friendship, kindness and devotion.

To Chris, life without humour is like tap dancing on cobblestones with bare feet. Thanks for giving me the right shoes. Love you more!

To the darling gay posse, miss you. Hope you are enjoying cocktails in Elysium.

Thanks Grandma Winnie and the Mackie family for all the laughter you have given me.

Thanks to my grandparents Charles and Uli for teaching me about Blake and magic tricks.

To Trevor, thank you for your companionship.

All photos used are from my personal collection. If I have accidentally forgotten to credit someone, please forgive me. Get in touch and I will be more than happy to acknowledge your contribution.

PROLOGUE

'Emily, Emily.'

They were the first words I heard as I slowly regained consciousness.

My vision was blurred but I could still make out the stark, pristine, white walls. The pervasive smell of antiseptic immediately hit me. These sensations led me to the realisation that I was in a hospital.

'Good girl, Emily, good girl.'

That voice again.

I mustered up all my strength trying to think of a joke but couldn't find one. The tube stuck down my oesophagus wasn't helping.

As you may have guessed, I'd had my stomach pumped. A nurse, the owner of the voice I'd heard, was still repeating my name, swiftly, almost perfunctorily, as she pulled out the tube.

I gagged, then smiled bravely and tried to assimilate the sea of faces surrounding me. Were they looking at me like that out of concern or because I was vaguely familiar?

I began acclimatising myself and tried to connect with some kind of tangible reality. It should have been an exciting time for me. I had been very much looking forward to starring in a British movie again – *Chicago Joe and the Showgirl* with Kiefer Sutherland – my first since *Wish You Were Here*. Some time later, while I was bantering with the other patients, my mother arrived with a bright smile on her face, masking her concern. I heard the doctor advising her that I would need time to recuperate before returning to work. My situation and what I had tried to do dawned on me.

Shit, I thought. *This wasn't good*. I was resolute. I needed to be back on set, regardless of the doctor's advice. As if to raise myself from this nadir, I lifted myself into a wheelchair. It felt surprisingly good to be upright again. I felt my energy levels returning. I started moving, realising I had no real sense of where I was going. I picked up speed and the other patients in the ward sat up and smiled as I hared up and down as if it was Silverstone racetrack. The nurses seemed amused but voiced their disapproval, my fellow patients looked entertained.

My antics were effective though. I convinced them all that this was only a minor setback and I was fit enough to return to work.

The following day I was back filming *Chicago Joe*, a bleak dramatisation of a real-life crime spree in 1944 that ended with the notorious 'cleft chin murder'. I was playing Betty Jones, the showgirl of the title who dreamed that one day her life would mirror the excitement of her favourite movies. I arrived on set, fragile, my throat sore and bruised, but my spirits surprisingly intact. The scene was set, the first assistant director (AD) said: 'Rolling! Rolling! Going for a take.'

I said my lines with as much confidence as I could muster.

'Speak up!' the director Bernard Rose yelled.

With a mixture of quiet defiance and suppressed emotion I did. 'Speak up!' he yelled again.

My body began to grow tense as I gulped, trying to suppress the reservoir of tears that had started to well up.

'Ok, cut!' the director yelled once more. 'You are not speaking loudly enough!'

He was the only one on set who knew what had happened to me. His pompous tone prompted in me an urge to verbally retaliate but I decided to let it slide.

A week passed. Somehow I struggled on, giving everything to my performance. But when a dance scene dragged on for eight punishing hours, leaving my feet blistered and bleeding, I was fit to drop.

A few nights later I was working on a night shoot at a grim location in London. The rain poured down incessantly and, after a gruelling number of takes, at 3am I began to feel as though I was disintegrating. My mother was on set and, noticing my demeanour, became concerned. I watched her wading through the thick mud towards the director, who was on the boom, and heard her shout: 'I think she's had enough.'

'Fuck off,' the director snapped at her.

At which point, to my intense relief, the more sensitive producer stepped in and said: 'Enough, it's a wrap.'

The shoot was over. Returning through the mud, my mother and I gave a sigh of relief and smiled at each other.

My mother said: 'I think I need a vodka.'

'I think I need my bed,' I said.

CHAPTER ONE

While Mum was pontificating to a group of bemused infants
and bellowing, 'Don't put your back to the audience,' à la Peter Hall,
one boy was swinging from a coat hook just moments before we
were due on stage. My nerves were jangling.

Before I get round to telling you all my adventures and adversities I thought if you got to know where I came from it might explain a lot.

My dad is Roger Lloyd Pack, an actor of some renown, but you might know him best for the role for which he was most famous – playing Trigger in *Only Fools and Horses*. Sometimes you'd be forgiven for thinking that's the only role he's ever had – certainly that's all anyone reminds me of these days – but since he left RADA, the Royal Academy of Dramatic Art, he's enjoyed a rich and varied career. He's been Owen Newitt, the lonesome and slightly scary farmer in *The Vicar of Dibley*, but kids the world over will probably recognise him as Barty Crouch Senior in *Harry Potter and the Goblet of Fire*.

My mother is Sheila Hughes, a former theatre agent and one-time secretary to the legendary playwright and Nobel Prize winner Harold Pinter.

Before they met, my Dad was a bit of a hippy, sporting a Zapata moustache and flared trousers, while Mum was a Biba-loving babe who didn't go anywhere without a spring in her step and showing off with something by Jean-Paul Sartre in her back pocket. I guess they thought they looked cool.

Their planets collided when Dad was working for the Royal Shakespeare Company at the Aldwych Theatre in London's West End. He had landed a minor part in a production of *The Staircase*, by Charles Dyer, and then was asked to stay on in the company for its Christmas show of *The Thwarting of Baron Bolligrew*, with Roy Kinnear.

At the time Mum was employed at the theatre as a dresser and was working on the same production. They say love is blind, and it maybe had to be on this occasion for it's hard to see what first attracted my mother to my father when she first clapped eyes on him. Dad was playing a jester in the story of the brave knight sent off to slay a fearsome dragon and was therefore kitted out in a skin-tight leotard, very long, severely pointed shoes and a nightcap with a bobble on the end. As he waited to go on stage, Mum studied him from the wings. She first thought what a ridiculous costume he had on. But then what struck her was his shy smile.

According to my Dad, one evening he and another actor, Ray Callaghan, went out dancing on a double date with Mum and another dresser, Annie Prior Palmer. Dad was supposed to be partnering Annie, but somewhere along the way he and Mum ended up together. By then Mum was finding him rather attractive and was drawn to his sense of humour and his interest in theatre and politics – not to mention his long legs.

They went back to her flat in Clifton Road, in Maida Vale, and, as Dad puts it, he never moved out. They hit it off despite being from

CONTENTS

vastly different backgrounds. He had been educated at the renowned Bedales private school in Steep, Hampshire. Although it was famous for its liberal approach to education, the school was attended by well-heeled, middle-class pupils. Mum felt Dad had had an altogether more sheltered upbringing, whereas her experience of life so far had been more varied.

When the London season finished, Dad stayed with the company for the summer at Stratford and moved up there into a rather miserable-sounding caravan, where he stayed on his own for a few weeks. Mum then went up and joined him and they found what seemed to be a very romantic house in the woods, by the Avon, about four miles out of the town, at a place called Welford. It was during this time together that they decided to get married.

While they were in Stratford, Mum had dressed Vivien Merchant, by then a big star for a performance in *Alfie* that earned her both an Academy Award and Golden Globe nomination. Vivien thought that Mum would make a good secretary for her husband Harold Pinter, and so when the season was over she started working for him. However, Mum and Dad were now homeless, because Mum had given up her room in the London flat when she'd gone to join Dad in Stratford. So Harold and Vivien let them stay in their mews house at the bottom of their garden in Hanover Terrace, near Regent's Park, until they could find somewhere of their own to live.

Back in London, they set about planning their wedding and tackled the daunting task of meeting their respective parents. Mum says Dad's mother was quite aghast at meeting her for the first time, particularly appalled by her false lashes and mini-skirted attire.

A wedding led to a home in Islington and it was there where Mum fell pregnant with me. She recalls being slightly shocked when she found out. She was a little older than he was, and for both of them having children wasn't exactly a priority.

Health-wise, Mum was in good shape and she continued to work for Harold. In fact, during this time he had written the film script for *The Go Between* and began shooting in the summer of 1970 in Norfolk. Dominic Guard, Julie Christie, Alan Bates and Edward Fox were the leads in the adaptation of LP Hartley's novel, but Dad also had a cameo role. I guess you could say I got my first taste of a movie set there, not that I knew much about it. Mum was still working for Harold so she helped out on the set.

Joe Losey was directing and he asked Mum to be in one scene. She was reluctantly propped against a tree, wearing a Laura Ashley smock while I apparently kicked away in her tummy in sympathy. Losey handed my Mum a pad and pen and in his American drawl asked her to do some sketching. Even to this day Mum is hopeless at drawing but, not thinking it was vital, scribbled some matchstick men. However, she can still recall Julie Christie and Edward Fox looking to see what she had done and turning their noses up at her artful attempt. Sadly the drawings – and the scene – ended up on the cutting room floor.

I made my grand entrance on 29 September 1970 in the Royal Free Hospital, in Liverpool Road, Islington, without too much fuss it seems. The only thing my Dad can recall was that he had to put on a green smock for the occasion. Mum, on the other hand, remembers him mucking about while she was in the middle of the contractions, dislodging a seat and spinning around the room.

Mum embraced motherhood completely but, looking back now, she says she feels Dad was perhaps too young and not yet ready for the responsibilities of having a child. Within months of my birth, cracks were beginning to appear in their relationship but Mum was so busy caring for me, rushing through days and continuing to work, that she wasn't conscious of Dad growing unhappy and them drifting apart.

It's sad for me to hear how their relationship floundered. They split for good when I was 18 months old. It means I don't know a life other than one where they are living apart and I have no memories of them being together (the flipside though is that it did mean two sets of Christmas presents!).

Instead, my earliest memories are a snapshot of strange days and odd occurrences. One involves the concrete playground in the square outside the Victorian house where we lived on Milner Square. I remember playing in the park. One of the children, I'm sure unprovoked, said: 'You have a dirty face.'

Her derisive intonation – she would have been only two or three – was enough to cut right through me and I remember being quite hurt and embarrassed. I so desperately wanted to retaliate, as children do, but couldn't think of a suitably witty retort (I was equally only about three) and so I ran home to my mother and cried. It sticks in my mind because it was one of the few times I cried as a child.

I wasn't a baby. My sister, on the other hand, who was to come along shortly, would cry at pretty much anything.

I don't seem to have been one of those kids who make a fuss for no reason and got on with my lot. My Mum thinks I was quite a brave child but that's a hard thing to say about myself. Having said that, I can't really remember the tears coming that often. I liked playing football in the playground and was a bit of a tomboy, kicking around with a local boy and quite liking it.

It's funny the images that stay in your mind but another of my earliest memories is the time I was skipping along holding my mother's hand. I remember I couldn't have been much older than five and was wearing scuffed, red Clarks shoes and didn't seem to have a care in the world until I came across a small snail right in my path. I hesitated for only a brief moment and then stamped on the poor creature with all the force I could muster. I've no idea what I was thinking. Maybe I didn't realise a tiny life was hiding inside that shell. All I know is that my mother shouted at me, tugged my arm and pulled me away. That memory still haunts me to this day (but not half as much as I imagine it haunts the snail!).

Mum and Dad might have divorced but I still saw him and from the age of three I used to go and stay with his parents, Charles and Ulrike, who we always called Uli. They had a lovely house in South Kensington. It was always first names with them, never Gran and Grandfather.

Uli was from Vienna and had come over to England in 1938 as a refugee with, my Dad says, nothing but endless envelopes full of photographs. She used to tell him stories about what life was like for her when she was a child in school, at the time Germany was annexing her country. There were poorer people in her class that she used to give her milk to, but literally the day after the Anschluss in 1938, when Austria was annexed into Nazi Germany, a girl took it and spat in it, saying, 'I'm not going to drink a glass of milk from a Jew'. Attitudes changed overnight for her. Soon her family had no option but to flee.

She was from a rather upper class background in Vienna, whereas Charles was very much of working class stock from Wapping, in east London. Charlie Pack, as he was in the early days, was an actor. As most of the plays of the time had a very middle-class theme and every actor possessed a double-barrelled name, he thought he needed a name change to fit in. He added the 'Lloyd' and it's a name that's remained in the family ever since. It's been passed down the generations like a family heirloom.

Uli first caught sight of Charlie in a theatre in Windsor where he was appearing with a local repertory company. She didn't speak much English and actually thought Charlie was rather posh. She might not have realised what she was getting herself into. Neither, for that matter, did he.

Uli was very strict and formal and quite intimidating, but she was kind-hearted and loved having her grandchild to stay. As soon as I arrived for weekend visits she'd have me out of the clothes Mum had dressed me in and into garments of her choosing.

She was strict about everything being in its place and set the table meticulously for dinner. One day I tried to test her powers of observation by deliberately moving a salad leaf while she was fetching more plates from the kitchen. On her return she took one look at the salad and froze.

'Have you touched that?' she asked. I shuddered.

Charles had a great pedigree from Hammer horror films like *Dracula* and *The Revenge of Frankenstein* and appearances in hit TV series' like *The Avengers* and *The Prisoner*. But in those days he was around the house a lot and was forever playing chess on a little electronic set. I would sit on his knee and he would recite William Blake's *The Tyger* poem. I miss him.

Mum might have been raising me by herself but I never felt like I was missing out. Her mother, who we've always affectionately called by her last name Mackie, had moved from Brighton to London to help with childcare, while Mum went back to work for Harold Pinter and was having to pick her way through the minefield that was his acrimonious marriage split from Vivien. Pinter had been having an affair with Lady Antonia Fraser and when he moved out Mum found herself caught in the middle, with divided loyalties. Eventually she felt she was nothing more than a messenger, passing on nuggets of information increasingly vitriolic in nature. On one occasion Vivien was at the end of her tether and threatened to kill herself. Harold's caustic response will live with Mum forever.

His only reply was: 'Just tell me where and when.'

She carried on working for Harold for six months but eventually he let her go. Then, with Vivien barely working, there was little point helping her out either.

The bitter collapse of their relationship must have placed a huge emotional strain on Mum but she rarely let it show and had problems of her own. It's impossible to overestimate how difficult it was for single mothers back in the early 1970s.

Cultural diversity wasn't a philosophy widely practised in Islington then but our little quarter in Milner Square had more than most. A mixture of homeowners and council tenants meant married middle-class families rubbed shoulders with working-class families, ethnic minorities and so-called broken homes like ours. That said, people generally stuck to their own and some neighbours looked down their noses at a single parent struggling to make ends meet.

I don't know whether Mum strived to have a male influence in my life but she met and fell for a telephone engineer called Martin Ball. They got married fairly swiftly and Mum fell pregnant but the relationship was floundering even before she was ready to give birth.

I was five when my little sister Charlotte arrived. Her birth sticks in my mind mostly because of the toy Mum bought me – a little sweet shop – to make sure I didn't feel left out. I was quite proud of our new addition to the family, at least, I certainly don't remember being jealous.

Two months after Charlotte's birth, Mum and Martin split up. Mum said it was a mistake and it was over before it began. If people had been snooty about a single mother with one child to support, it was nothing compared to how they reacted when they had a twice-divorced mother of two living in their midst.

Mum wasn't immune to the local condescension but didn't let it bother her. In fact, despite our economically challenged situation, she was determined to give me the best start in life. We might have lacked a father figure but we were not short of eclectic influences. Mum's friends ranged from theatre chums, gay friends, artists and writers. The house always seemed to be buzzing with people, with music and laughter a seemingly constant soundtrack. She practically operated an open door policy and kids from all over the square were encouraged to play in our house, which wasn't always the case with other families, with some parents of white kids not keen on their children mixing with black children.

It was great for us as youngsters because it meant we had lots of playmates but my grandmother Mackie despaired when she came to look after us. She would literally sweep the kids who'd gathered on our front steps off into the street with a broom. In some ways she invoked the same fear in youngsters as the Child Catcher in *Chitty Chitty Bang Bang*, only Mackie repelled kids rather than enticed them.

While aspects of our upbringing might have seemed unconventional it was also enriching. Although like many kids I loved TV favourites like *Andy Pandy, Bagpuss, Snoopy, Hong Kong Phooey, Scooby Doo* and *Top Cat*, Mum also introduced me, from a young age, to classic films and musicals. In some ways, having actors for a dad and grandfather removed the mystery of movies, but at the same time sparked an early interest in the performing arts. I remember seeing Elizabeth Taylor – who would go on to star with my grandfather in *The Mirror Crack'd* – in *National Velvet* when I was still five. She was so captivating and radiant that I decided there and then that I wanted to be an actor. The fact that Charlie also managed to acquire Elizabeth's autograph for me only served to show that her impossible glamour was attainable.

Those dreams would have to remain on hold. I still had nursery to navigate. Being able to interact with other kids from a young age was good grounding for nursery and that was put to the test not long after Charlotte's birth, when I attended my first school. It was a Montessori Children's House in Islington, which focused on giving children a strong start in life, even though we were still only five and just wanting to play.

I enjoyed being there but we were frequently given assignments to do. Very quickly I developed a habit of going round the class checking all the children were doing their work. I was so preoccupied with this task that I failed to remember I too had work to do. On many occasions I was not allowed out to play because I hadn't finished my assignments.

It took me a while to grasp the structure of school life. To be honest I'm not sure I ever did and it was almost a shock to my system when I started at primary school. Our local, Thornhill, had adopted the controversial Initial Teaching Alphabet system of teaching, where words were spelled phonetically – *wot woz thay thinkin*?

The highlight of my time there, however, was definitely Mum's drama production. The school asked her to write and direct the school play because of her theatre connections. She took it incredibly seriously. The school told her 'no favouritism', so naturally she cast me in the lead role of the princess in the production of *Arabian Nights*.

When the big night came round, there was chaos backstage. Whilst Mum was pontificating to a group of bemused infants and bellowing, 'Don't put your back to the audience', a la Peter Hall, one boy, Nicholas, the son of Labour MP and future government minister

Margaret Hodge, was swinging from a coat hook, proclaiming, 'Look what I can do!' just moments before we were due on stage. Needless to say my nerves were jangling.

Before long it was my turn to come on stage and I appeared in a white chiffon dress, my two front teeth missing. Mum said even at that age when I opened my mouth I had presence. A talent for acting, it seems, was something latent in me, waiting to be nurtured.

What I didn't realise was that soon I'd be performing the role of my life – trying to convince people I was a normal, happy child.

CHAPTER
TWO

*When we got home I had a feeling of liberation. I can remember
jumping up and down on my mother's bed shouting 'freedom
at last'. My mother was holding my hand and joining in.*

Like many children I was raised on a diet of fairy stories. Mum read
to me constantly and I was enthralled by Grimm's tales of *Snow
White, Hansel and Gretel* and *Rapunzel* and Hans Christian
Andersen's *The Snow Queen, The Little Match Girl* and *Thumbelina*,
among others. Yet, as well as the customary tales, she regaled me
with the adventures of Br'er Rabbit, from Uncle Remus's stories
of the American South, and the fables of Aesop, like *The Boy Who
Cried Wolf, The Hare and the Tortoise* and *The Goose that Laid the
Golden Egg*.

My room in our maisonette in Milner Square was below a high-
ceilinged sitting room and a kitchen that looked onto a small garden
where overgrowing ivy and honeysuckle ruled unchecked. It was a
place where I could indulge my fantasies; lose myself in the fairy tales.
I was encouraged to read from an early age and can remember the
delight I felt while beginning to explore these adventures for myself.

But just as I found that the fairy stories I immersed myself in were filled with darkness and horror, so too would my little fantasy world be shattered by a truly terrifying episode when I was still five. This is something I have never spoken of publicly before. Even forming the words here causes me to feel contaminated.

Mum had so many demands on her time and was trying so desperately to make ends meet that she entrusted babysitting duties to Mackie and a number of friends. One family friend was an older man whose keenness to help out was a lifeline for Mum.

What she didn't know was that he was a depraved predator who relished the chance to be alone with a young girl. For so long I've blotted much of this period from my mind that I worried what impact revisiting it would have. I think it's important, however, to explain, even in part, what I went through.

The man, once invited into the family home, betrayed that trust in the most sickening way imaginable. He would pick his moments carefully, mostly when he was alone in the house with Charlotte and me. She was still a baby – it was only me he was interested in. He would come into my room after I'd gone to bed and subject me to acts so abhorrent it's too painful to recount.

Even if I could remember all the things he did to me I wouldn't repeat them here but, from what I've learned about abuse and the control perpetrators like to exert over their victims, I know they were accompanied by the classic threats. If I told a soul about what was happening, worse would happen.

I felt dirty and worthless, invaded and helpless. I'd love to say it was an isolated incident but it wasn't. It went on for weeks, perhaps months. It felt like years – a never-ending suffering. I think the only thing that enabled me to cope day-to-day was the belief that if I kept quiet I was protecting Charlotte and, to a degree, Mum. As long as

I handled it myself we would be together – nothing would break us up. I think that's what got me through.

I never disclosed what was happening. I never dared. He was a friend of the family and I was too scared of the consequences to air what had been happening. I can't remember it even crossing my mind. Who would believe a five-year-old girl over a grown man? It seemed better just to lock it away. Whatever was right or wrong, that seemed the most sensible decision, the one less likely to disrupt things further.

I had no concept of what I was doing at the time, of course, but in effect it was my first acting role – trying to pretend nothing was wrong. The longer it continued the deeper down I pushed my feelings. I tried to carry on as normal but it wasn't easy. As well as being terrified that the horror would continue I was also unhappy at school. The peculiar method of teaching left me bamboozled and I felt myself slipping behind the other children – a horrible feeling when you're that age.

Another incident not long after my ordeal didn't help to lift my spirits. I was playing outside in the square at the front of our house. It was snowing and I was trying vainly to construct a snowman when a group of boys who lived in the houses nearby came out and made straight for me. Without warning they pushed me in the snow and started kicking me, really quite hard. Although I was just outside my front door I was on my own and had never felt so far away from home. I don't know whether the boys got bored but after what seemed like an eternity they gave up and left me alone, lying there in the snow. When it appeared unlikely that anyone was coming to my aid I got up and ran home in tears. I'm still not sure what motivated them to attack me like that. I'm sure I didn't do anything to provoke them but, coming after what I'd recently been through, it only added to my general unhappiness.

After just over a year at Thornhill, I was so miserable that Mum decided to move me to another school. A new independent private place was opening up nearby called Dallington and spaces were available for parents on a low income. Mum managed to secure a subsidised place for me.

Dallington was almost unique in that when it started there was only one class of about 20 pupils, run by an enigmatic headteacher called Mogg Hercules. She took the class and insisted the children call her by her first name. Her ethos was to inspire progress and wouldn't hold children back. Her methods were considered radical back then but although she was slightly unorthodox she was a stickler for discipline and ruled her class with a firm hand, if not an iron fist.

It's difficult to work out why and when things happened to me but the school didn't provide the change in fortunes we were all hoping for. Right from the start it seemed I was destined not to be one of Mogg's favourites.

It didn't help that around the same time I started to develop the first of some behavioural quirks. Looking back it's perhaps clearer now what sparked this but at the time my Mum hadn't a clue why I was acting the way I was. I started developing routines for all sorts of things. At night I'd give her a running commentary.

'Just switching off the light now Mum. Just turning over my pillow now Mum.' That sort of thing. It started off innocently and she perhaps considered it charming but quickly it became obsessive. Soon I could not leave the house without performing a sort of ritual. I had to dress a certain way, touch certain things before I left the house, walk a certain way to school, making sure I touched certain parts of a wall or lamppost. Of course today we recognise this as obsessive-compulsive disorder but then such erratic behaviour was less easily defined.

It's easy to say now that this was because of the trauma I'd suffered – that my behaviour was a manifestation of the ordeal I kept hidden – compounded by the fact there was a history of OCD on my Dad's side of the family. We didn't know that then though.

Dallington, it transpired, wasn't the type of educational establishment to embrace such oddity in its pupils. By the time I was eight the school had expanded in size and my sister got a place in the nursery, and Mum even landed a job there as a secretary. It should have been an ideal situation with us all close at hand to each other but things didn't work out that way.

One day Mogg asked the class to draw a picture of the moon. A simple enough task you might think. I drew a smile on mine. We hadn't specifically been told we weren't to humanise it but I soon discovered this was not what the teacher had been looking for. I was made to stand in the corner of the classroom. In an intimidating discussion with my Mum, Mogg said she felt I had behavioural issues and suggested I see a psychiatrist. Intriguingly she said I lived in a fantasy world.

Given what I'd been through it may be that the teacher had detected some deeper malaise within me but Mum, oblivious to what had been going on, was furious at the suggestion.

I befriended Mogg's daughter Abigail, who was also in my class, not with any strategy in mind but even that didn't help ingratiate me to the teacher. When Abigail and I had a falling-out, Mogg, somewhat unsurprisingly, sided with her daughter and started reprimanding me. When Mum found out she confronted the headteacher and let's just say they shared a difference of opinion.

From that moment on it was clear that class was only going to become more distressing for me, and Mum not only took Charlotte and me out of the school but quit her job too. When we got home

I had a feeling of liberation. I can remember jumping up and down on my mother's bed shouting 'freedom at last'. My mother was holding my hand and joining in.

I had more cause to feel relief. Almost as quickly as it began, the abuse stopped – the monster moved out of London. Night-times no longer meant fear and alarm, wondering if the terror would continue. But although the immediate danger had gone, I was left with reruns in my mind of what I had suffered. In many ways that was worse.

Dallington went on to become a fine school and developed an excellent reputation for giving kids a good start in life. My fellow classmates, like the singer Dido and novelist Jojo Moyes, are testament to that. It's just I didn't fit in there and that was a concept I was beginning to get used to.

While Mum set about finding me a new school, Mogg's words about the psychiatrist stayed with her. That, coupled with my increasingly erratic behaviour at home, prompted her to try and find out if there might be something darker lurking inside my head.

CHAPTER THREE

When it was time to leave I turned to the psychiatrist and, gesturing to my mum, said: 'Doesn't she go on?' I'm not sure he appreciated my attempts to lighten the mood.

As I sat in the sparsely furnished room while the man and Mum conversed endlessly about me, I had the feeling this wasn't normal.

Mum had told me that the special doctor – a psychiatrist – would be able to explain why I had been behaving the way I had. As soon as we entered the little clinic in Islington I sensed it would not be a pleasant experience. The questions were endless, probing and intense. Why the routines, what did I feel when I did things? It went on and on. I responded, mainly, with shrugs and guarded answers. Mum was doing a lot of the talking too, filling him in on my peculiar quirks and her own theories as to what was behind it all.

Then he turned to me again and asked: 'Has anything happened to you?'

The suddenness of the question surprised me. I looked at Mum.

Should I say? I tried to consider the consequences of either course of action.

A voice came into my head.

'Don't tell. Bad things will happen if you do,'

Fear gripped me. I shook my head.

'No, nothing,' I mumbled.

Mum continued talking.

I tried to think how a normal child would behave. What was normal? I hadn't a clue. When it was time to leave I turned to the psychiatrist and, gesturing to my Mum, said: 'Doesn't she go on?'

I'm not sure he appreciated my attempts to lighten the mood.

I don't know what, if any, conclusions were reached. By this time I'd grown pretty used to dealing with things in my own way and wasn't about to start gushing forth. Nothing untoward had happened since the abuse and I was determined to keep it that way.

My inner turmoil revealed itself in other ways. I began writing poetry. The words flowed like torrents. Some I hadn't read for years until I discovered them while researching this book. One, which I wrote aged eight, sums up the disconnection between my day-to-day life and my internal dialogue.

Entitled, appropriately, *My Head,* it reads:

Thoughts drift by
Through my head like white feathers floating
Imagination races away
'Time for school'
But my head's far away
Thinking of moments of the day
Behind my head comes a deadly pain
Between my head lays the golden key

A substance of black absorbs my mind
A bewildering blood stream rushing by
I turn my head but only to meet, the time going by.

I desperately wanted someone to crack my coded messages but the more I acted that everything was okay the better I got at deceiving people.

My parents believed that any abnormality in my behaviour was down to not being settled at school and their priority was deciding where to send me next. I looked at two schools with them. One was Prior Weston, a modern-thinking school, and Canonbury, a more traditional school in Islington. My Dad wanted me to go to Prior Weston. My Mum and I preferred Canonbury. My Dad got his way.

My displeasure at the outcome of their argument was compounded when I arrived to find I was being placed in a class with children a year younger than me, with a syllabus I'd already studied.

Having changed schools so frequently and still only eight I resolved to begin on the right foot and attempt to make some friends quickly. I didn't get off to the best of starts. One of the boys in my class who sat behind me slipped me a love letter one day. Another girl in the class, Rosie, must have liked him too because from then on she and her friends ganged up and refused to speak to me. It made for an unhappy time.

My erratic behaviour continued, the quirks more pronounced. Mum was worried my unhappiness was showing itself through my rituals. Convinced she'd conceded too willingly on the school issue, she went back to my Dad and persuaded him we needed to reapply to Canonbury.

At last I found a place where I was happy. It took me a while to settle but once I did I began to make my mark, in more ways than one. By this stage my mother was imposing herself on me visually. She was always very fashion conscious. The school didn't have a uniform so children could get away with wearing anything they liked, within reason. She bought me a pair of yellow banana boots, which were just coming into fashion. The other girls hadn't heard of them and started making fun and calling them names. I turned around and said, 'Shut up, they're outrageous,' betraying another influence on me at that stage – Mum's gay friends who would often come round the house. I had the last laugh, however, when my friends all started wearing them six months later.

Although I was more settled at school, I couldn't switch off memories of what had happened to me. Outwardly I continued to try and maintain that everything was normal but my thoughts continued to come out in poems. One, from when I was about nine, speaks of darker images not normally associated with children that age.

A World of dangers,
Fearful War, Peace,
Protective till the moment of fear,
Hoping to keep from the danger of hurt,
Screams of horses,
The past and future to come,
Cellars hidden below,
Oil, swords, and death the worst,
The breeze of today knowing all, but cannot say,
Now peaceful, but who knows what is to come,
Sorrow, loneliness of Widows,
Standing on the wrecked castle,
Mourning for their sweethearts.

After I'd been at Canonbury for about a year I made good friends with another girl called Emily. By this time we were both very popular and friends nicknamed us 'the two Es'. Emily's dad had a boat and he took us out on it once to catch mackerel. We did everything together. For a school production we dressed as tramps in bowler hats performing Flanagan and Allen's *Underneath the Arches* and entered a fancy dress competition with me as Ginger Rogers and she as Fred Astaire.

By this stage I was used to performing because Mum was always encouraging Charlotte and I to dress up for song and dance numbers. Mum wanted us to express ourselves and on the occasions she had theatre friends round for parties, we were allowed to join in the fun. Even at a very young age I loved being part of that world and immersing myself in the colourful language and outrageous clothes.

I remember falling asleep on the settee in our house one time and had that sensation of waking up and feeling like I'd missed out on something. When the time came for me to be dismissed to my room for bedtime, I lay awake and listened to the music and noise from above, wishing I were still part of the action.

As Charlotte got bigger she became more of a companion for me and joined me in dressing up in Mum's clothes. The emphasis was on fun and the more laughs we had the less I dwelled on the pain I'd previously suffered. It sounds sad to think now but for a while I thought I'd got over it.

That wasn't to say that we weren't capable of more melancholic moments. Raising two children on her own while trying to find work sometimes overwhelmed Mum and there were times when I'd find her sitting on her own upstairs in the kitchen, quietly sobbing. On one occasion I silently tiptoed downstairs and whispered to Charlotte that we needed to do something to cheer her up. We donned some of Mum's clothes and draped jewellery that was so long around our necks that I expected we'd trip, tottering back up the stairs in Mum's own high-heeled shoes. We hastily arranged a little dance routine and clippity-clopped our way back towards her.

It may have been our impressive performance or just the appearance of us at that moment but it seemed to do the trick. Mum brightened, dried her eyes and gave us both a huge hug. Comforting each other in times of trouble would turn out to be something at which we would all eventually get quite good.

Money was still a scarcity. One day I came home to find the house adorned with copious bouquets of roses. An admirer was trying the subtle approach to win Mum's affections. She was standing there shaking her head.

'I can't afford to pay the electricity bill, yet he buys me a houseful of flowers.'

Despite the economic reality of our situation, I grew happier in my own skin and loved to lose myself in books, graduating from fairy stories to more advanced works like *The Secret Garden*, *The Wind in the Willows* by Kenneth Grahame, *Five Children and It* by Edith Nesbit, *Black Beauty*, *The Hobbit* and *Charlie and the Chocolate Factory*.

For the most part these were happy times. Friends loved coming round to our house to join in the songs and games. We had music on constantly – soundtracks from musicals like *West Side Story* piping out around the house, much to the annoyance, no doubt, of our elderly curtain-twitching neighbours, Mavis and Fred, who were always moaning about the racket below. They were very judgemental and hated the fact that we were always out on the front step. We had a communal hallway and used to hear them whispering through the intercom. Knowing they were listening, we'd say, 'Don't they have anything else going on in their life?'

Mum never pestered us to help with housework or tidying, instead she encouraged us to recite poetry, learn musical instruments and appreciate art. That's possibly why Charlotte and I find domesticity so alien today.

While we enjoyed the same TV shows most children did, like *Swap Shop, Why Don't You?* and *Grange Hill*, Mum also schooled us in musicals from *Bugsy Malone* to *High Society*.

Every week a piano teacher that we nicknamed 'Stinky Steven' would come round and give lessons to my sister and me. Although we didn't have much in the way of mod cons, one luxury we did enjoy was an old upright piano. We'd giggle about the whiff from Steve while he chomped his way through the chocolates Mum would leave out on the piano top. I enjoyed learning music and seemed to pick it up quite easily but never had the self-discipline to practise and eventually gave it up.

I was, though, dedicated to a drama class we attended. When I was about 10 years old me, my sister and about 11 friends joined an acting class, at a local place called Dance Works. The teacher was called David Jaeger. We went every Saturday, kitted out in our leg warmers. He was inspiring and creative and charged hardly any fees. He put on a production of *Abigail's Party*, Mike Leigh's acclaimed play about the suburban middle classes and *Kes*, Ken Loach's film based on Barry Hines's seminal novel *A Kestrel For a Knave*. I played the lead role in *Kes*.

There's a point in the play where the kestrel dies and I remember I said the line, 'look what they've done to him', in a Yorkshire accent, with real tears streaming from my eyes. My sister, who was then only six, played Max's mother. She only had one line, in reply to my line, 'Mack, Mack, is he up?'

She had to say, 'bugger off you little sod', which still cracks me up to this day whenever I think about it.

We tried ballet but the male teacher and I didn't hit it off and after a lesson where he was particularly nasty, likening me to a rhinoceros, Mum had a massive row with him and cancelled the classes for me. As she'd shown at Dallington, Mum would be fiercely loyal when required.

I was always looking for ways to express my creativity, with mixed results. Charlotte was really into Barbie dolls, in a way that I couldn't stand. I had one Sindy doll but saw her as a lone crusader against Barbie's objectification of the female form. We were supposed to share an old fashioned dolls' house we'd been given but Charlotte had claimed it as her own. When she was out I decided to give it a makeover with some psychedelic colours. When Charlotte came home she was devastated, and viewed my act of kindness as one of vandalism.

My sister has never really shared my love of performing. Studious and shy, even from a young age, she would always be forced to join in our regular shows. On her birthday we worked out a routine from *Bugsy Malone*, a film we knew off by heart. She was Tallulah, the gangster's moll and club singer played by a 13-year-old Jodie Foster in Alan Parker's musical with an all-child cast. Under great protest she put on a blue sparkly top, sat on a boy's lap, took off his glasses and sang 'My name is Tallulah' before pointing at all the other assembled children. She then joined me for our own take on the famous ice cream adverts singing 'Just one Cornetto' to the tune of *O Sole Mio* in a dodgy Italian accent.

Although she found the idea of them excruciating, I think Charlotte found the little performances fun when she got into them. We marked all birthdays in this way and the local kids loved them. All the rest of them were going to places like McDonald's and they liked coming round to see what we'd do.

On one occasion, Charlotte and I were performing a particular routine in the living room with gusto. Singing and dancing by the ground floor window, we had attracted quite an audience of local boys. One in particular seemed to be extremely engrossed. Only when we paid closer attention did we realise he was staring down to the basement and not at our performance. Mum was getting changed in the room below, curtains open, blissfully unaware her own little show had attracted such attention.

One of Charlotte's friends was a rather portly boy called Kevin. We persuaded him to do the 'caterpillar' break dance move. Let's just say he was not the right body type and nearly went crashing through the floor. Another of her friends, Michael, rapped, although I suspect his bravado might have been for my benefit.

It was a female dominated existence and anyone who came into our world had to face the consequences. Even my poor cousin, Ben, we used to dress up as a girl.

Lots of the local children used to love hanging out at our place and not just for parties. After school my sister and I used to play with the kids from the square, who were mainly from working-class backgrounds.

We played games like 40/40 Run Out, a variation on hide and seek where not only did you have to find the other players but get back to base before they did. We also drove the neighbours mad with Knock Down Ginger, our version of knocking on a door and running. We'd squeeze every last moment out of the day, until Mum's shrill posh tones could be heard echoing around the square calling: 'Time to come in now darlings.' It never ceased to embarrass us and made the other children titter.

At school my friends were more middle class. It was only when I went to their houses that I began to feel the first pangs of envy that there were some people with more to their lot than we had. It didn't get me down though. I was always grateful for what we had. There was a different energy with the boys at school. I used to like winding up the Arsenal fans that I preferred Tottenham Hotspur because that was the team my Dad supported. They'd tear after me and I can still recall the thrill of the chase before I locked myself in the girls' toilets, while they tried to kick the door down outside. However, I support Arsenal now.

There were still constant reminders of how tight things were for us. After Dance Works classes on a Saturday I'd go to Selfridges with my sister and her friends. They were nuts about Hello Kitty and My Melody toys but we could never have afforded to buy them. So, I'd surreptitiously switch the prices on them and managed to get them much cheaper.

In a bid to alleviate our impoverished status, Mum started working with Arlington Enterprises, a presenters' agency, in Charlotte Street in Fitzrovia, helping to look after a roster of TV presenters and actors. Although the job meant she was away from us a lot, the upside was that she practically never returned home without a gift for us from Pollock's Toy Museum in Goodge Street, not far from her office.

Although it never got quite so desolate that we were depending on the kindness of strangers, the kindness of friends and family didn't go amiss. It was one such gesture that brought about our first foreign holiday. Mum's boss at Arlington kindly paid for us to go to Majorca when I was nine. Being able to play in the warmth on a daily basis was heaven for Charlotte and while the trip was noticeable for Mum's introduction to Sangria, I became adept at bartering for trinkets from the market stalls on the shore front and found it thrilling whenever I was able to skim a few pesetas off the price tag.

Mum's job meant Mackie, her mum, looked after us again – and that was not without its mishaps. My mother always said Mackie was nosey and one day she was poking around the wood shed in the garden for a broom. She found the broom but also stumbled upon a wasps' nest. The next thing my sister and I saw from the window was her running for her life, covered in swarming wasps. Ten minutes later she looked like the Elephant Man.

Mackie's real name was Winnie. My sister and I used to run around her singing and chanting 'Winnie Mandela, Winnie Mandela'.

For added company we pestered Mum to let us have a pet. In the event we got two, a dog and a cat, both rescue animals. The trips to the RSPCA kennels were heartbreaking experiences and we'd weep and want to give homes to them all before finally settling on the ones to take back.

Amy was a little black Labrador and Spaniel cross, while Bo was a little black cat. We'd take Amy to the park but nearly every time she would run straight back home again and we would have to run after her.

One Christmas, a man my Mum was seeing at the time gave us a copy of a humour book called *One Hundred and One Uses for a Dead Cat*. Charlotte and I were amusing ourselves with this when Bo staggered into the room in an inebriated-like manner. My mother took him to the vet. It turned out he'd swallowed a Christmas cracker toy. He was quite a greedy cat. The toy, however, had punctured his lung. He didn't survive the night. As we mulled over the tragedy of a cat who died of his greed, the book's humour suddenly lost its impact.

We added to the family a white cat called Blanche while Mackie acquired a Yorkshire terrier called Billy. Mackie was brushing my hair one morning when I suddenly noticed she was using the dog's brush. I urgently brought it to her attention.

'Oh,' she replied nonchalantly, 'he doesn't mind.'

In the three years after that visit to the psychiatrist, my OCD was still apparent but causing less of a concern. I washed my hands repeatedly and still performed rituals before going to places but it became part of who I was rather than a hindrance to my development.

When I was 11 I had to leave Canonbury, where I'd been so happy, and prepare for secondary school. The school my parents chose was Haverstock in Camden, a renowned educational establishment that would go on to earn a reputation for producing future leading lights in the Labour Party, after Oona King and both David and Ed Miliband attended.

Coming from the relative sanctuary of Canonbury, I remember finding the big comprehensive a bit of a culture shock. It seemed quite a tough place to be. During a French class one day someone threw a rubber band ball so hard at the window that it smashed. I sat, shocked, expecting the teacher to unleash her wrath on the miscreant responsible, but instead she just carried on with the class.

The shock of a new regime coincided with a shock of a different kind. My best friend Emily hadn't joined me at Haverstock, her parents choosing to send her to private school. I'd introduced her to another friend, Saskia, who accompanied me to Dance Works. Recently they'd been giving me the cold shoulder. Then I them spotted in the street together, walking arm in arm, with identical bows in their hair. Trivial it may be but for an impressionable girl on the cusp of being a teenager it was crushing.

I was only at Haverstock for a year when my grandfather Charlie died. A few days earlier I had wanted to see him but wasn't allowed. I felt rejected and a sense of isolation. And when I was told he had died I felt bereft and forlorn.

He wasn't very wealthy but he had left me some money. My only consolation was that I grew close to Uli as I got older. Uli said she would pay for me to attend a private school. Mum was all for it but because I was trying to make the switch during term time my options were limited. One of the few schools that could accommodate me was the International Community School, based at Baker Street in Marylebone.

I had to sit an exam but it was fairly straightforward and I passed. The school was essentially a private place for the children of wealthy foreign businessmen to attend while their parents made obscene amounts of money in the City. The Sultan of Brunei's nephew was in my class. I was one of the few English girls there.

The school did help broaden my horizons, however. I was part of a group that went to The Hague as a mini representation of the United Nations. We were each assigned a country. I was Guatemala. My only line in a short production was: 'I refute that allegation categorically.'

On the way back I fell asleep on Musa, whose father was an ambassador for the Sultan of Brunei. Someone took a picture of me but to compound my embarrassment my teacher pinned the picture up on a wall on my return.

Also at that school, during a short production of Macbeth, they cast me as Lady Macbeth. I didn't have to memorise the whole part, but did relish the famous 'Out, damn'd spot' scene.

While I was there I became friends with an American girl called Darcy, who was over in London from San Francisco. To me she was the epitome of cool as by then I'd become quite addicted to American TV shows, pop bands and films. I watched the Oscars religiously with Charlotte and Mum and obsessed over movies like *Fame* and *Flashdance* and shows like *Cagney and Lacey*, where naturally I would play the glamorous blonde Sharon Gless character, Christine, to Charlotte's rather dowdy brunette Mary-Beth.

Darcy talked about me going over to her place in California but it seemed such an unattainable dream. I felt a pull to the United States though and hoped that one day it would be a reality.

My desire to spread my wings led to friction with Mum. She allowed me to go into town to watch *The Rocky Horror Picture Show*. Darcy's parents gave her a £50 note — the first one I had ever seen — to spend. We got to Baker Street underground station and promptly lost the note. Instead of revelling in the risqué of Rocky Horror, we spent nearly three hours on our hands and knees trying to find the missing money.

When I explained my miserable evening to my Mum she was less than sympathetic and refused to let me go again. I responded by daubing graffiti all over the pink walls of my bedroom. I scribbled hurtful messages like: 'I hate my Mum,' in what I believed was a defiant statement of intent, but what was really just a bout of teenage rebellion.

Typically, Mum shrugged it off. 'That's healthy,' she said, enraging me even more.

I began a campaign to persuade Mum to let me fulfil my dreams and go to a school where my creative energies could be nurtured. I think at first she resisted, believing I'd be better focusing on a mainstream education.

Eventually, Mackie said to her: 'For god's sake send her to acting school.'

Mum agreed.

I was ecstatic. My dreams of being an actress might just be realised.

CHAPTER FOUR

To add insult to injury we were then asked to do the splits.
The other girls glided gracefully to the floor. I was the
only one suspended half way.

I am so grateful my grandmother suggested and advocated (sorry, dear reader, that's a tautology – didn't sleep much last night!) that I continue my education at drama school. Perhaps she sensed my discontentment and restlessness at my current school, or more importantly, my yearning and irrepressible desire to act. My mother precipitated the move by helping me to apply to three drama schools – the Sylvia Young Theatre School, my preferred choice of Arts Educational, which had as much to do with the straw boaters girls wore as to its impressive reputation for nurturing talent like Julie Andrews, and last, but not least, Italia Conti.

The first audition was for Sylvia Young, which opened in 1981 but had just moved to new premises in Marylebone and would go on to help launch the careers of Amy Winehouse and Billie Piper. I met Sylvia, the blonde rather matron-like owner of the theatre school and liked her immediately. I had to do a tap dance routine, which I'd had no previous experience of, and demonstrate my singing, not exactly another forte of mine. Needless to say I didn't get in.

My next audition was for Arts Educational, a much more established school at the Barbican with an impressive track record, particularly in the field of classical ballet. I was to audition at the same time as some other girls in front of a rather serious-looking panel of overly superior examiners. When it was my turn to go up I read *Dolly on the Dustcart*, Pam Ayres' lament about a classical toy discarded following the advent of newer, more sophisticated models. Someone had suggested it as a suitable verse so I learned it off by heart ahead of the audition.

Summoning my best Somerset accent I delivered it perfectly: 'The dustman see, he noticed me, Going in the grinder. And he fixed me on the lorry, I dunno if that was kinder.'

I thought things were looking up, but any ray of hope I harboured was quickly quelled as soon as I finished by the disapproving glares from the panel. To add insult to injury we were then asked to do the splits. The other girls glided gracefully to the floor. I was the only one suspended half way. Next were the dreaded pirouettes. I tripped up and twisted my ankle. Alas, you can guess I was not accepted. It had been my first introduction into the competitive, cosseted, cellophane environment of stage schools. I left the audition feeling deflated and depressed.

I did not have time to wallow, however, for next up was Italia Conti and for this we tried a change of tack. In preparation for the audition a gay friend of Mum offered to choreograph me a dance routine. He was very old fashioned in his style, though, and showed me a tap routine to Cab Calloway, the jazz singer and bandleader most famous for *Minnie the Moocher*. The song was the only redeeming feature. The dance was stilted and arcane. My mother and I changed it to Chaka Khan, *I Feel for You*. The song I chose to sing was *Look at Me I'm Sandra Dee*, Betty Rizzo's wicked send-up of Olivia Newton-John's straight-laced Sandy, performed by Stockard Channing in *Grease*.

When it came to the big day the audition was in front of a judging panel of four teachers, including Mr Vote, the bearded Australian headmaster. I had a vague sense of Jennifer Beals in *Flashdance* as I began my routine, which included a moment where I pointed seductively at each of the panel.

The audition also called for an acting piece and a speech. I read, as Titania, an excerpt from Shakespeare's *A Midsummer Night's Dream* and for the speech, recited the scene from *Kes* from my time at Dance Works. Again, the audition was in front of a panel but to my relief the examiners seemed slightly more approachable and receptive.

Two months later a letter arrived in the post. Mum stood over me expectantly. I eased out the letter so she couldn't see what it said.

'Oh no,' I said, my face falling. As Mum prepared her best 'not to worry' face, I came clean.

'Only joking. It's a "yes".'

We were all ecstatic. In my head I could hear Debbie Allen, the leg-warmer-wearing taskmaster in *Fame*, barking: 'You got big dreams? You want fame? Well fame costs, and right here is where you start paying… in sweat.'

My *Kids from Fame* adventure was due to commence in September, but before all that I had a summer holiday to negotiate and two exciting trips to look forward to. Monica, the daughter of a friend of my grandmother Uli, had invited me and another English girl to stay with her on Elba, the Mediterranean island famous for providing Napoleon with a place of refuge following his abdication in 1814. In my short history, however, Elba would become famous for being the location for my first meaningful kiss. His name was Matteo, he was fairly good looking and he wanted more. As much as I enjoyed the experience it was an episode that ended with a demure, but definite, slap.

Much more exciting to me was the prospect of a trip to America. Darcy, my Californian friend, had invited me to live with her for a month in Santa Cruz, near San Francisco. The small drawback was that I had to fund the trip myself.

I'd taken on a Saturday job in a shoe shop called Hooves in Upper Street, Islington, in the hope it would provide me with necessary cash for the flights. It only paid £10-a-day. I enjoyed working there and revelled in the opportunity to engage the customers in conversation. The stands were filled with gorgeous shoes but they might well have been glass slippers so out of my price bracket were they. One pair of boots in particular seemed to speak to me. I desperately wanted them but, on £10-a-day and with a flight to pay for it would have taken me weeks to earn enough to afford them. One Saturday I discreetly moved them into my bag and took them home.

The following week the owner, Tracy, a lovely woman, called me into her office. This is it, I panicked. She knows I took the shoes.

Tracy sat grim-faced. I fidgeted, trying to avoid her glare.

'You know what this is about, don't you,' she said.

I'm sorry, I wanted to wail. I didn't mean to. I'll pay them back, I promise, I promise.

'Don't know,' I mumbled.

'It's not working out Emily, I'm afraid. You spend all day talking to the customers. You're not meant to be their friend. You're meant to sell them shoes.'

That was a turn-up I thought. I wanted to point out that Mackie had been practically keeping the shop going by purchasing 10 pairs of shoes in the last few weeks but thought better of it. Better to quit while I was ahead and consider the boots as a pay-off.

I found another job working in a chemist not far from Hooves. It seemed an ideal solution. The people were friendly, the shop was busy but there was so much stock it was impossible to become an expert on it all.

This was demonstrated when a man came in one day and rather quietly asked for a tub of KY Jelly. Not having a clue what this was, I shouted across the store: 'Where's the KY Jelly!'

By the time I'd turned back to the customer he'd shot off to the other side of the store.

The job was fine but I needed to come up with an alternative source of funds. In addition to the piano lessons I'd had when I was younger, I'd also tried my hand at a number of other instruments provided by the various schools I'd attended. There had been a trumpet, even a huge cello, but also a clarinet, which, for some reason, I hadn't returned. I couldn't even remember which school had lent it to me. Realising I was about £100 short of my total for the plane fare I took the clarinet to a second-hand music shop near Oxford Street and promptly sold it for the cash I needed.

I could scarcely take it in. The promise of the trip had been on the table since Darcy and I became friends and by the time I left I'd been saving for a year to make it happen. Ever since I was a young girl I'd dreamed of going to America. By then I was really into the films of Eddie Murphy, the aforementioned *Kids from Fame* and *Grease* as well as *Dallas* and *Dynasty*.

Even though I was still only 14 I took the transatlantic flight alone, never thinking for one moment that it would be something I'd get pretty used to by the time I was 20.

I joined Darcy at her high school in Los Gatos, about 20 miles east of the Pacific Ocean, just south of San Jose, for a month. It was an amazing experience. I was only there for a relatively short time but the people were friendly and welcoming and her school seemed fun and exciting. I felt instantly like I belonged there. It also helped that I got a lot of attention from American guys. I had a crush on one boy, a 17-year-old called Luke. Summer 1985 was when *Back to the Future* was hitting the cinema screens and, just like Michael J Fox's Marty McFly in the film, Luke's favoured mode of transport was a skateboard. I thought he was unbelievably cool.

Darcy invited me to a friend's house party and walking in the door felt like I was walking into my own American teen movie. There were unfeasibly gorgeous kids everywhere, the music was pumping out loud and everyone was helping themselves to a keg of beer. My fantasy grew wilder when it transpired Luke seemed to have the hots for me too. We ended up kissing in one of the bedrooms.

When it was time for me to leave all the boys signed a Back to the Future-style hooded top I wore constantly. Some of them left fairly flirty and risqué messages on there. By that I mean, 'bitchin' and 'radical dude'.

When I came home and Mum saw the very forward things the boys had written I could almost see the thought bubble appear above her head as she pondered: 'What did she get up to out there?'

It was tough coming down from the high of my American adventure. For weeks afterwards I must have driven Mum and Charlotte mad by continuing to speak in a faux American accent, obsessed with all things Stateside. They were probably delighted when it quickly became time for me to attend Italia Conti and I was grateful for something else on which to focus my attention.

I remember the thrill of buying my school uniform. I'd never had one before. By the time I'd put on the dark and pale blue shirt, tie and jumper my spirits were high, but mixed with trepidation and nervous excitement.

I wasn't especially aware of this then but the added stress brought out my OCD. What should have been a five-minute walk to the bus stop on that first morning took nearly half an hour, as I went through my various rituals. I couldn't step on cracks, had to go back to touch a lamppost, touch a wall on the right place. This was all to prevent something bad happening to me, I figured. Exhausted, I finally arrived at the bus stop only for two boys to randomly throw eggs at me. So much for warding off bad things.

I arrived at Italia Conti dishevelled, my shoe laces trailing and tie skewed, in complete contrast to the other girls who were pristine in their finery.

Quickly I discovered that most of the pupils had been studying dance since the age of five, so I felt I was playing catch-up. When I was accepted my dance experience was minimal so Margot Fonteyn I was not.

My class was full of people who were either already featuring on television or destined for great things. It was impossible to ignore Naomi Campbell because even then she had legs up to her shoulders and always looked beautiful. Even then though she had a reputation for throwing tantrums. One girl got into a spat with her and after one unkind and faintly racist comment Naomi hurled her tap shoes in her direction. Perhaps it was a sign of things to come.

Fleur Taylor appeared in *Grange Hill* as school bully Imelda Davies shortly after I arrived. Lee Ross, who would go on to star in Mike

Leigh's *Secrets and Lies,* was starting to pick up smaller roles and Lionel Blair's daughter Lucy was also in my class. There were only about five boys in the whole school and we suspected that most or all were gay. One boy I made friends with called Paulo came round to my house and I wasn't sure if he liked me or not. When he came into my room I asked: 'What shall we do?'

When I turned around he had my powder puff out and was applying it liberally. That was the moment I thought, yes, he might well be gay.

Mornings were when we studied the academic curriculum while the afternoon sessions were dedicated mostly to dancing and singing. The school was named after the Italian actress who founded it in 1911 but I wondered if the original Italia Conti would have been satisfied that the modern school only set aside one hour a week for drama. Even then some of the classes left me cold. In one lesson we had to pretend we were a chocolate in an assortment box.

I stood agog as my normally languid classmates suddenly jumped to life the embodiment of enthusiasm.

'I'm a strawberry chocolate,' one girl gushed.

'Oh, I'm a coffee crème,' another purred.

The spontaneous surfeit of sugar turned my stomach.

Shaking my head at the banality I was witnessing I made for the exit.

'What do you think you're doing?' the teacher asked me.

'I'm stale,' I replied and walked out.

As with most schools the teachers seemed to be there for our amusement. One, who we dubbed Morticia from the *Addams Family*, COULD NOT SAY ANYTHING WITHOUT SHOUTING. She once sent me out of class because someone was talking. I wasn't actually the culprit, it was the guy sitting next to me. I'm not saying

I didn't have my garrulous moments. A certain teacher constantly criticised my work. One day I had had enough and I called her a frustrated lesbian. It didn't go down a peach but in the end she seemed to take it in good spirits – perhaps she thought I was one too!

It was difficult being a latecomer into a place like Italia Conti. Looking back, perhaps I was too instinctive an actress to fit the mould.

Certainly that was never more apparent than in the first end-of-term production in which I took part. It was to be a performance of *A Chorus Line* and there was a lot of pushing and shoving among the students to play the leads. Those who were eventually selected predictably developed overinflated egos and scarcely hid their self-importance. During rehearsals I remember thinking their heads would become so big they might topple off the stage.

At first they considered me to sing *Dance: Ten; Looks: Three*, with the lines 'Tits and ass. Bought myself a fancy pair. Tightened up the derrière. Did the nose with it. All that goes with it.'

But then they took it away from me. Instead they put me in the front of the chorus line. We had to dance by reaching for the sky, but as the rest of the line's hands went up mine went down and vice versa. To quote my sister, 'I have always danced to my own beat'.

The director, however, took a dimmer view and considered my dancing out of synch with the choreography. So they moved me back to the second line and then the third and, when I was feeling completely demoralised, they relegated me to the back.

By way of compensation they gave me two measly lines to sing: 'I really want this job, please God I need this job. I've got to get this job.'

Oh well, I thought. At least I get to sing. Then I was told to mime it. Mime it?

41

The night of the performance arrived. The audience was packed with pretentious stage school parents all cooing at their starstruck offspring who pranced across the stage as if they were at Juilliard.

I was almost beyond hoping my mother and sister, who were there, would even manage to get a glimpse of me but then I heard their warm, comforting laughter at my miming and going in the wrong direction to everyone and I knew how amusing it was.

To give you an idea of how competitive it was at Italia Conti – or Cunti's, as it was affectionately nicknamed – a friend of mine, Vicky, landed the song I had been due to sing. Just moments before she was due on stage another girl, Lara, put tomato ketchup in her shoe. There was no time to change. Vicky had to carry on regardless.

At the end of my first year I began to be aware that the school's productions weren't the only way for teachers to show their favouritism. Often casting agents and production companies approached the school looking for the best young talent to audition for teenage parts. *Grange Hill* and the soaps were often on the lookout for new actors but very occasionally a good film role would also come up. If I had waited for the school to put me forward for an audition I doubt I'd ever have become an actress.

Luckily I had other avenues. Mum left Arlington Enterprises and set up on her own. She got wind that a production company were casting for a Neil Jordan-directed film called *Mona Lisa*. She tried to get me an audition but when that tactic failed she stuck one of my photographs through the casting director's door. And she says she's not a pushy mum! It worked though. She got a call and it shows you do what you can to get a foot in the door.

The casting director invited me to audition. It was my first and it couldn't have been more daunting.

I arrived at the studio to be told I'd be reading a scene with

Robbie Coltrane who was also starring in the film. Effectively it was a screen test and it was going to be filmed too.

I remember having to cry and pretend I had been beaten up. The scene seemed to go fine and I recall one of the crew coming up to me afterwards and saying 'have you really been hit?' I guess it was a compliment.

I waited for ages to learn if I'd got the part. Even though I wasn't holding out too much hope it's only natural to start dreaming that you've got it. Eventually Mum rang up for some news. It turned out I'd got down to the final three but in the end the part went to Kate Hardie, who would go on to marry the photographer Rankin.

I was disappointed but tried to take positives from the fact I seemed to have done well. My worry was that I might not hear of another audition for a feature film for ages. Incredibly, however, Italia Conti was notified that the hunt was on for a teenage girl to play a part in a film called *Hope and Glory*, a wartime comedy drama, directed by John Boorman. The school must have got wind of my audition for *Mona Lisa* because they selected me as one of about 10 girls who travelled to the studio for the audition.

On the train there one of the girls turned to me and said: 'Well, you're not going to get this because you are not a dancer.'

It's always nice when you have the encouragement of your peers.

We entered the studio to find a room full of girls. Clearly Italia Conti wasn't the only school to get the call. The company intended to whittle down the candidates by a process of elimination. We were all to stand in a line and John went down the line of girls picking those who were to be considered for the next stage. I stood there nervously. When he came to me he looked me in the eye and tapped me on the shoulder. I wasn't sure if that meant I was through or if I should go home. It was a bit of both. I was through to the next stage but it meant I'd be called back later.

About 30 girls then read for the part. I can't remember much about the audition but I'm indebted to John Boorman who, in his autobiography, recalled that I was a good mimic, which was kind of him to say.

Once again I was down to the final three but lost out to Sammi Davis, who funnily enough also landed a role in *Mona Lisa*. Our paths would cross again later in my career.

It was tough to come so close once more but I tried not to be too despondent because I could feel I was getting closer to achieving my dream of becoming an actress. Once again, however, I wondered how many of these great parts would come my way. With the exception of *Grange Hill* there wasn't a lot out there for young teenage girls.

I was surprised, therefore, when not more than three months later, Mum mentioned to me that David Leland, one of the writers of *Hope and Glory,* was directing his own film. He required a sparkling young actress to play the lead role of a precocious teenage girl in a movie set in the 1950s. The film was called *Wish You Were Here*.

CHAPTER FIVE

The spoonful of soup I just put into my mouth splattered on to the table and I felt a huge surge of happiness. It was as if my 15-year-old expectations of life had just been given wings.

'Listen,' Mum said as she fussed over my outfit. 'First impressions are paramount. You have to look the part. They are looking for a sexually precocious teenager for the role.'

I stood in front of the mirror.

'Well, you've got that right.' I thought to myself.

A leather mini skirt barely cleared my backside and the azure blue crocheted top underneath my denim jacket was so cropped you could see the fluff in my belly button.

'Trust me,' Mum said, clearly detecting my unease.

As far as first impressions went, I was already on my second attempt. After Mum had heard about the casting, a call had come through Italia Conti looking for suitable 'actresses'. Several of us had tried our luck but were dismissed because we were deemed too young for the role.

But since then Dad had heard from an agent friend that the

casting director had changed. Susie Figgis was now in charge of finding the female lead. My Dad's agent then also confirmed the producers hadn't yet found the girl they were looking for.

I arrived for the audition in a studio in Dean Street, Soho. I was taken to Susie and nervously introduced myself.

'I'm Emily Lloyd Pack. I'm here to read for the part of Lynda.'

Susie took one look at my provocative attire.

'You look like jail bait,' she said. 'Go home.'

I stood there unable to move. Inside I could feel my heart freezing. Any moment it would smash into a million pieces.

Susie's eyes softened. 'Come back this afternoon in something more suitable.'

I could have kissed her. A third chance? Even with my extremely limited experience I reckoned this was unheard of. I rushed back home to change and returned wearing my favourite jeans. After a few minutes a shortish man with light brown hair and a serious expression appeared and extended his hand.

'I'm David. Thanks for coming, Emily.'

He introduced himself fully as David Leland, the director of *Wish You Were Here*. From that first introduction he was warm and considerate. He showed me into a room and talked me through the role. Lynda, he explained, was a confused but bright and garrulous young girl who railed against her environment but was essentially misunderstood. He showed me a script and asked me to read. It was a scene in a café where Lynda was reeling off from a menu but inserting rude suggestions of her own. I remember being curious about the expression 'up yer bum'. That was one I'd never heard before.

I read the scene and David seemed pleased with me. He invited me back for a screen test. This time George Akers, the editor, joined David for the audition. The scene they wanted me to read involved Lynda in a psychiatrist's office. Even then I was growing captivated by the sharpness of the script, particularly when I read that Lynda was to rebuke the lecherous doctor with a stern 'you dirty bugger'.

As if we were shooting for real, a woman appeared with a clapperboard and snapped it shut so close to my face I thought she'd taken the end of my nose off. For a moment I thought I'd freeze but instinct took over and the dialogue jumped off the page. I gave it my best shot and when the scene finished I detected George whisper something to David. Later I'd learn he was saying: 'The camera loves her.'

Afterwards David told me he was screen-testing five girls for the part, all between 17 and 19. I was the only one under sixteen. The general consensus was that they needed someone older for the role but thankfully David was less convinced. He just wanted the right person. From 1,000 girls he'd auditioned, he said, he was down to a final five.

David asked me to come back the following week when they would give me a wardrobe test with some outfits to further assess my suitability. I was getting closer. In a costume house near the Barbican centre I tried on endless Fifties-style dresses while a photographer snapped away and a costume designer asked which ones I liked.

'All of them,' I replied.

By then there was only one other candidate in the running, an older girl. I was down to the final two but after what happened with *Hope and Glory* and *Mona Lisa* I was filled with contrasting emotions – trepidation at the prospect of another rejection, combined with a rising surge of hope.

The fashion parade over, David asked if I wanted to join him for some lunch. Over a bowl of soup he talked more about the film and explained how it had grown from a TV movie for Channel 4 with a budget of £750,000 to a cinematic release with more than double the funds behind it. Working Title Pictures, he told me, believed in the project and was allowing him a six-week shoot.

'So,' he said. 'Would you like to play Lynda?'

'Yes,' I replied through a mouthful of bread, not realising the implication of his question.

'You've got the part.'

The spoonful of soup I just put into my mouth splattered onto the table and I felt a huge surge of happiness. It was as if my 15-year-old expectations of life had just been given wings.

It was only after filming that David revealed to me the character Lynda was loosely based on the early life of Cynthia Payne, the notorious madam who had been prosecuted for running a brothel from her home in Streatham, in South London, in 1980. Payne had been hosting sex parties where elderly men paid in Luncheon Vouchers to dress up in women's clothes and be spanked.

David had felt if I'd known the background to the character too early it might have put too much pressure on me or influenced my performance. It was to be the first of many concessions he made for me which would help make my first movie experience a memorable one.

David, whose work on the screenplay for *Mona Lisa* would earn him a Golden Globe nomination, wrote *Wish You Were Here* pretty much by accident. He had written *Personal Services*, a film about the scandalous period of Payne's life, which was in production starring Julie Walters and had the idea to do another focusing on her earlier years, when she came of age. He infused the story with his own memories of growing up in a village near Cambridge, which had its own bowling club and a British Legion. He recalled a pretty young girl who seemed to continually ride around the village on her bicycle with the wind in her skirt. It was to become an iconic image.

Once *Personal Services* was in the can, he put himself up as director for *Wish You Were Here*. David Rose, the head of drama at Channel 4, instantly backed his plan to make the film, having known David from his time as director of the Crucible Theatre in Sheffield.

By the time I was cast everything was in place – the set was designed, the rest of the cast were hired. They'd just needed a Lynda. That meant that when I signed up they were ready to start rolling. Filming would take place on location in Worthing and Bognor Regis, Payne's hometown.

David's close direction was invaluable for me. Although the budget had been increased, it was still small by cinema standards so we didn't have the luxury of filming several takes for each scene. That meant rehearsing as much as possible before the cameras started rolling was key. We practised scenes in a hall in Highgate, London, before we headed down to the south coast. Not only did it give me valuable acting time, it also allowed me to get to know some of the other cast before filming commenced.

Nevertheless, heading down to Worthing was both daunting and exciting. I will always be indebted to the efforts by Sarah Radclyffe and the rest of the Working Title team who made every effort to support me at each stage of the process. In each department Sarah employed people she thought I would like and feel at home with.

David wanted me to rehearse and concentrate on my lines at the end of each day's filming so I was in a hotel away from many of the other cast and crew and the distractions that went with them. I wasn't complaining. I was being paid £4,000 for the part, which wasn't a great deal by anyone's standards but seemed like a king's ransom to me. I didn't want to let anyone down but at the same time, at that age, it's impossible not to wonder what you're missing out on.

My first day on set just happened to be 29 September 1986, my 16th birthday. I can still remember the wonderful sense of excitement in the air. It felt like I was coming of age in more ways than one. No sooner had I taken my position for an early scene, then the cameraman, Ian Wilson, who unbeknownst to me was the jester on the set, asked me if I liked chocolate cake. His facial expression amused me as he realised he had inadvertently let it slip that I might be able to expect a small celebration later. Sure enough, when we finished filming for the day I was touched to see the crew had arranged a cake and party for me. They'd even got me a present – a yellow, waterproof Walkman. I still have the picture of me being presented with the cake, wearing the dress Lynda wears in the final scene in the movie. It was an unforgettable end to my first day as a professional actress.

A week into filming and the cameraman Ian had become my best friend. We were constantly playing pranks on each other. The cameramen called me 'Trouble'. Hair and make-up dubbed me 'Demon Minx'. Some days we started at six in the morning. 'Oh God,' the girls said, 'it's Demon Minx. Get the ear plugs in'.

While working on the film, I experienced many magical moments and images that will always stay with me: cycling along the grey seafront in Worthing, the steel railings which seemed to give me strength as I leant on them, learning the art of flirting with Lee Whitlock who played Brian. The feelings of serenity, strolling past the still lake pushing a pram in my yellow dress, in harmony with David's gentle direction, bonding with the rest of the cast and crew. So many good memories.

It was such hard work though. We rehearsed and rehearsed and David would give me close pointers on how he wanted each scene played. Most of the scenes were shot in chronological order, apart from the first and last days of filming. We shot the last scene – the Sea of Tranquillity, where I walked past the lake with the pram – on the first day. With what was to come it was a somewhat gentle introduction into what would be a demanding but uplifting six weeks.

There was a family feel about the shoot – David's own daughters Chloe and Abigail featured in the film – but that didn't really extend to my relatives. Dad came down to see me one day but the production company actually advised me to keep them away so I wasn't distracted.

The one time when that was unavoidable, however, was when Mum and Charlotte joined me on set. David's script called for a flashback to a younger Lynda and he felt Charlotte was ideal to play the younger me. The only trouble was my sister has dark hair. The solution was to dye her hair blonde, film the scene, then restore her natural colour. The mere thought of being blonde – even for a day – appalled my sister.

All went well, however, when Charlotte emerged from the salon a bubbly blonde. Now all she had to do was cry on cue for the cameras. She was petrified at the prospect.

'What am I going to do Emily?' she asked me repeatedly in the run up to the filming of the scene. 'You're the actress, not me. How can I cry on demand?'

'Dunno,' I replied. 'You'll just have to act.'

I could detect Charlotte wasn't entirely reassured with this advice but when it came to her time to shine one of the crew put drops in her eyes and, voila, instant tears.

There was nothing artificial about her sobs, however, when she went back to the salon to have her hair returned to its former glory. She emerged from the boutique – one of London's finest – with a barnet several shades lighter than usual on top, with her darker shade below.

'Great,' she exclaimed. 'I look like a cowpat.'

There was no arguing with that but, hey, that's showbiz, I counselled.

Back at work, I developed a crush on Lee Whitlock. By then he was a recognisable star, appearing in the successful television series *Shine on Harvey Moon*. The script called for us to kiss and I was nervous beforehand about getting it right. The moment came but afterwards Lee said I wasn't doing it properly. I was mortified. He said it felt strange because I was too young for him. I wanted to point out he was only 18 and by then I was 16 but it didn't seem worth it. Besides, Lynda was supposed to be inexperienced, that was the point. David was happy with the results and that was the main thing.

One of the pivotal scenes in the movie was inside the cinema when Lynda is hoping for a romantic date but discovers Lee is only interested in having a quick fondle. The old Dome cinema in Brighton was the location for the scene. I can recall running up and down the steps for a crane shot. My shoes were a couple of sizes too small and the more I ran the more my blisters throbbed.

The final 'cut' was music to my ears and when David coupled that with a 'well done Emily' it was amazing how quickly the pain subsided.

We were blessed that the film was packed with so many memorable scenes but the one that attracted a lot of attention when the movie was released was when Lynda is in the garden, shouting 'up yer bum' repeatedly to her horrified neighbours before mooning at the shocked faces at the windows. Before we started filming I demanded that everyone on the set had to do it as well.

'I'm not doing it on my own,' I said. Everyone who watched the scene had to moon. Before the shot took place I looked over my shoulder. On the roof where the camera was situated all the electricians were mooning. I was the butt of the joke!

One of the trickier scenes to film was when Lynda was under the bed and a dog came in and snatched the used condom. While I remained pinned under the bed, the dog steadfastly refused to pick the condom up. Who could blame it I suppose? In the end the assistant director suggested putting a sausage in the condom. Sure enough it did the trick. The dog scampered off and I could finally emerge.

Many scenes were emotionally demanding. One, on a bridge, was being shot when it was freezing cold. My voice was going and I had to say, 'All you see is tits and arses', which was harder than it sounds.

My Mum was worried about whether I'd be able to handle the sexual nature of some of the scenes. I reassured her that it was acting and it wasn't me there, it was Lynda. I surprised myself, actually, by how well I seemed to adapt. Given what I'd experienced at the hands of an older man I guess I could have gone to pieces but something in my head was able to separate the fantasy world of the movie from reality.

Only in one scene did I feel particularly uncomfortable. For many, it's a difficult scene to watch – the one where Lynda is groped by the older Tom Bell. I knew the script called for Tom to put his hand up my dress but he got a little too close for comfort and I jolted in shock. I was a little upset that David chose to capture my real reaction than trust me to act the scene.

For the most part, though, David looked out for me. Often he said: 'If it's too draining you can have some respite by walking along to the beach and having a swim.'

I never did though, regardless of my anxiety. I took encouragement from my ability to get a scene right in a limited number of takes. I think my longest was three and that spurred me on. Other than that, though, I had no idea how well I was doing.

The last day of filming was quite difficult. It was the scene in the shed with Tom Bell, an intense but generous older actor who'd made his name in the so-called 'kitchen sink dramas' of the 1950s playing characters with a sinister edge. His character Eric in *Wish You Were Here* was no exception.

It was the moment Lynda lost her virginity. David had deliberately saved it until last because he knew it would be especially challenging and difficult. There was a last day of term atmosphere about the set and the crew were cracking jokes in an attempt to lighten the mood but I was tenser then than I'd ever been on the rest of the shoot. While everyone else was demob happy I really had to concentrate.

Thankfully they captured the claustrophobia and unease. In hindsight, I wish they hadn't left it until the end of the shoot and dealt with it earlier. I would have preferred to have a scene that was more in the spirit of the set on that last day. Sadly Tom Bell died in 2006, aged 73, following a short illness. Despite the awkwardness of some of our scenes together, I will always remember his help and guidance.

There was a wrap party after filming was finished. My party piece was pretending to pull my lips up with invisible thread, and turning my eyelids inside out. The bubbly flowed but for me that meant lemonade. I started a drinks fight and before long we were splashing fizzy stuff all over each other.

As the party drew to a close I knew that the following day I would have to rejoin the real world. The second assistant said: 'Well, ladies and gentlemen, that's the end of *Wish You Were Here*.'

The tears were streaming down my face.

CHAPTER
SIX

*I felt as if I had been transported into an exhilarating, stimulating but
unreal world. An aeroplane circling the blue skies of Cannes came into
my view. A banner was attached to the plane displaying the
words in large letters 'We Love Emily'.*

The transformation in my fortunes was instantaneous. Not from a
fame point of view – the film had not yet been released – but
from the change in attitude of my teachers at Italia Conti towards
me. In the past they had always been unimpressed with my work and
parsimonious in their praise.

Before I filmed *Wish You Were Here* my reports portrayed me as
unfocused, inattentive and quirky or untalented. Astonishingly
my new reports were gushing accolades. Teachers now enthused
that I was naturally gifted and was fulfilling potential they had
always recognised.

It was very amusing but at the same time infuriating. It wasn't that
I felt superior – far from it – but I felt they were still trying to mould
me into a run of the mill stage school actress who emotes on cue
and acts by numbers. I felt I was more instinctive an actress and I

don't think that computed with their accepted model. They weren't letting me be myself, I felt. It led to further friction in class. During a ballet lesson I was thrown out for showing my belly button – very Lynda-like behaviour.

Among the students there were a couple of green-eyed monsters but my friends genuinely seemed pleased at my success. There were other times when I felt Lynda's impulsiveness and recklessness had invaded my personality. One of my Italia Conti friends, Joanne, who was far more sophisticated than I was, particularly when it came to boys, invited me to her house. She knew some 17-year-old boys who had a car. One day they were heading to the beach and offered to give us a lift. That wasn't enough for me. I climbed onto the back of the car, hauled myself up to the roof and clung on to the open sunroof. The boys took off and we were heading at quite a speed. I felt myself being thrust backwards and it was quite an effort to hold on. The wind rushing against my face and the screams from the occupants in the car as I dared the driver to go faster and faster sent my spirits soaring. I was alive.

Shortly after another Conti friend called Sarah came round to my house for a sleepover. Previously I'd asked Mum if she could stay and for some reason she'd refused. Ignoring her out-of-character stance, I smuggled Sarah in to my bedroom. All was going well until we heard Mum coming down the stairs. I hid Sarah under the covers just as Mum wandered into my bedroom, in the mood for a girly chat (she had a habit of doing this from time to time).

I began to sweat. The conversation focused on my friends and Sarah's name came up. To my mortification Mum asked, 'And how is silly Sarah?'

'You're sitting on her!' I said, suppressing laughter. Sarah's head popped up from under the duvet and my mother turned pink, but quick as a flash quipped: 'Oh hello, silly Sarah.'

What I found hard to accept before the movie came out was that I remained the struggling actress in many casting agent's eyes. It was all very well saying you were the lead in a forthcoming British movie but until people could see the evidence of your talents you were still considered an unknown quantity. That was certainly the case with me.

The challenging parts I'd auditioned for in the last year seemed to have dried up. Instead I was being offered commercials. It's not that I was precious, it's just that once I'd experienced acting in a wonderful role I felt my ambition was being realised. I wanted to stretch myself further, explore what I was capable of.

I accepted that I still had no real formal training and much more to learn so dutifully I auditioned for a commercial for a fingernail treatment. The whole experience was degrading. Candidates had to stand in a line holding a plaque with their name on it. I felt like a cow in a meat market.

My hands could not have cut the mustard because after a lengthy wait I was told I would not be needed. I don't know what I was expecting after *Wish You Were Here* but I knew that wasn't it. I came home and burst into tears. Mum tried to comfort me but I was inconsolable.

'I've played a lead in a film,' I wailed, 'and now I feel humiliated and worthless.'

Shortly after that I learned of another acting role – this time for a TV series called *Tickets for the Titanic*. I landed the part of Polly, daughter of a man played by Jonathan Pryce, for one episode. Steven McIntosh played my brother.

It felt reassuring to act again and play a different character.

My time as Lynda wasn't over, however. The editing process had begun and I was called to attend a studio in Dean Street, Soho, to loop some scenes. This is when the sound doesn't quite match the images so I had to redo the lines to synch them with the scenes.

One of the scenes that needed work on was the soon-to-be-infamous 'up yer bum' incident in the garden. In order to emulate the same energy and ambience David directed and encouraged me to jump around the editing suite and shout 'up yer bum'.

It had been two months since I had finished filming, and seeing myself on screen in the rushes at the studio I tried to remove myself from the performance but found it impossible. You might think that it would have been a profound experience, savouring the moments and marvelling at David's skill behind the camera. Funnily enough, the only thing I seemed to focus on was: 'Oh my God. My nose is *so* big.'

The movie's official release in the UK was still some months away but in May 1987 the producers learned it was to be included in the prestigious Directors' Fortnight competition at the Cannes Film Festival. Not only that but the festival organisers requested me to attend, and were willing to pay to fly me there. It was unheard of for an unknown actress to actually be at the festival, let alone be there at its request. I was beyond ecstatic. As I was looking forward to visiting Cannes and unchartered territories a predicament presented itself. The festival clashed with my 'O' level exams.

I counselled opinion from my Mum and Dad. Roger was adamant. Celebrity could wait. It was important to continue my studies, sit my exams so that I would have something to fall back on should my acting career die in its infancy.

Mum was equally single-minded. 'Darling,' she said. 'Acting is your love. You *have* to go to Cannes.'

Although I had revised for my exams I never sat them. Cannes beckoned.

So began the craziest week of my 16 years. One of the producers provided me with accommodation in the hills outside the town. Perhaps the idea was to keep me away from the frenzy as much as possible but if that was the case then it went out the window once the film received its showing. I had no idea, although the words of encouragement from David during filming gave me hope, whether the work we had all created would resonate with cinema audiences. When I heard the peals of laughter at the first screening I could finally assimilate the response to the movie.

It was fascinating to see which scenes the audience responded to. One scene they seemed moved by was Charlotte's – the flashback to when Lynda's mother died. The film cuts to a shot of her from behind, but as the camera pans round it reveals her crying, then fades to me as the older Lynda in the same position and also quietly crying.

The audience appreciated the film so much they gave it a 15-minute standing ovation. Suddenly the buzz was that I was the 'toast of Cannes'. It was manic. I was doing 30 interviews a day. One was with Barry Norman, whom I had always admired and who was kind and considerate.

Meetings were arranged with Mel Gibson, on his boat, and with Peter Ustinov and Charles Dance.

I was sitting on the Croisette, the 2km stretch of road on the sea front where all the most exclusive hotels and designer shops were, and talking to people on cue every day. The photoshoots were endless. One day they wanted me to ride a motorbike along the Croisette so they could get a picture of me. No one perceived I'd never ridden one before. When my film company advisers finally realised one commanded: 'Get off the motorbike now.'

I felt as if I had been transported into an exhilarating, stimulating but unreal world. During my stay there, I was slightly taken aback when an aeroplane circling the blue skies of Cannes came into my view. A banner was attached to the plane displaying the words in large letters 'We Love Emily'. It was unbelievable but I really wanted to be sitting next to the pilot.

Princess Diana was in town for the festival, with much fuss given beforehand as to whether she would appreciate the more risqué elements of *Wish You Were Here*. As it turned out our film wasn't one on her itinerary but it was still suggested that I would present the princess with a bouquet. I had to choose an outfit and selected a black ra-ra outfit with a tailored-in jacket with a little bow at the back. The reaction from the film company was something akin to me suggesting I would greet her in my birthday suit. Apparently it is not etiquette to wear black when meeting royalty so suddenly that was out of the question. I was rather peeved about this at the time as I thought a teenager should be able to wear what she liked.

David had to hurriedly take me to buy an alternative. A white puffer suit was deemed more acceptable.

When the time came to meet the princess she was more beautiful than I had possibly imagined and had the warmest of smiles. She had a luminous star quality about her.

She said to me: 'Aren't there a lot of cameras?'

I wanted to say: 'Surely you must be used to it,' but thought better of it.

I remember a French journalist interviewing me on the beach and her saying to me: 'Up your bum? What eez "up your bum"?'

'I haven't a clue,' I answered. To tell you the truth, some 26 years on, after having it shouted to me in the street on a fairly regular basis I still have no idea what it means.

That *Wish You Were Here* could signal a landmark in British movie making wasn't the only buzz around Cannes. Agents started to swarm around me like bees around a honey pot. At first the attention was flattering but quickly I discovered it would take all my efforts just to make sure I wasn't stung.

CHAPTER
SEVEN

*One of Hollywood's most powerful agencies were offering to buy
me a horse if I signed with them. I rang Mum back home in our
council conversion to tell her. She replied: 'We only have
a small garden, darling.'*

'She's already done something I've seen happen so rarely in films
that I count it in single figures. Julie Christie did it swinging
insouciantly down the street in *Billy Liar*, Julie Walters did it again
much later on, stomping independently over the college cobbles to
"better herself" in *Educating Rita*. Just by inhabiting a role, not
playing it, by using instinct not training, by relying on natural looks
not make-up, by projecting an inner verve and not just dialogue, in
short simply by being there, these players serve notice as soon as they
appear on screen that they're here to stay. Emily Lloyd lugs herself
directly into your feelings.'

Those kind words were from movie reviewer Alexander Walker in
the *Evening Standard* in May 1987 and initially it was difficult to
comprehend they were being said about me. Praise wasn't just
reserved for my portrayal. The rest of the cast also received good

reviews and David's careful direction was recognised for its soaring realism and for accurately showing how a young mademoiselle grew up to be the madam Cynthia Payne. For an actress to receive instant acclaim in a first feature was a dream realised.

On returning to London from Cannes, the tides of fortune changed and smiled on me. The phone was constantly ringing off the hook from mainly American agents courting with offers to represent me. It was overwhelming and difficult to differentiate between whose motives were genuine in guiding my career and supporting my wellbeing and those who wanted to take advantage of a new and potentially bankable name.

A tidal wave of attention threatened to engulf me and I had no one to tell me how to ride the crest. There was no time to even acclimatise to this new world I found myself in because a month after Cannes I went to New York for the American launch of the movie, which would come before the UK release in December.

Mum had to stay at home to look after Charlotte but although the prospect of facing a rapacious media alone in the Big Apple filled me with apprehension, at the same time I relished the chance to break out on my own. Everything was happening far sooner than I had ever dreamt of and with such an intensity I never thought possible. No one gets to choose when fame and success come calling. It's how you handle it that is the test. In the end a compromise had to be reached because both Mum and Dad weren't happy with me being in New York on my own, so my Aunt Janice came along as my chaperone.

We checked into a suite in the Sherry Netherland Hotel in Manhattan for a round of interviews before travelling through to Los Angeles for the premiere and more publicity. In New York the buzz around the movie was incomprehensible. My days started at 8am and sometimes didn't finish until midnight and consisted of a seemingly never-ending run of television appearances, press lunches and more interviews. It might sound glamorous but it was exhausting, Quickly it became clear that the focus of the attention was me rather than the film, something I started to feel uneasy about.

I made it to a few clubs at night, once the work was done, just to unwind, listen to some music and dance – anything to make me feel like a normal teenager. It's not that I was complaining, it's just that it seemed so surreal. Word of the clubbing got back to the press in the UK, however, and I started to earn a reputation for partying. If only they'd known the truth they'd have seen how fatigued I was.

One night, in an unbelievably pretentious club called Nels, where people just gathered and stood around waiting to be seen or discovered, I noticed Bruce Willis who was among the celebrity names on parade. I was still so unaccustomed to seeing Hollywood stars in the flesh that I half-expected his *Moonlighting* co-star Cybill Shepherd to appear. It was an altogether strange experience. People ignored me but when someone from the film company explained who I was suddenly they were fawning all over me.

One evening, when I was having dinner at Nels, I met Sting, but think I made a faux pas. I asked him if he had enjoyed filming the love scenes in his latest movie *Stormy Monday* with Melanie Griffith, not realising there had been rumours their on-screen passion had spilled off set. He said he was always thinking of wife Trudie.

When it was time to fly to the coast for the premiere in Los Angeles, Jonathan Daner, head of Atlantic pictures, who had bought the film for America, said to me: 'We're pulling out all the stops for you Emily. It will be the full works – Emily Lloyd hits LA.'

I wasn't sure whether his words were intended as a promise or a threat.

After a while, Aunt Janice had to return to London, so my American friend Darcy visited from Santa Cruz with her mum, who kindly offered to keep an eye on me. We checked into the Sunset Marquee hotel.

When I hit Tinseltown the wave of interest was like a tsunami. I was even on the television news. I don't want to complain, as in many ways it was wonderful that the film and my performance was garnering such accolades but I was beginning to feel isolated and pressurised. In a city like 'La La Land' that is obsessed with cultivating young starlets, I still could not comprehend why there was the particular fascination with a 16-year-old from Islington. Being undecided regarding the choosing of an agent, I had no protection. Looking back, someone should have been there to say: 'Stop. She's had enough.'

Atlantic booked me to appear on the legendary *Tonight Show starring Johnny Carson*. It was the trendsetter as far as chat shows went and since its launch in 1962 had featured anyone who was anyone in showbiz. Since 1972 it had broadcast out of Burbank, California. Before filming began, thinking of the well-known actors I was following in sitting on that armchair filled me with trepidation. I was backstage having my hair and make-up done when a man snuck up to me, thrust a bit of paper under my nose and begged me to sign. He was an agent who'd blagged his way in saying he already represented me.

For a moment it threw me off my stride but by the time I was due out in front of the lights I had managed to regain some composure. I must have done because I challenged the veteran host to a game of Knuckles, one of my favourite icebreakers. It's a game of quick reactions because if you don't move fast enough it's pretty painful.

Next I heard that the boss of Creative Artists Agency (CAA), one of Hollywood's most powerful agencies, were offering to buy me a horse if I signed with them. I rang Mum back home in our council conversion to tell her.

Calm as you like, she replied: "We only have a small garden, darling,' as if this was the most natural offer in the world.

Someone from Gersch – another respected agency – said they would rent out a whole ice rink for me if I joined them. Then a rumour started circulating that Triad had bought me a gold watch if I went with them. But it wasn't true. Jonathan at Atlantic actually bought me the watch, from Tiffany. It became embarrassing because Triad were making a big play for me. When I eventually signed with them some of their clients, who believed the rumour, requested a watch.

On a superficial level it's flattering when people are being nice to you. When the outlandish promises were made I felt inclined to accept them, but I managed to keep a level head and took time to choose who I felt would be best for me creatively.

Ilene Feldman at Triad adopted a more subtle approach. When I met her in LA she said she was throwing a barbecue for me. I arrived at her sumptuous villa in the Hollywood Hills to find she'd invited many of her hot young male actors. The feeling was that this was a crowd I could be part of. As I mingled with these bronzed, artificial looking creatures that seemed a different species from the boys back in London I had the sense her strategy might be working.

Ilene's partner was Nicole David, an actress who had starred with Elvis Presley. I liked her and Ilene instantly and felt a connection to their personalities.

Mum came out to visit me in Los Angeles. I think she was slightly numb about the impact the film was having but that was quickly dispelled the moment she disembarked the plane. For a start, Triad, the front-runners for my signature, had lined up a limousine to take her from the airport to their offices in Hollywood. She felt like

Thumbelina on a giant's foot. *Wish You Were Here* was being heavily promoted in LA at the time and Mum recalls emerging from the labyrinth of LAX's car parks and exit routes to find the boulevards lined with gigantic posters of her daughter promoting a quintessentially English movie. It's unsurprising to learn she thought she was dreaming.

While I was being wooed in LA it was like being in a sweet shop and being able to have anything you wanted. My Mum gave me a lot of freedom and trust. She felt that the agents were trying to win her over in order to gain influence and encourage me to sign with them. It was almost too much for her.

She came with me to meet Ilene and Nicole from Triad. Mum's preference had been for me to sign with CAA who she felt had more clout. When she learned that Warren Beatty was in the building and wanted to meet me it only served to strengthen that opinion.

Eventually, though, Nicole and Eileen convinced her to a degree that they had my best interests at heart, but she was still worried she was handing her daughter over to these ruthless Hollywood movie types. Her flight home was scheduled to leave later that day and she had to leave from Triad's offices. She was desperate to stay but I was quite relieved. Try telling a teenage girl she needs her Mum in one of the coolest cities on earth. Mum was in tears when we said goodbye. 'Trust me,' I told her. 'I'll be fine.'

She was still visibly upset by the time the limo appeared to shuttle her back to the airport, but the information that it was a car once used by Elizabeth Taylor and the appearance of a very cute chauffeur in a crisp, starched white uniform seemed to hep dry her tears – that and the presence of a vodka-heavy minibar inside.

How she got on the flight back to London I'll never know. When she regaled her best friend Barbara about the trip she was so overwhelmed and effusive about her experience in Hollywood

Barbara told her to come back down to earth and stop getting so carried away.

My first experience of the downside of fame came when I discovered I was so well-known no one would serve me in a bar because they all knew I was underage. Atlantic laid on a dinner in my honour and invited Frank Zappa's children, among other guests. In one respect it was kind that someone had thought to ask along younger people for me to meet. They were charming and I felt they might have something to say about growing up in the public eye, given they had names like Moon Unit and Dweezil. But even by then my anxiety was mounting. I was growing suspicious of people's motives and couldn't help wondering if the film company were trying to choose my friends for me.

The impact of the movie continued to surprise me. Steven Spielberg asked me to meet him in his offices at Amblin Entertainment. Once again it was like I was living my wildest dreams. Like a kindly uncle, he told me he'd seen the film and loved my performance. He told me not to get too sucked into the industry.

'Stay young,' he counselled. 'Have fun. Be a kid and go to Disneyland.'

'I'll try,' I replied, suspecting that if the theme park wasn't down on my already packed itinerary there would be little chance of that happening.

As I was whisked from event to party, I met Mickey Rourke, who railed against the Hollywood machine, and Al Pacino.

In the Sunset Marquee I bumped into English pop stars Curiosity Killed the Cat – then probably the hottest band in the UK after their debut album *Keep Your Distance* had gone in straight at number one. They were in America promoting it. It was a relief to meet some fellow English people who shared my observations about LA.

We had a laugh together and I broke into the Jacuzzi late at night with some of the band. We sat there in the bubbles sipping Daiquiri cocktails. It was all innocent fun but by the time word got back to Mum about our little escapade, the Chinese whispers had transformed it into a tale of debauchery where I was taking Quaaludes, a drug that earned popularity in the Sixties and Seventies for supposedly heightening sexual pleasure. Not that I ever got to find out. Not only was I not taking drugs but I wasn't attracting any romantic interest either, although I did suspect that the band's rather handsome bassist Nick had taken a shine to me. I tried telling Mum she was getting the wrong end of the stick but she was determined to fly out again and sort me out.

I managed to bat her off this time and convinced her she could trust me but it had been such a release to break out from the monotony of regimented interviews and appearances that I planned a little escape.

Atlantic planned a leaving party for me and then promised me a holiday to recuperate. When I discovered the holiday was just a plane back to London I rebelled and with Darcy hatched a plan to give my minders the slip.

A limo driver arrived to take me to the airport. As I stood in the elevator with my bags, Darcy, her mum and the driver, I suddenly said: 'Oh, God, wait. I've left a bag in my room. Hold the lift and I'll meet you back here.'

Darcy and I ran out of the lift, out of the hotel, hailed a taxi and checked into the Hollywood Highland motel. It was only then that I was breaking free of the film company's shackles and I wasn't ready to go home. I wanted to taste Los Angeles for myself.

All hell broke loose. You'd have thought we were fugitives on the run rather than teenagers wanting some fun. But after a couple of days Ilene offered to put me up at her house and that seemed to reassure Mum.

Under Ilene's tutelage, we went round the studios to see what was on offer. I ended up signing a development deal with United Artists. Despite reports back home suggesting it was a three-picture deal worth $2 million, there was no money involved. It was an open-ended contract that seemed to be flexible. If I found a script I liked I had to take it to them first and while they said they would source 'suitable vehicles' for me, I didn't have to do it if I didn't like it.

There was barely time for me to catch my breath and it was off to Japan for the Asian premiere. I felt like Alice in Wonderland in Tokyo, exposed to another new cultural experience. My friend Jane, who was a year older, came out from London to keep me company. The premiere was funny. It was a gala occasion but when the announcer came on to make the introductions his thick Japanese-English accent meant something got lost in the translation.

'Ladies and gentlemen,' he said, 'we would like to introduce you to Hemorr Hoid.'

Jane and I were in hysterics but no one could figure out why we were giggling so much.

We were staying in the Capital Tokyo Hotel and Michael Jackson was in the suite next door. His 10 security guards dwarfed my one school friend and his presence there upstaged me considerably.

For the first time I might have started letting the fame thing go to my head and must have been stropping around like a diva, because I remember Jane getting annoyed with my histrionics. We got into an argument and she snapped: 'You're not Sofia Loren yet you know.'

Mostly though it was another mesmerising, if eye-opening, experience in a seemingly never-ending succession of such events. My 17th birthday fell while I was out there and the film company laid on another cake and small celebration. Could it really have been a year since I was nervously standing on set for the first time?

Jane and I took kimonos from the hotel and went to the Hard Rock Café. Everywhere we looked strange sights greeted our eyes. Japanese girls were doing an aggressive version of *Grease* and the fighting seemed too real to be pretend. Meanwhile businessmen who would otherwise have looked respectable in immaculate well-fitted suits were passing out on the pavements. Too much Saki, apparently.

My old friends Curiosity Killed the Cat happened to be touring Japan at the same time I was there. We joined them in a karaoke bar where less time was spent on singing and more time arguing the respective merits of James Brown's classic *It's a Man's, Man's, Man's World*. Nick and I picked up where we'd left off in Los Angeles and we had a little scene together – all very innocent.

It was a surreal time and for the most part seemed like the fulfilment of my wildest aspirations. When I'd been younger and my OCD had been at its most pronounced I couldn't leave Milner Square without touching the surrounding wall at a particular point.

'Touch the wall and you'll be famous,' I used to say to my sceptical friend, who refused my demands for her to touch it too.

When I returned from my exploits in America and Japan she said to me, 'I wish I had touched that bloody wall.'

The interest showed no sign of letting up as the London premiere approached. Selina Scott, then the doyenne of morning telly with the Princess Diana hair, whose presence on the BBC's *Breakfast Time* guaranteed that most men rose with a smile, came to interview me at Mum's house. She revealed her tip for handling nerves was to dip her feet into cold water. Sure enough, throughout our interview she had her feet bathed in a basin under the table.

We filmed in Chapel Market, near Angel, where my Uncle had a stall. Given the attention I'd received in Los Angeles I half expected more of the same on my home patch but all the traders were interested in was my glamorous interviewer. 'All right Selina?' came the shouts as we moved through the bustling marketplace.

The London premiere of the movie came in December. A limo arrived to take my family and me to the venue. My hair was styled and I had a gold Emanuel dress especially for the occasion. I felt every inch the movie star. It was an incredible experience to be part of such a celebration in my home city. It was there I met Cynthia Payne. Seeing her in the flesh it was hard to compute that she was the embodiment of the character I portrayed. David had been right to keep from me the fact that Lynda was based on Cynthia. It might have been too much for me to handle.

'I've already seen it and I cried my eyes out,' she told me, adding: 'When my family saw *Personal Services* they didn't speak to me. Now, after *Wish You Were Here* they are speaking to me again.'

When I said to Cynthia, 'You must meet my Mum,' quick as a flash she responded, 'and your Dad.'

She said she felt I was wonderful as her and couldn't be bettered. Of all the praise I had been fortunate enough to receive, this was about the best.

We posed together, saying 'sex' for the cameras. Later, at the after show party we would dance together and I changed out of my gold dress into one more suitable for riding a helter skelter that was inexplicably there.

When all the hoo-hah of the film finally started to die down, an event reminded me that celebrity doesn't shield you from the pain of everyday life.

Amy, our rescue dog, was dying. She'd been with us for eight years and although she'd often driven us mad with her antics she'd been part of the family. Her legs could no longer get her out of Milner Square let alone propel her back home again from the park. I helped Mum carry her to the vet, praying for some sort of miracle, but inside knowing that our time together was drawing to a close.

She looked up at me with moist, sad eyes, like she too knew what was coming. She seemed resigned to her fate.

The vet spared us further torment by taking her away to perform what needed to be done. I was left feeling empty and bereft. The door slamming shut behind him was the only closure we were offered.

I barely had time to compose myself when it was back to work. Nicole had been in touch regarding a film she thought would be ideal for me. Susan Seidelman, who'd directed Madonna in *Desperately Seeking Susan*, was casting for a female lead for her new film *Cookie* – the tale of a gangster's daughter who tries to connect with her wayward dad. Nora Ephron, whose script for *Silkwood* earned her an Oscar nomination, had written the screenplay. It was a role coveted by some of America's finest young actresses, Nicole said, among them Jodie Foster. I gulped. The idea of going up against the girl who as Tallulah in *Bugsy Malone* had kept me entertained during my childhood seemed unthinkable.

Although I was English, such was the buzz around me that there was a chance they'd take a gamble and cast me over a more obvious American candidate. I was to go back to New York to audition. Once again I packed my bags for the airport.

At the age of 17, I was about to be leaving to live on my own in New York. An incredible adventure was about to begin, but it would also be the start of some very hard times.

CHAPTER EIGHT

Suddenly he grabbed my head and gave me a full on smack round the face. I hesitated and slapped him back. I got terribly English and said: 'You don't hit an actress.'

'You gotta eat somethin',' the big Italian mamma yelled at me for the umpteenth time that week, thrusting the over-flowing plate of pasta back in my direction.

'I don't wanna eat nothin',' I shouted back, pushing the plate away.

It could have been a scene from my latest movie but this was no film set. It was real life… well, my version of reality. For two weeks I had been living with an Italian American family in deepest Brooklyn. Susan Seidelman, my director on *Cookie*, was hoping that time spent with an authentic Brooklyn family would soon have me speaking like a native New Yorker. I'd beaten 5,000 girls to the lead role, including Miss Foster, I was told.

'The whole world is falling in love with Emily Lloyd,' announced Nora Ephron, while Susan Seidelman explained her thinking in choosing an English actress over an American.

'The original goal was to find an American Emily Lloyd,' she said, 'but that was before we knew Emily had such a wonderful ability to pick up accents. It's not so much that she has great experience or technique but she has an amazing amount of energy. There's a kind of unpredictable liveliness about her.'

The platitudes were lovely, but apparently I still needed to work on my accent.

Although, for the most part, I had enjoyed my time living with my temporary mother, Theresa, her husband Joey and their two young daughters, latterly it had become a war of attrition. My hostess meant well but seemed to be on a mission to fatten up this limey.

I often lay in bed at night in the cramped apartment, listening to the sounds of the city outside, pondering whether all movies stars went through this. Since *Wish You Were Here*, I'd been labelled the new Marilyn, the new Greta… were they sent off to live as archetypal characters in order to hone their acting skills? Unlikely, I thought.

Nevertheless, my challenge, set down by no one but myself, had been to come to America and try to make it as an actress. Not for the first time, I started to wonder whether I should have stayed longer in England, established myself more. What was it those Royal Shakespeare Company thespians had been saying? That to covet Hollywood was something beneath a serious actor. Maybe they were right, maybe the stick I was getting was justified. Then Mum's dulcet tones popped into my head.

'What the hell do they know? They'd all be on the first flight over given half a chance of a starring role.'

From mamma Theresa's house, it was onto the set and into the Mayflower Hotel, overlooking Central Park on the Upper West Side. Already the whole city felt like a movie set, with every street corner throwing up an instantly recognisable vista. In surroundings like these it was impossible not to feel you were just permanently playing a walk-on part.

Initially, everything was exciting. I instantly struck up some friendly banter with Mikey, the hotel doorman and an Irish American whose mongrel accent reminded me of Michael J Fox's attempts at the lilting brogue in *Back to the Future*.

We quickly built up a rapport, enjoyed some banter and played tricks on one another as I came and went. 'Curly' was his affectionate name for me and when he greeted me with a smiling 'How's tricks, kid?' as I departed for my first day on the set I left with a spring in my step.

Any thoughts I might have had that life on film sets was universal after my experience on *Wish You Were Here* were dispelled the moment I reported for duty. It was another world. For a start there was a cast of thousands. People everywhere, bustling about doing jobs it was impossible to define. The noise and activity created a chaotic atmosphere, with everyone beavering around looking important.

It all felt very Hollywood, particularly when I was informed I would be having my own chaperone, because I was only 17 and on my own in New York. She would look after me and act as my very own gopher, attending to my every whim. This is the life, I thought.

When I was introduced to her, however, it appeared the reality was going to be quite different. Her name was Vi, which I'm sure was short for Violet, but it might have been violent. She was about 60 but a formidable mountain of a woman. Now I realised why the Winnebago motor homes that littered the film lot were so big. This woman clearly hadn't made a habit of skipping lunches.

'Hello,' I said, with a cheery smile.

Vi looked me up and down – perhaps assessing if I'd make a decent snack – and seemed completely disinterested. She must have seen a million precocious teenage film stars over the years and appeared to have already made her mind up about me.

Then it was an introduction to my dialect coach, Tim Monich, one of the best in the business. He seemed much more friendly and became someone I grew very fond of. He was going to be on set with earphones and after every take would give me notes on my pronunciation.

Once filming started the hard work began. We were shooting in November, it was bitterly cold with sub-zero temperatures – even snowing at some stages – and we were filming for 18 hours a day.

Peter Falk, the legendary *Colombo* star, was playing my father. He was a mobster called Dino who, after 13 years inside, was hoping to reconnect with his illegitimate daughter by hiring her as his driver. Only by driving him around does Cookie learn about his gangland ways and overhears a plot to kill him. The film was also starring Academy Award winner Diane Wiest and Jerry Lewis, who my mother revealed had tried to seduce her many years earlier.

It was good knockabout fun. But perhaps Peter took this rather too literally. He was a method actor, so very intense, and I found him difficult to get close to between takes. During takes we sometimes got a little too close for comfort. In the middle of shooting one scene, we were having a heated argument. Suddenly he grabbed my head and gave me a full on smack round the face. I hesitated and slapped him back. I got terribly English and said: 'You don't hit an actress.'

Susan Seidelman had to step in to break up the fight. The crew was stunned. No one knew if he was trying to provoke a reaction or acting out his frustrations. Whatever, it was actually a turning point. Clearly remorseful, Peter sent helium balloons to my trailer by way of an apology, which was strange. I was expecting flowers, maybe, or chocolates or even a bottle of Champagne, but that was Peter for you. Maybe it was an invitation for me to fly away.

Dad came to visit me for a few days and I think was somewhat taken aback by the change in circumstances for his little girl. In the absence of a bank account or credit card, I had no option but to carry cash on me, but this meant I had shoeboxes over-flowing with dollar bills. It was a steep learning curve for both of us. Dad had always tried to instil the value of money in me, compared to my Mum who says, 'If you got it, spend it.'

Dad met with the British director Stephen Frears, who was developing an adaptation of the French novel *Les Liaisons Dangereuses*, which would become *Dangerous Liaisons*. At the same time, coincidentally, I met the acclaimed director Milos Forman, who was planning his own adaptation of the same novel called *Valmont*. As we sat in his Manhattan office, while he was making soup, I noticed that on the wall were hanging posters for *One Flew Over the Cuckoo's Nest* and *Hair*.

'Those are good films,' I said. 'Who directed those?'

When he replied, 'It vaz me!' in his distinctive Czech accent, I realised I had much still to learn.

As the days rolled on and the temperature plummeted, the demands got greater. I started to feel ill, was feverish with a rasping throat. I knew it was far worse than a common cold but the financial constraints of the movie meant they weren't going to take kindly to halting production until I got better. Eventually I was diagnosed with mononucleosis – glandular fever, as we would say, but 'mono' as the Americans called it. The response from the production team was to give me one day off to recover.

I got a lift though in the shape of my mother and Charlotte who came to stay with me. Mum even came to visit me on set.

We were about to shoot a scene where I walk into a bar to confront my father about his infidelities. The setting was a coffee shop bar. My mother was excitedly watching.

'Ok,' bellowed the first AD, 'Rolling, rolling, we're going through a take.'

There was silence apart from a pair of tottering high heels echoing through the room and I heard a voice in a high-pitched tone say: 'Can I have an orange juice please?'

To my dismay it was my mother. She was under the impression it was a real bar. Everyone cracked up.

'Cut, cut!' the first AD screamed. 'Get that woman off the set.'

One of the crew looked at me and said: 'Who is that woman?'

'That's my mother,' I sheepishly replied.

Afterwards, my mother was mortified but revealed that she'd had to go looking for a drink for me because Vi had clearly considered it beneath her. She'd clearly got the actress–gopher relationship all muddled up. There were times when I was running around fetching her hot soup while she sat there like the Queen of Sheba. She was later sacked – which might have been on my mother's say-so – but her replacement seemed to share her work ethic, and fondness for food.

As if I needed anything else to ingratiate myself with the crew, I then, following a later scene, went to the toilet, partly to get away from the cacophony of constant talking amongst the crew and the monotonous drone of the AD's walkie-talkie. When I emerged the crew was staring at me. I suddenly realised why. When I was in the toilet I hadn't turned off my radio mic. As I approached the set, one of the teamsters said: 'Feel better now?'

Blushing and embarrassed and not knowing where to look, I simply said: 'You gotta go, you gotta go.'

It might have been antics like these, or the simple fact that I made it my business to try and speak to everyone on set, from the runners to the drivers, but I got on well with the crew. They played tricks, like pretending to bind me up in cables, to relieve the stresses of the job.

During my time off I was able to forget about the pressures of work and have some fun with Charlotte. We climbed the Empire State Building and, for a brief time, behaved like any normal teenagers would do on being let loose in the most exciting city in the world.

I was further elated when word came through that I had been nominated for two prestigious awards for *Wish You Were Here*. In the Evening Standard Film Awards, I'd been deemed good enough to bypass the Best Newcomer category and was fighting it out with some incredible luminaries in the Best Actress category.

To my amazement, this was followed by a similar nomination in the BAFTAs, a significant honour, given it had been my first movie role. I was ecstatic and slightly disbelieving of the recognition of my work.

When it came to the night of the Evening Standard award ceremony I was still filming *Cookie* and couldn't make it back to London. However, I was informed beforehand that I'd won and that Christopher Plummer, of *The Sound of Music* fame, had been chosen to present the award to me. The award ceremony was presented by Joan Bakewell and attended by lots of lots of celebrities and her Royal Highness the Duchess of Kent. The nominees were as follows:

Vanessa Redgrave, for *Prick Up Your Ears*, Sarah Miles for *Hope and Glory*, Julie Walters for *Personal Services*, which incidentally David Leland, the director on *Wish You Were Here*, co-wrote with Terry Jones, and, lastly, me.

There was a camera crew in the hotel suite. Christopher introduced me by saying: 'I am presenting an award to a young actress – a very young actress indeed – whose amazing achievements have resulted in her hurtling past the newcomer award to be voted unanimously this year's best actress. The young lady is starring in her first American film. London, get her back fast before Hollywood grapples her to its heart.'

Then he presented me with the award, I shook his hand and kissed him.

I had prepared a little speech: 'I'd like to say thanks a million to the *Evening Standard* for giving me this award. You've really made 1987 a great year. And thanks to David Leland for believing in me and the cast and crew for putting up with "Trouble" as they nick-named me. Also, especially, thanks to Tom Bell who was great to work with. And thanks to my family. Hopefully I'll be back there in three months so you can warn the airports I'm coming and hope-fully I'll get the chance to act in more English films.'

I added: 'I just want to say, "Hi", to my grandma Mackie and I wish I was there. Or should I say, I wish you were all here. And rock on London. Bye.'

After the award presentation we all had drinks at the Mayflower Hotel. Christopher Plummer and a journalist from the *Evening Standard* joined us. They were both great raconteurs and observing them compete for the funniest stories was like watching two racing drivers striving side by side as they made for the finish line.

Interesting stories were exchanged but out of the corner of my eye I noticed Michael, the journo, flirting with my mother and then Christopher asked her and me to dinner. After a sumptuous meal was consumed, Christopher Plummer made to leave but as he departed the restaurant my mother and I both stood on the table and serenaded him with an impromptu version of *Edelweiss*. Although our rendition was delivered in far from the dulcet tones the song required, it was, nevertheless, sung with gusto and a lot of character. Plummer left chuckling. That wasn't the end of the night's hilarity. It later transpired that the drunken journo knocked on my mother's door, hoping for a nightcap.

I assumed such a liaison could lead to good reviews for me the next morning but, alas, she opened the door and politely declined.

The story was almost repeated some weeks later for the 41st BAFTA ceremony. But while the circumstances were similar, as a film crew set up in the hotel suite because I was still filming *Cookie* in New York, the mood was altogether more sombre. This was serious business now.

The idea was that I was to be filmed by satellite, while my rivals for the prestigious gong sat in London. My three agents were with me as well as my new chaperone, who, as well as a fondness for food, had also developed a predilection for the hotel minibar and seemed on the prowl for some man action. She was in the corner of the room, glugging vodka and masticating on whatever morsels were available, while eyeing up any male who came within a few feet.

Before long the big moment came. I had an earpiece on. A camera was fixed on me to capture my reaction and I was wired to a mic. Unlike the Evening Standard awards I had no idea of the result.

This was it. I could hear the nominees being read out to the live audience in London and the watching millions on TV. The names I could hear were Julie Miles for *Hope and Glory*, Julie Walters for

Personal Services, Emily Lloyd for *Wish You Were Here* and Anne Bancroft for *84 Charing Cross Road*.

I could only hear very faintly what was going on in the UK. The suspense was escalating and so were my nerves. Just at the moment when the presenter announced the winner my agents started gesturing to me whether I had won.

I faintly heard Anne Bancroft's name and, registering my disappointment by pulling a face, put my thumbs down to indicate: 'No'.

But, unbeknownst to me, the cameras were still rolling and when the programme was aired in the UK there were two boxes of actresses all clapping on the screen, no doubt demonstrating the conventional false delight for the winner, and in the corner right box there was me putting my thumbs down in response to the result!

My father didn't speak to me for a week.

My mother was very proud.

CHAPTER NINE

Matt Dillon ordered soup and when it arrived offered it to us rather
suggestively. He passed it to Gaby who very seductively took the soup.
He did the same to me. The soup missed my mouth and
spilled down my top.

'Oh, that's great. Just there. Yes, like that. Oh, just great, great.'
No, this wasn't the script for a hardcore film I'd been offered but the world renowned photographer Annie Leibovitz, lovingly caressing the long lens in her hand as she barked increasingly insane orders at me.

'Quick, jump on that fire truck. That's the shot, yes. Speak to me.'

By now I'd been used to the demands of the photo-shoot, the hours of preparation for hair and make-up, the vast array of outfits supplied and the manic shouts of the excitable photographers. Mostly, though, these had been in a studio, a controlled environment where overworked assistants scuttled around adjusting lights and backdrops and pop music blared at deafening volumes.

But Annie Leibovitz was different. By 1987 she had earned a fearsome reputation as one of the world's top celebrity photographers.

Making her name at *Rolling Stone* magazine, she famously snapped John Lennon and Yoko Ono in a stunningly original vulnerable pose just five hours before the ex-Beatle was shot dead.

I had turned up for the shoot in a downtown Manhattan street not knowing what to expect. I didn't even know what magazine the photos were for. Nicole just told me to be there. Two hours later I was standing on the sidewalk as Annie scanned the neighbourhood for suitable backdrops.

Like a mad professor she crackled with inspiration, suddenly becoming energised and barking orders.

'Quick,' she shouted. 'Into the traffic. I want to capture your energy.'

You want to capture me dead, I thought, as I glanced nervously towards six lanes of traffic that were roaring nose-to-tail up the avenue towards Midtown and me.

'Now!' she yelled, her blonde hair flying out behind her, the sun glinting off her oval glasses. I paused at the kerbside. This was like Russian roulette, only with hulking Buicks and SUVs instead of bullets. Here goes. I darted out into the traffic to a cacophony of horns and engine roars. I got halfway and turned to face her but she was already snapping away furiously.

'Now, back,' she screamed over the din. I spotted a gap and ran for it trying to keep my eye on the lens while at the same time keeping watch for any articulated lorries. If I wasn't careful I could end up like a human-sized dolly on the dustcart.

Annie seemed delighted. 'Great, great, I got the shot,' she said, before adding, 'Do it again.'

I wasn't brave enough to say, 'but I thought you said you'd got the shot'.

Back I went, running in as quick as I could and out again. How I didn't get run over I'll never know. All the time Annie was orgasmic, flicking away furiously.

She must have captured my energy because when it was all over I was knackered. I never did see the finished pictures but hers was just one of a series of bizarre shoots. *Vogue* magazine dressed me up as Pierrot the clown and had me dancing with a broom wearing a bowtie. Patrick Demarchelier had me in a trilby and gloves for another cover shoot. For another I posed with big cats at the Shambala Preserve, the Californian animal sanctuary belonging to Tippi Hedren, the star of *The Birds* and the mother of Melanie Griffith.

New York seemed to be one insane experience after another. I couldn't work out whether this was peculiar to me or whether the city served up these episodes to all its citizens on a daily basis.

Ilene was on the phone. 'Matt Dillon wants to meet you.'

Of course he did. This was the most natural thing in the world. It was perfectly normal that people who stared at you from posters on your bedroom wall would want to take you out for dinner.

The Outsiders, Francis Ford Coppola's movie based on the novel by SE Hinton in which Dillon played a gang member alongside Tom Cruise, Emilio Estevez and Rob Lowe, was one of my favourite movies. My friends at Italia Conti and I used to send notes to each other pretending to be the tragic outlaw characters Ponyboy Curtis and Johnny. We would quote lines from the movie.

Dillon also starred in *Rumblefish*, another favourite of mine and another Ford Coppola adaptation of a Hinton novel. Dillon loomed large on my bedroom wall alongside Ralph Macchio and Rob Lowe. If anyone had said to me then that in a few years I would be meeting him there's no way I would have believed them.

The idea was that he was to meet me at a very ostentatious

restaurant in a swanky part of town. Gabrielle Anwar, a friend of mine from Italia Conti, who was trying to make her name as an actress, was staying with me at the time. I took her along for some moral support and I didn't see anything wrong with taking a glamorous friend along to dinner with a heartthrob I had a crush on.

That was my first mistake. Matt arrived and was charm personified. His teeth were blinding and his manners impeccable. We shared a drink and some stilted conversation before the starters arrived.

Matt ordered soup and when it arrived offered it to us rather suggestively. He passed it to Gaby who very seductively took the soup. He did the same to me. The soup missed my mouth and spilled down my top. I was mortified. Wishing the ground would swallow me up and realising three's a crowd, I made a hasty exit and left them to it. They say you should never meet your heroes. That's probably true. You should never spill soup down yourself in front of them either.

I stepped out into the Manhattan night and, unsure what to do with myself, took the subway to Harlem with some notion to shake off the stifling atmosphere of the ostentatious restaurant I'd just left and find the real New York.

I was walking along the pavement when I encountered two tramps, or bums as they're called in America.

'Spare a dime, sweetheart,' one said.

I reached into my pocket but the only money I had was a hundred dollar bill. The two down-and-outs could scarcely believe their eyes as I unravelled the crumpled note and inspected it before them. This was a modern dilemma they don't warn you about. How to satisfy two tramps with only one $100 note.

'I don't suppose either of you has change for a hundred,' I said. 'Then you could split it.'

They both looked at me in amazement. While I still worked out what I was going to do, the two men decided to resolve it in their own way – by fighting to the death!

They started rowing over who should get the cash. It looked like it might get out of hand so I stepped in to calm things down… just at the point when one of them swung for the other. Bang, I caught the punch square on the eye.

'If you want it that much just take it,' I said, handing over the cash and rubbing my now throbbing socket.

Now I had a nice black eye and an empty pocket to go with my soup-stained top. At least I'd found the real New York!

I was at a party in a Manhattan nightclub shortly after that when I became aware of a commotion. Someone was clearly important enough to be surrounded by an entourage of heavyweight minders and airhead glamour girls. Curious to see who it was I squeezed my way into the ensemble and asked who the VIP was.

It was Mike Tyson, then the undisputed heavyweight champion of the world. I did wonder why someone who billed himself as the 'baddest man on the planet' needed this level of protection. Maybe he wasn't as hard as he made out. I was granted an audience and, as I was discovering regularly in America, once you fought past the squad of minders, people were quite down to earth. So it proved with Mike.

'I know who you are,' he said, although I suspected this was because he'd been whispered the necessary information moments earlier.

What do you do when you're granted an audience with the hardest man on the planet? Challenge them to a fight? Well, that's what I did. Not 15 rounds of Queensberry Rules boxing, but my favourite, Knuckles. He seemed fairly bemused when I broached the subject with him but he got the message once I'd bashed his knuckles a few times. And by the time he'd practically broken my hand I realised he was getting the hang of it pretty quickly. It was time then to call a halt to the proceedings but I claimed a moral victory. I liked Mike. He was very affable and there was a vulnerability and gentleness about him.

By now I was being admitted to nightclubs without too much fuss. Either the initial interest had died down and doormen had forgotten I was underage or they turned a blind eye. It didn't matter. I wasn't a big drinker and interviewers were always amazed when they saw me sipping an orange juice and munching crisps rather than downing cocktails. I did develop another party piece, however, which was ripping off beer bottle tops with my teeth.

Episodes like those with Tyson and Dillon might give the impression that I was having the time of my life, but the reality was that living on my own in Manhattan at 17 was harder than I imagined. After filming finished on *Cookie* I moved into a loft apartment on the corner of Hudson and Houston near Soho. Without work or my family and friends to keep me occupied I was reminded how lonely I was and the fun we'd had when they'd visited only exacerbated the isolation I felt. I tried to combat it by making out I was having the time of my life but, behind the pranks and the laughs, I was miserable. This is your dream, I told myself, and this is what you wanted. What I didn't have an answer for was what to do when your dream doesn't turn out the way you planned.

It was the time in my life when I should have been hanging out with friends my age, gradually experiencing greater freedoms and exploring my sexuality. Instead I had been thrust into adulthood, my formative teenage years vanishing in the glare of publicity. I was expected to make grown-up decisions and in many ways I still felt like a child, having missed a crucial part of my life. Memories of past traumas haunted me and the behavioural traits that had blighted my personality when I was younger now returned. Often I wouldn't be aware of it but in company I'd drift off in the middle of conversation, I developed nervous ticks and heard voices in my head telling me to do certain things. I needed help but had no idea how or who to ask for it. Even if I did I could imagine the reaction back home: 'She's only been in movies for five minutes and now she's acting like the prima donna angst-ridden film star.'

I looked like I had it all. I had the means to hop on a plane to London but mostly I made transatlantic flights for work commitments and engagements and, while often it was fun, it was also exhausting. In June 1988 I returned to London to appear at a concert to mark Nelson Mandela's 70th birthday. By then he had been imprisoned for over 25 years and the event also called for his release. My parents had raised me to be politically aware and to have an opinion on current affairs. My role at the Wembley Stadium concert was to introduce one of the most politically charged sets of the day by *Simple Minds*. I joined Denzel Washington on stage. A year earlier he had won acclaim for his portrayal of Steve Biko, the anti-apartheid activist killed in police custody in *Cry Freedom*. We experienced some sound problems on the day but it was an honour to be involved and to have the chance to mingle back stage with renowned musicians, actors and artists from all over the world.

I probably could have benefitted from an extended break at home to recharge my batteries, but I had to return to New York to prepare for my next project. The privilege of an actor's life, I was to find, is that it can temporarily lift you out of the doldrums and make you believe the fantasy is real.

I had still been working on *Cookie* when Ilene told me about a new film called *In Country,* an adaptation of Bobbie Ann Mason's novel. She thought it would be a good vehicle for me. Norman Jewison, who'd directed *In the Heat of the Night* with Sidney Poitier and Rod Stieger, who I was later to work with, and *Moonstruck,* starring Cher, was in the chair. The part I would be going for was that of Sam Hughes, a 17-year-old whose father Dwayne was killed in Vietnam before she was born. She lived with her uncle Emmett, who was going to be played by Bruce Willis, rather than her remarried mother, who Joan Allen was cast to play. Sam, a fresh but quizzical teenager, seemed to be the pivotal character in the story. By supporting Emmett and searching for the father she'd never meet, it seemed she was conducting an inquest on behalf of America into the war that cut deep into the country's emotional heartland.

As with *Cookie,* I would have to convince the director I was worth taking a gamble on ahead of equally capable American actresses. I met Norman in New York and tested for the part. It's fair to say he was sceptical from the outset. I was too conditioned to the Brooklyn accent for *Cookie* and hadn't properly worked on trying to nail the very distinct Southern drawl. Norman thought the accent was a problem but I persevered and over the next few weeks tested again for the part. Gradually I got the hang of the Southern twang, enough, anyway, to impress him.

He tested dozens of girls but felt that all the actresses eligible to play a teenager were too worldly wise. They didn't have Sam's innocence. Lack of experience and innocence were things I had in abundance. Eventually, I believe it was between myself and Winona Ryder for the part. She'd won plaudits for her role in the dark high school drama *Heathers*. Norman chose me, but it would not be the last time the fortunes of Winona and I would be intertwined.

Accepting the role meant I had to turn down the part of Mandy Rice-Davies in *Scandal*, the British movie on the Profumo affair, but I felt it was a small price to pay for hopefully further enhancing my reputation in America. The thought of working with Jewison appealed – as did the pay check, which was going to be more than I received even for *Cookie*.

Rehearsals began in New York in the sweltering heat of the summer 1988. I immediately warmed to the script, penned by Frank Pierson, who wrote *Dog Day Afternoon*, starring Al Pacino, a copy of which I was given, leather-bound with my name inscribed in little gold writing. Kevin Anderson, the good-looking star who would go on to save Julia Roberts from her psychotic husband in *Sleeping with the Enemy*, played Sam's love interest, the character of Lonnie Malone.

I'd met him some months earlier when I'd flown with Ilene to Iowa to meet the actor/director Gary Sinise. He, Kevin and John Malkovich were all in Steppenwolf Theatre Company, based in Chicago, but Gary wanted to sound me out about a movie he was directing called *Sylvie*.

That was a story in itself. I arrived at the shoot to find Kevin playing basketball with Richard Gere, who was also in the movie. As I had time to kill before my meeting with Gary, I took the opportunity to shoot some hoops with the guys. Naturally I won.

Anyway, I digress. Back in rehearsals for *In Country*, I connected with Kevin immediately and clearly there was chemistry between us when we commenced shooting for real. Norman continued to have reservations about my accent and linked me up with Tim, the dialect coach who'd been invaluable to me on *Cookie* and who'd kindly said

I had an ear like a sponge. It was reassuring to work with such an expert again and one who seemed to have taken a shine to me – so much so he called his new baby daughter Emily.

I arrived in Paducah, Kentucky, to find the heat even more oppressive than that which we'd just left in New York. My home was going to be a detached country house surrounded by woods. There was a pond full of goldfish at the back of the house and there was a gym with a large pool at the end of the road.

I had two weeks there before the shoot started to acclimatise and further immerse myself in Southern culture and to get over the jet lag. I went to the local schools to talk to students and went on my own to the local mall to tape the local girls to hear how they spoke. One of my favourite challenges was to strike up a conversation with a random stranger and speak to them with a Kentucky drawl and see if I could fool them. Nine times out 10 I pulled it off.

As a large part of the film's subject matter was relating to the Vietnam war my character's quest was to find out about her father. Sam had an unquenchable curiosity. Some people suggested I read up on Vietnam or watch documentaries before filming started but I decided against it. Sam didn't know anything about the war and I felt it was better that I channel my own curiosity through her character.

Anyway, it was my belief that the suffering of soldiers is universal, regardless of the conflict. To be faced with a barbaric vision of men destroying other human beings and then having to come home and chat to their wives about mundane matters like what colour curtains to choose must have been impossible.

Instead I talked to a lot of ex-veterans who told me some moving yet disturbing stories. One told me that after they came back from the war they would go into the woods and randomly shoot things.

Maybe they found some comfort in belonging to the group as they found it difficult to fit in and be accepted by society when they returned from the war.

Filming began in 110F heat. Sam had this boundless energy and loved to run so the first scene we shot involved me running through a graveyard. As it was going to be a feature of the film I had to practice my technique and off camera jogged around the set, accompanied by the trusty yellow Walkman I had from *Wish You Were Here*.

I was on my third feature and I was growing much more confident in my understanding of camera language. I think Norman found my style unpredictable but he seemed to like me. Other actors have described him as an old curmudgeon but I liked him and felt he understood me on the same level David Leland had.

He later said he hadn't thought much of my accent when I'd first auditioned and directing me was 'like trying to catch quicksilver' but grew to see me as Sam. 'She had this energy,' he said. 'She reminded me of Judy Garland – not in her vulnerability, but in her innocence and glow.' Praise indeed.

With the stifling heat kicking in we were supplied with copious amounts of water, which we gulped like parched people stranded in the desert.

Supposedly looking after me in Paducah was Johnny, my gay friend who was meant to be my assistant. He was the Danish boyfriend of Malcolm, my mother's closest friend.

In the house the film company rented for me were two bathrooms. Johnny had allocated himself the largest bathroom and the best bedroom. I came home from filming exhausted on that first day and asked if there was any food.

In his Danish accent, he said: 'It's in the fridge. Get it yourself.'

When my Mum came to visit she walked into one of the bathrooms, which was filled with Clarins, Clinique and Lancôme toiletries.

'I love your bathroom, Em,' she said.

'No, that's Johnny's,' I said, 'this one's mine.'

Johnny spent most of his time in the gym when he was supposed to be collecting me from the set but he did have his uses.

He looked after a Siberian puppy I impulsively bought after seeing him cooped up in a pet store. I called him Oscar. He was gorgeous, with one blue eye and one brown eye. I took him on set but when he started getting in the way I left him at the house for Johnny to exercise.

Johnny also ensured I didn't get into trouble on set day. After I'd been a little late arriving on one or two occasions he put the clocks back and changed my alarm so I would get up on time.

The schedule was punishing. I remember doing one scene in a swamp. I was reading my father's diary and the script called for tears to be shed. In order to invoke the emotion before every take I listened to Marvin Gaye's *What's Going On?*, with the line, 'war is not the answer', which I considered pretty apt. This was enough to make me cry.

Bruce Willis was something of an enigma on set. He didn't exactly ingratiate himself with the production crew when he moaned about the size of his trailer shortly after arriving. This didn't make him very popular with the teamsters either, who made their feelings known by producing baseball caps and sweatshirts saying '*In Country* starring Emily Lloyd'. He looked like he was going to spend a lot of time in his trailer.

Die Hard had just opened in the States when we were filming and he was yet to become the global superstar. At the time of *In Country* he was only really famous for *Moonlighting*. Gradually though he opened up and revealed himself to be a surprisingly considerate but complex character.

My Aunt Janice arrived with my cousin Ben, who was then 11. When Ben joined us on set he hung out with the teamsters, who built a mock shooting range with vegetables from the mobile canteen. Bruce, though, came out of his trailer and showed Ben how to aim correctly. He was firing pellets happily when Demi Moore, Bruce's wife who'd joined him on set with their newborn baby Rumer, popped her head out and asked him politely to stop.

I think Bruce and Demi took a shine to me. They invited me bowling and it was nice to see how they interacted with each other away from the set. The only sickly thing was that she called him Duke and he called her Bunny. I was nicknamed Wolf and his assistant showered me in *Die Hard* gifts. But on set Bruce continued to rub people up the wrong way.

One time we were filming a scene where I was telling my mother I wanted to go to college. It was supposed to be an intimate scene played with just me and Joan, but Bruce felt he should be the one I told so he wrote himself into the scene, leaving the rest of the cast a tad perplexed.

I don't know what it was with me and birthdays but, just like it had been on *Wish You Were Here*, my birthday fell on a day when we were filming. It was my 18th. I was touched when Norman presented me with a pair of pearl earrings and the crew bought me a handmade American quilt. Bruce Willis gave me a little silver pig inscribed with a line from the film: 'Fuck the Tyre Plant'.

During the eight-week shoot the days were long and the heat made it doubly difficult. To keep myself amused, I tried to stay active and passed the time between takes by winding up the crew, lobbing mud pebbles around, pinning rude messages on people's backs and launching into impromptu waltzes across the set.

Kevin was a permanent fixture at my house. I talked over potential film projects with him. At that time I was inundated with scripts. Those that caught my eye included a film called *Mermaids* and an early script for a sci-fi adventure called *Johnny Mnemonic*. During breaks in filming Kevin and I took a drive over the border to Indiana. We had what I term 'a little scene' together but, while it was all very innocent, there seemed to be a strong connection there.

These were the days before mobile phones and when we returned Janice wasn't happy. Given she had offered to look after me in the absence of a chaperone, she wasn't best pleased that I'd gone AWOL.

But the time we spent together off set was welcome respite from the often-monotonous schedule of filming. We bought Freddy Krueger masks and gloves and terrorised Ben with them. We rented movies from Blockbuster but only permitted my young cousin to watch the likes of *Robocop* and *Good Morning Vietnam* if he agreed to dress up in my clothes.

Oscar proved to be quite a handful. Despite me believing I was rescuing him from a life of misery in the pet shop window, he had other ideas about what freedom meant. He ran off and we spent three days looking for him. Someone finally found and returned him but he did another runner the following morning. I had befriended a local girl called Tiffany – a pneumatic blonde who wouldn't have looked out of place in *Playboy*. She drove Kevin, Ben and I around in her vintage red convertible Cadillac until we found him.

Tiffany took us to Churchill Downs horse race track in Louisville, home of the famous Kentucky Derby. My Aunt Janice, who I admit had been given a testing time looking after me, was finally able to relax as we took in some races and enjoyed a flutter on the horses.

That was until our elation at winning in one race proved short-lived when I discovered I'd lost my betting slip. She thought it was a sign of my increasingly frivolous attitude to money, exacerbated when she saw the bundles of dollar bills stuffed into shoeboxes and drawers in the house.

It wasn't that I was throwing money away, it was just that I was never very good at looking after it – a failing that would cost me dearly in later life.

But if I intended to show my Aunt I could be responsible, I didn't immediately show it. Not long after, we had lunch with the larger than life American actress Peggy Rea, famous for her stints in *The Waltons* and *The Dukes of Hazzard* and who had a part in the film. I'm not sure how it started but a food fight ensued, causing Peggy and my Aunt to duck for cover.

Back on set, I tried to knuckle down to the task at hand but some things just set me off. One scene showed a heron flying. A trained bird was provided for the shot. I had to say the line: 'Damn it, Emmett'. For some reason this tickled me and I could not stop laughing.

My antics seemed to wind Norman up and often he liked me to be beside him so he could keep an eye on me. He later said he wished that I had more dramatic training or theatre experience to fall back on. He acknowledged that I worked hard but found I was surviving on raw instinctive talent. He felt that sometimes he had to help me focus because I didn't have that training to fall back on.

I could understand what he was saying – it was one of the few criticisms levelled at me at the time. I wasn't sure what I was expected to do about it, however, go off and do rep theatre for 10 years? And if I did have the necessary experience, wouldn't that have just made me like the dozens of 'jaded' actresses he'd encountered who were old beyond their years? I always tried to take on board criticism, but sometimes it seemed the world was expected of me.

From Kentucky, we travelled to Washington to shoot the film's most moving scenes, when Bruce Emmett visits the memorial to honour his fallen comrades. My Dad joined me in Washington for the crucial part of filming. I walked up to the Vietnam memorial. It was shattering to see row upon endless row of names of war dead and the anguish of these grown men who had come to pay tribute to their friends. One man, when he touched a name, let out this animal noise of sheer desolation and I just stood there with tears streaming down my face. It was so sad. There were letters from girls my age just left there saying things like, 'I know you're there Dad, I love you' and, although I have no experience of war, I began to understand a little when I saw all that pain.

With filming finished it was time to move on. I hadn't given much thought to what I would do with Oscar after leaving *In Country*, but Bruce Willis's assistant had taken a shine to him and owned a farm herself with plenty of space, so I gave him to her. I wasn't going back to New York but I still felt a dog was an added responsibility I didn't need. I was going straight to Los Angeles where my friend Gaby had found a place in Laurel Canyon, not far from the Hollywood Hills. We'd talked about getting somewhere together since we were 17 and had gone to see Daniel Day Lewis in *The Futurist* in a theatre in London. Inspired by the ideology we'd vowed to live together, start our own theatre company and even a political party. We thought we were taking on the world.

CHAPTER TEN

Cher stared and stared at me through her ridiculous sunglasses for ages and then finally screeched: 'You don't look genetically like me.' I looked at her and said: 'Well you don't look genetically like you.'

It was Gaby who discovered them. At the back of our house, up on the hill that flanked the canyon, were mysterious stones, arranged as if for some kind of druid ceremony. The stones were quite large and had obviously been laid for a reason – a sacrifice perhaps. Certainly many a young starlet's dreams had been dashed on the altar of Hollywood, which lay just a few minutes' drive away on the other side of the freeway.

The sight of them disturbed us. Gaby had stumbled across them while she was out running and when she took me up to show me the sun was setting over the hill. The sound of dogs howling in the distance only added to the spookiness. Laurel Canyon had always attracted a bohemian element. Jimi Hendrix, Jim Morrison, Joni Mitchell and Frank Zappa were among the musicians who had homes there and it was a favourite haunt for artists and actors who preferred a more relaxed environment than the garish glitz of Beverly

Hills. However, like most of Los Angeles, its darker side was never too far from the surface.

The small house Gaby was renting was on Wonderland Avenue, the location for four unsolved murders in 1981 that exposed a seedy underbelly of drugs and porn and belied the fairytale of La La Land. Ours was a bungalow seemingly surrounded on all sides by huge mansions and villas. The canyon boasted a distinct community but I was bemused that no one walked anywhere. People would jump in their cars for even a two-minute stroll to the shop. Gaby and I couldn't drive so we took cabs everywhere. They were a luxury I could afford but I would have much preferred to be able to walk places.

Unfortunately Gaby and I were not destined to be the ideal roommates. I'm inherently disorganised while she was fastidious − not an ideal combination. After a few months she made it clear that it might be better for both of us if I found somewhere else. My business manager found me a place in Benedict Canyon, an area of Beverly Hills north of Sunset Boulevard.

As I tried to settle into life in Los Angeles I went to showbiz parties that sound very glamorous but the reality of these get-togethers is that they're all motivated by money. People hung around like dollar disciples, weighing up whether it would be financially beneficial for them to speak to you. You could stand there being ignored and then someone would introduce you and explain who you're working with and suddenly they'd become interested. The city was built on social climbing and networking and it all seemed alien to me.

The stereotypical image of Hollywood is that it is all sex, drugs and rock'n'roll and in my experience it was a bit like that − just not quite in the hard-living way many people might imagine.

I hadn't been in LA long when I was in a club one night and a prominent actor started chatting to me. He seemed perfectly charming and genuinely interested in me. When he invited me into a private room so we could continue our conversation in quieter surroundings I thought nothing of it. Once we were inside the small room, empty but for us, he closed the door and locked it.

My suspicions barely had time to arouse but something else certainly had. The actor whipped down his trousers and exposed himself. He was clearly excited and it was obvious what he expected me to do.

At first I stood motionless. Thoughts flashed through my mind. I couldn't quite take in what was happening. Was this the same man who'd been making polite conversation just seconds before? I would have been shocked had any man behaved this way but the fact that this was a famous star, part of a renowned family of actors, made it all the more shocking.

I regained my composure and told him, politely, where he could put it.

It was an unsettling introduction to the ways of Hollywood. I always suspected the casting couch culture was something of a myth, but some people must have believed starring in movies gave them the power to treat women as they saw fit. Some actresses might have thought, 'have I made a faux pas by rejecting him?' But I wasn't dancing to his tune.

Drugs might have been commonplace in Hollywood but in the early days I saw little sign of them. Money was the drug on which they were all hooked.

It was all about work, the business and networking. And self-obsession was practised like a religion.

A woman I knew who worked as an assistant to an acclaimed

British director told me of the time she'd been chatting to an A-list star when she revealed she'd been diagnosed with multiple sclerosis.

'You think that's bad,' the actor replied. 'I haven't worked for a year.'

There was no escape from the business. Even the cab drivers tried to get in on the act. You couldn't jump in one for five minutes without a driver announcing that he was a second cousin to Meryl Streep's uncle, or that he'd penned a film script that was a sure-fire hit if only someone would take a chance on it.

I don't mean to sound scornful. The money I was earning was more than I ever dreamed of, but although it made life comfortable I wasn't receiving anything like the sums being speculated about back home. Some newspapers said I had signed a £2 million picture deal or had earned as much as £750,000 in the last year. I wish it had been that much. It was much less, especially once you deducted 10 per cent to the agent, 5 per cent to the business manager, 5 per cent to the lawyer and £2,000 a month for the publicity people who for that sent me photocopies of interviews I'd conducted. Then there was tax at 35 per cent in America with British duties on top. I wasn't complaining. I knew how lucky I was.

The parties could be fun and the best part about them was the food – there was so much of it – wonderful concoctions like chocolate-coated strawberries. Everyone else was either too polite, too fearful of upsetting their rigorously enforced dieting regime or too busy sealing their latest film deal to take advantage. Meanwhile I sat in the corner and stuffed my face.

Although LA was now my base I could fly to New York or back to London when I needed to. This only brought more chaos, and rather than give order to my disorganised scheduled it only served to fuel it. I was leading a gypsy life, albeit an intercontinental gypsy

– but I lost bags and tickets with increasing regularity, and more often than seemed normal I had to sleep in airports until the next flight was available. Luxury it wasn't.

I needed a break when a friend of mine called Ellie, a third AD from New York, suggested we take a trip to Anguilla, a tiny island in the Caribbean. What should have been a relaxing trip became anything but when halfway through I ran out of money. We were spending cash as we went and I had no concept of how much a trip like that would cost. The concept of credit cards was still beyond me at that time and I had to phone my business manager who wired some money to me. While I waited to be again flush with funds, we had to sleep on the beach. Even by the end of the trip I remember coming through passport control in New York in my shorts and t-shirt with sand still in my shoes. I turned up at the Ritz Carlton, where I'd booked in, looking like a beach bum.

New York was where I was discussing my next movie role. After reading the script for *Mermaids* in Paducah I was keen to be involved. On paper it sounded an exciting project. Orion Pictures were keen to produce the movie, an adaptation of Patty Dann's coming of age novel (of the same name). Published in 1986, the book charts the story of teenager Charlotte Flax and her unconventional upbringing in smalltown Massachusetts in 1963. I'd been approached by one of the screenwriters who felt I would make an ideal Charlotte, the narrator of the story as she explores her relationship with single mum Rachel and sister Kate, while negotiating a path through adolescence. They were in talks with Cher to play Charlotte's mum, who she calls Mrs Flax. When I'd first read the script a director hadn't been attached to it but it immediately appealed. The relationship between the women intrigued me. By the time I signed the contract, Orion still hadn't found a suitable director but they assured me – and it was inserted into the agreement – that the part was mine regardless of who took the helm.

A short while after I signed for the film the project became even more enticing when I learned Swedish director Lasse Hallström would be in the chair. *Mermaids* would be his American debut after winning acclaim and an Academy Award nomination for his Swedish language film *My Life as a Dog*. Lasse began his career directing videos for ABBA but was keen to cement his growing reputation as a moviemaker in the United States and *Mermaids* seemed to be the perfect vehicle.

It was a prolific time for me, my agents kept telling me, with offers flooding in for a variety of projects. Many of them clashed with the scheduling for *Mermaids* and I had no option but to turn them down. In all I turned down roles in five movies, one of which was the part of a prostitute opposite Richard Gere in a film called *Pretty Woman*. The role instead went to Julia Roberts. I wonder what happened to her?

I met Lasse in New York for rehearsals and I felt we were working well together. Lasse was intense and direct but knew what he wanted and I was encouraged by the early signs that we could make a good movie. The problems started when we began shooting and Cher arrived. She had an ego as big as her hair but at that time, in early 1989, probably with good reason. She'd effortlessly made the transition from pop idol and television personality to movie star, earning praise and Oscar recognition with performances in *Silkwood*, *Mask* and Norman Jewison's *Moonstruck,* for which she won the Academy Award for Best Actress.

The moment she arrived we knew we were in the presence of a diva. She waltzed in with a big pair of shades on and never took them off. Cher stared and stared at me through her ridiculous sunglasses for ages and then finally screeched: 'You don't look genetically like me.'

Coming from someone who'd reputedly spent thousands modifying her looks I thought this was a bit rich.

I looked at her and said: 'Well you don't look genetically like you.'

It was unlikely we would bond after that. Initially I didn't pay too much attention to her complaints. Rarely is the likeness between a screen parent and child an issue, and Cher only had to look at her own children to see that their blond hair and fair complexions bore little resemblance to her.

An issue, though, it was most certainly to become. Had they never heard of hair dye? As the shoot continued Cher repeatedly clashed with Lasse. Something had to give and it was the director. Lasse was fired, apparently at Cher's insistence. The setback didn't seem to affect his career. Lasse went on to receive his second Academy Award nomination for *The Cider House Rules*, a movie that earned Michael Caine an Oscar for Best Actor in a Supporting Role.

On *Mermaids*, Frank Oz was brought in as Lasse's replacement. Oz was an actor, director and puppeteer best known for his work on *Sesame Street* and *The Muppets*, creating, among others, Miss Piggy and Oscar the Grouch. Maybe it was felt his expertise with plastic monsters would be invaluable. I never got the chance to find out. Shortly after Lasse's departure I had a meeting with the studio executives.

One said to me: 'Look Emily, I give you my word. We're not going to fuck you over. This is your job.'

Frank Oz didn't last long either. He was out, replaced by Richard Benjamin. He was probably best known for being the prey to a psychotic robot in *Westworld* and he may have needed to draw on that experience to survive *Mermaids*. I didn't realise that the new director had been given cast approval. A few weeks later I too was told I would no longer be required.

Given the faith I'd shown in the production it was a slap in the face. My agents and management were furious. In Hollywood there's an unwritten rule that when things like this happen you just smile and get on with it. I would have been happy to but my lawyers believed I had a strong case to sue. In addition to breach of contract, they sued Orion and Mermaid productions for mental injury, nervous pain and suffering, symptoms of which I could certainly show them.

Winona Ryder, ironically the actress I'd beaten to the role of Sam Hughes and the possessor of Cher-friendly hair, replaced me.

I barely had time to digest the fallout from *Mermaids* before I was back on the publicity trail for *Cookie*. The film was released in summer 1989 to mixed reviews. Many critics felt the script lacked originality but those that praised my Brooklyn accent gave me heart. The film didn't do as well as the producers had hoped, but sometimes it's hard to put your finger on exactly why. Roger Ebert, the renowned critic of the *Chicago Sun-Times*, suggested that the director and scriptwriter, Nora Ephron, who sadly died recently, were more interested in the dynamic between Dino and his mistress and his wife, rather than his daughter. That might have been a factor. She had also been working on another script around the same time for a movie called *When Harry Met Sally*, which was later released to widespread acclaim. The most crucial aspect for me though was that I had proved I could carry myself in an American movie and to a certain extent proved any doubters wrong.

With the release came the customary media interviews. Normally the monotony of answering the same questions over and over means these blur into one. One, however, sticks in my mind for its absurdity. An interview with a UK showbiz magazine was scheduled to take place in my hotel room in New York. When the journalist showed up he informed me he'd just dropped an ecstasy tablet and wanted to conduct the interview on the bed. I attempted to humour him and went along with it for the sake of a good write-up but just minutes into our chat he fell asleep. I didn't have any experience of drugs but it seemed to me he should have asked for his money back; either that or my conversation was particularly soporific. I left him dozing and went out to a party.

During a rare break in my publicity commitments, I went for a stroll near my hotel in Midtown. A French street vendor said to me in a really sexy voice: 'Oh you look lahk somebodee.'

I thought he was going to tell me I was like some glamorous French actress but instead he told me I looked like Emily Lloyd.

I replied: 'But ah am Emilee Lloyd.'

He didn't believe me.

'No, no you are not, you look lahk her but you are more common than her.'

No matter how much I tried to convince him I couldn't. As I walked away I turned around and shouted: 'Well, anyway I'm better than Emily Lloyd!'

Sometimes my life felt like a page from a Woody Allen script.

During another photo shoot and interview on the streets of Manhattan for a British newspaper, I recognised a police officer I used to see around when we were shooting *Cookie*. I had on me a water pistol, which I had a habit of carrying around. Previously it had got me into trouble when I squirted a man in a swanky nightclub in New York, at a party for Isabella Rossellini, not realising he was the manager. That incident hadn't put me off though.

Anyway, as I approached Nick, the cop, I shouted 'Freeze!' and pulled the trigger, showering him in spray. Instinctively he reached for his holster before realising it was me.

I could visualise the headline: 'Cookie crumbled by New York cop.'

While being interviewed I was conscious that my lack of formal education would show in my answers. In an attempt to overcome my insecurity, I took to carrying around a dictionary and read voraciously in a bid to broaden my vocabulary.

Once the media merry-go-round ran its course I was leaving America to return to the UK. I had signed to star in *Chicago Joe and the Showgirl*, a British crime thriller based on the true story of the 'cleft chin' murder – a notorious crime spree conducted by ex-soldier Karl Hulten and his lover Elizabeth Jones. The project had much to recommend it. It was going to be directed by Bernard Rose who, although a relative novice when it came to making his own movies, had coincidentally worked with Frank Oz on *The Muppets* and *The Dark Crystal*, and more controversially had been behind Frankie Goes to Hollywood's video for *Relax*, which was banned in the UK.

I was appearing alongside Kiefer Sutherland, whose star was most definitely in the ascendency following the success of *The Lost Boys* and *Young Guns*.

My character, Betty Jones, was born in 1926 and at the age of 13 she ran away from home and was eventually sent to an approved school because she was considered beyond parental control. Kiefer's character enlisted after the attack at Pearl Harbour but described himself as an officer and a Chicago gangster, both of which were false. He was in fact a private. The friendship only lasted six days. During that time they knocked over a nurse cycling along a country lane. They robbed her, knocked her unconscious with an iron bar and threw her into a river to drown, though she survived. Finally they murdered a taxi driver named George Edward Heath and robbed him of £8.

Betty then announced she wanted a fur coat. Hulten attacked a woman in the street and tried to snatch her coat. The police came and Hulten only managed to escape in a stolen car.

He was eventually caught. In the meantime Betty had gone to the police and admitted the crimes to ease her conscience. During the trial they implicated each other and were both sentenced to be hanged. Hulten was executed in Pentonville prison on March 8, 1945. Jones was reprieved and released in May 1954. Her subsequent fate is unknown.

In the film she was a stripper with a deluded fantasy worldview formed by watching a steady stream of Hollywood film noir movies and gangster pictures.

My Dad warned me off it. 'She sounds like a psychotic whore,' he said.

But I was fascinated by Betty's character from the moment I read the script and I was excited about the prospect of making a movie in England again. Filming would take place in London and at Pinewood Studios and the film company rented me an apartment in Kensington for the duration. After a year of living out of a suitcase and the previous months trying to settle in Los Angeles I was pleased to be coming home.

I had no idea that the torment I thought I'd been able to suppress from the moment I embarked on my movie career was about to engulf me.

CHAPTER
ELEVEN

*My next memory was waking up in hospital, the tube down
my throat and the nurses calling: 'Emily, Emily.'*

One of the most frustrating aspects of my malaise, or mental illness, call it what you will, is an inability to accurately recall sequences of events at important times in my life. A combination of medication, lack of sleep and perhaps a self-defence mechanism resulting from the traumas I suffered as a young child make it hard, looking back, to piece together the key causes and effects that led me to a certain course of action.

I offer this as a way of explaining why, when it comes to describing the moment I came to stare at a bottle of pills prescribed to combat depression, I can't quite remember what led me to think it would be a good idea to take the lot.

As is the way with most people who consider taking their own life, it's never the result of one thing. More often, it is a culmination of events, a gathering storm that eventually erupts with devastating consequences.

So it was with me.

In the summer of 1989, just short of my 19th birthday in September, I suffered a breakdown, minor only in that in the subsequent years it would be overshadowed by far more serious events. To the outside world I may have appeared like a girl with everything to live for – a Hollywood career, a jet-set lifestyle, invitations to premieres and parties. In my world, however, I felt burdened with expectation and a victim of circumstance.

It is impossible to know exactly why, when I was 18, I felt an overwhelming need to finally confront what had happened to me when I was five. All I know is that it felt like my mind was a pressure cooker and I had to release some of the stress or it would explode.

A major factor was also my increasing awareness of my sexuality. Since adolescence I'd had my share of innocent fumblings but, as I grew older, it felt like an unstoppable force threatening to overwhelm me. The more I worried about it the more it awakened dreadful memories I had suppressed since I was five.

How could I feel comfortable after what I'd experienced as a child?

How could something that was supposed to be pleasurable come from something that had caused me such pain?

The voices struggling against each other in my head prevented me from falling in love and all that goes with it, which most people take for granted.

Add to this turmoil my feelings of self-doubt and flagging confidence, my isolation in New York and the pressure to succeed in Hollywood and it was a lethal cocktail of emotions.

I returned to London that summer in preparation for *Chicago Joe and the Showgirl*. The film company had agreed to rent a flat for me for the duration of the shoot, but my Mum's boyfriend at the time, John, had a friend who was looking for someone to take a short lease of his flat in Knightsbridge and it seemed an ideal solution. Although

I was living on my own, being in close proximity to my friends and family brought me solace, at least in the short term.

In addition to spending time with them I also hung out at the house of my Mum's best friend Malcolm. He was gay, older than me and was more of a cool uncle to me than a friend of the family. His flat in north London was frequently a location for dinner parties with myriad interesting guests but, even when he wasn't entertaining, his was an open door and I could pop round whenever I wanted. Malcolm was Johnny's partner and the two made a fun couple.

You don't suddenly decide one day to confide in someone that you were the victim of sexual abuse at a very young age, but my growing unease made it increasingly likely. The more time I spent at Malcolm's the more reassured I felt that he might be the person to whom I could unburden myself. I trusted him.

I can't remember the exact circumstances, nor can I remember how I broached the subject but I can recall the relief when I finally articulated the words, releasing my feelings into the open. Malcolm was understandably horrified, instantly sympathetic and completely devastated on my behalf. It's a lot for someone to take in. From what I can remember he urged me to confide in my Mum, but I explained that was something I still found hard to do after all that time. He offered to speak to her for me. From memory, I'm not sure if I gave him explicit consent, but I might have indicated that he could do whatever he thought best. In any event, he told my Mum.

For a mother to learn that her child has been the victim of abuse must be among the most traumatic things a parent can be told. For her then to realise that she has unwittingly invited the perpetrator into her own house must be even more horrific. Again, my memories are foggy of the day my mother came to me, her emotions in turmoil after Malcolm's revelations, but what remains crystal clear is how upsetting it was to see her so distressed. It was decided we should also inform Charlotte – she was then 13 – but I was keen that no one else knew. Although I had spoken about it I remained intensely troubled and reluctant for it to become something discussed by the wider family. Also I was desperately keen that word of it did not leak out to the press.

My relief was short-lived. Mum and Charlotte's anguish brought a new emotion – guilt. I know it was irrational but I couldn't help but feel responsible for their pain. A problem shared might be a problem halved, but if the problem takes on new dimensions it doesn't feel that way. I tormented myself for inflicting pain on my family and chastised my own weakness for not being able to deal with my traumas on my own. I'd chosen to stay silent to protect Charlotte and my Mum. Now it seemed I had failed.

I felt worthless, as if nothing I did was right. Clearly I had good cause to feel upset, but when you are in the grip of a malaise it is impossible to be rational. I can vaguely remember going to my GP and complaining of a general unease. As I had done with the psychiatrist 10 years earlier, I avoided telling him the truth. Nevertheless, the symptoms I described were enough for him to conclude I was suffering from depression. These were the days before Prozac became a household name and the condition wasn't as accepted as it is today. He prescribed me anti-depressants, which he said would help stabilise my moods, but it was with a heavy sense of foreboding that I began shooting *Chicago Joe*.

My Dad's warning about the film turned out to be prophetic. Betty Jones, or Georgina as she changed her name to in the film, was a character unlike any other I had portrayed.

In preparation for the role the director Bernard Rose asked me to analyse her character by writing down as many personality traits for her as I could imagine.

Focusing solely on how to develop her for the movie, I discovered the more violent the crimes got the more excited she became. She was the manipulative one, the instigator, pushing her lover Karl Hulten on. As I did with every role, I tried to inhabit the character and think like she thought. I imagined what motivated her. She was obsessed with noir films and seemed to have blood lust, so I suggested to the director that after committing the murder she touched the blood and smelled it to illustrate her pleasure. He liked it and agreed. She was at odds with Hollywood's traditional attitude to female characters. Normally in films, even when the women are evil, they're given traits that make you like them despite their circumstances. Betty had no such attributes. She was psychotic and I didn't want the movie to flinch from showing that. A feel-good film this was not.

Kiefer Sutherland might have been one of the hottest actors, but when the filming started he was in the process of splitting from his wife Camelia Kath, the mother of his daughter Sarah. It would later emerge that when he had been filming *Flatliners* he had grown close to his co-star Julia Roberts. Their subsequent engagement would end with her jilting him three days before their wedding. He clearly had a lot on his mind, which might have explained his detached and preoccupied demeanour on set. Maybe it was just me but he seemed more engaged with Patsy Kensit, who played his other love interest, which accentuated my feeling of isolation.

Whatever the reason, he was aloof with me. Before shooting a scene he would come up and present me with notes on how he felt it should be done. It is healthy for actors to have some input to the roles they play, but his manner made him appear controlling.

Keith Allen played Kiefer's mate in the film but towards me he displayed little charm and offered no pleasantries, which hurt me. From the outset I could sense this was going to be a very different experience to my previous British movie.

Filming was on location in London and at Pinewood Studios in Buckinghamshire. Practically the only highlight was when I had a rare break and popped into another studio where an actor friend Jeff Fahey was filming *White Hunter, Black Heart*, starring and directed by Clint Eastwood. I sat there silently off camera while Clint was reciting his lines. He snagged on one where he had to say, 'I'm going to Africa…' As he stammered '…with, with…' trying to remember the name, he turned to me and said… 'with Emily'. We hadn't been introduced but clearly he knew who I was. In my already mesmerising movie career it was another defining moment.

The pleasure was fleeting. On my own set, the pace was demanding, the scenes relentless. One of the key set-pieces in the movie was in a dancehall where the whole room is jiving to the jitterbug. I rehearsed the scene with a group of professional dancers that specialised in the 1940s jitterbug style and gave me a sense of the rhythm and frenetic energy that was needed.

When it came to filming the scene the music was frantic, almost tribal in its hypnotic intensity. Somehow I managed to learn the steps. I had good teachers but perhaps the basic ballet training I had when I was younger helped me. Whatever it was I needed it.

For eight punishing hours we danced and danced. If I wasn't the main focus of the shot I had to dance so the cameras could pan to capture other dancers.

My character was on the edge and as the day wore on I could feel myself joining her. I wanted to give my all but after eight hours my feet – crammed into high heels – were bleeding.

My memories are blurry but after that scene was finally completed I went home and sat alone in the flat staring vacantly into space. This wasn't living.

I tried to articulate my despair in poetry. Among the verse I wrote at the time was this:

I breathe, I see, I learn, I live
I give, I give, I give
I bask in the sunlight and laugh in the rain
I play music and others sing
A melody who knows what will bring
A magpie looks searching for a crowned king
I feel the leeches embedded in my mind
I beg them to try and be kind
This web of despair
Devoid of care
I'm just not there
I try to refrain, there seems no gain
From this unending pain
I want to love again to feel to need
Maybe even to achieve
I try to eliminate the maggots in my brain
And realise I'm not insane

What was supposed to be a return to reality by coming back to Britain had turned out to be anything but. Heartache and pain seemed to be everywhere. There was no respite.

I must have stared at the bottle of pills and, as I contemplated everything spinning around in my head, something must have snapped.

I can remember staggering out into the street in Kensington, having downed however many tablets I had left. My actions must have scared me because when a stranger approached me I blurted out what I'd done and asked him to help me. My next recollection is John, my mother's partner, arriving, and carrying me to the Chelsea and Westminster hospital. According to my mother they had been on their way to my flat and were alerted to the drama by John's friend who owned the property.

My next memory was waking up in hospital, the tube down my throat and the nurses calling: 'Emily, Emily.'

What happened next is the episode I recounted at the beginning of the book. I later learned that when he heard I was in hospital the director stopped the shoot but only momentarily. His response was: 'Get her back on set.'

He needn't have worried. I was back the following day. My agents, Ilene and Nicole, came over from Los Angeles. I'm sure my wellbeing was their motivation for travelling but they were in the process of splitting up and each wanted to ensure they could count on my signature when Triad's future was settled. I'm convinced they were also making sure I fulfilled my obligations but there was never any question about whether I'd finish the shoot. Quitting wasn't an option.

There was little to like about the film. The characters were seedy, their actions deplorable and there was no warmth from the production. When word leaked about some of the racier scenes, the *Sun* reacted in mock outrage at 'Lloyd's Lust', claiming there was an outcry over *Chicago Joe*. It claimed some of the movie – which was to receive an 18 certificate – was soft porn. This was because Betty pushed Hulten against a wall and performed a sex act and because of my suggestion that she sniffed the blood of the murder victim to get turned on.

I struggled to the end of the shoot and when filming finished I collapsed, exhausted.

My overdose had been a cry for help. What I needed was some rest and a break from emotional turmoil. I had no idea what was waiting round the corner.

CHAPTER
TWELVE

*Sometimes I yearned for someone to have a gun so I could put it
to my head and pull the trigger. I didn't want to die. I just wanted
to end the pain inside my head, kill the person inside there
that was making my life misery.*

After the ordeal of *Chicago Joe* I moved in to my father's house in
Kentish Town, London, while my manager found me a new
place in Los Angeles. Living with Dad was an education for
me and an eye-opener for him. It was an opportunity to spend
time getting to know his second wife Jehane and their three
sons, Spencer, Hartley and Louis. I think he was shocked at
how undomesticated I was. Whenever I returned to Mum's
she fussed over me and never let me lift a finger regarding the
cooking or household chores. At my Dad's, I was expected to
learn how to operate the washing machine. I broke it twice in my
first month. I attempted to master the ironing but it seemed so
difficult I left it.

At the time I was friendly with Uma Thurman and had spent time
with her in Paris while she filmed *Henry and June*, Philip Kaufman's

adaptation of Anais Nin's novel. After shooting concluded, she visited me at Dad's house, much to his delight!

From a career perspective, I was still recovering from the ordeal of my last shoot. I was therefore grateful for some positive news and it came in the shape of reviews for *In Country*. The movie received its American release shortly after filming finished on *Chicago Joe* and by January 1990 was in cinemas in the UK. It garnered favourable reviews, particularly for the performances. Bruce Willis was commended for his portrayal of a Vietnam veteran while *The Guardian* praised me for 'the most complete thing she has done on the screen'.

Meanwhile *The Times* said: 'The film has Emily Lloyd whose sparkly vitality dominates the action. She has a quality of coming alive on screen and of convincing us that she is impelled by real thoughts and feelings. Even given the number of accomplished young actresses available in Hollywood it is easy to see why Jewison would cast this remarkable young English personality in a role which demands such varied reaction to the mysteries of adults and their history.'

The kind words were a much-needed boost to my fragile self-esteem. Shortly afterwards I had my first royal premiere in the presence of Her Majesty the Queen – not for *In Country*, I should add, but Steven Spielberg's latest film *Always*. As the film's stars Richard Dreyfuss, Audrey Hepburn and Holly Hunter were too busy to attend, Nigel Havers and I were asked to stand in to spare the company's blushes. I wasn't sure what you wear to meet the Queen but plumped for a gold shawl over a dress with matching gold boots. I was so nervous about what to say that I completely forgot how to present myself and probably broke royal protocol by standing, with my arms folded as Her Majesty came along the line. The Queen had a glazed look on her face as if she wanted to be anywhere else, but Prince Philip was much more lively, flirtatious even.

Pictures of me smiling nervously made the newspapers. Not for the first time I used work as a crutch to lean on and to help convince the outside world everything was normal.

I travelled back to Los Angeles where Nicole said she had scripts waiting for me to read. My manager had found me a house in Benedict Canyon. It was much larger than the place I'd been sharing with Gaby. This had four bedrooms and I had roommates for company, each displaying varying degrees of eccentricity. An older man called Jason had no concept of boundaries and thought nothing of going through my underwear drawer, although for what he wasn't entirely clear. He kept a tarantula in a jar. I felt sorry for the spider. Then a girl who claimed to be a 'B' movie star moved in. I doubted many of her scripts would have been more bizarre than the real-life drama being played out in the house.

Dutifully I thumbed the scripts Nicole sent over. A part she thought might work for me was in a Christian Slater movie called *Mobsters,* loosely based on the life of Mafia's *capo di tutti capi*, or boss of all bosses, Charles 'Lucky' Luciano. I knew Christian from the times I'd hung out with other young actors like Eric Stoltz. The project looked exciting. I had to audition, which by that time should have held little fear for me, had I been in a calmer frame of mind.

I was unsettled by a request from my agent to meet with a manager they recommended. I didn't see the need for yet more representation (for a start it meant another 15 per cent) but she was insistent. The would-be manager took me shopping and chose a $3,000 dress for me to wear for the audition. I felt I was being pushed in a certain direction – another part of my individuality being eroded.

In the run up to that screen test the voices in my head returned, compelling me to look up and stare at the sun. In LA, that's not an easy thing to do. The sun is blinding at the best of times but when you feel you can't take your eye off that burning star for a second it's terrifying.

By the time I went inside for the audition my eyes were so dazzled I couldn't even see the writing on the script.

The compulsion passed in a day or so but my chance had gone. So had the would-be manager.

I was fortunate though that at that stage in my career I was still in demand. I had the luxury of several scripts and opportunities.

Invitations to star-studded events were commonplace. One invitation I received was to a Warner Brothers event paying homage to the movie studio. Assuming I had been invited to make up the numbers, I rocked up wearing black cut-off jeans, a scruffy black top and matching black trainers. I mingled with actors I knew and enjoyed the festivities while someone started making an announcement.

Meryl Streep's name was called out and she arrived on stage looking every inch the screen legend she is in a glamorous evening gown. Then Harrison Ford was announced, then Jack Nicholson and both leading men joined Meryl on stage to huge applause. Then, without warning and to my utter dismay, the announcer proclaimed: 'Emily Lloyd.'

They were all impeccably dressed in black tie (I obviously hadn't read the invitation). I looked like a cross between a chimney sweep and a beach bum. I was thrilled I was included with these illustrious names. How could I be expected to join these immaculately turned out superstars on stage? It was only then I realised my *In Country* appearance qualified me to appear alongside these greats. Sheepishly I took to the stage and tried to skulk at the back. Mercifully, more names were called out and I managed to hide behind Matthew Modine.

Among the manuscripts I received, one appealed to me. American theatre director David Beaird was adapting a play he'd written in 1985 called *Scorchers*, an ensemble drama set in Louisiana. Originally his idea was to tell three interweaving stories but narrowed it to two.

I immediately warmed to the script and responded to the dialogue and the sensitivity of the piece. It was set in the French quarter. My character Splendid was, as they say in the South, a 'scorcher', a sexually passionate young Cajun belle but she was scared to death of losing her virginity on her wedding night. She went to great measures to try and get away without having sex with her new husband. Her hang-up was because her mother died in childbirth and she associated sex with death.

He had no one attached and needed a name on board to raise financial backing for the film. I found it flattering that I was considered a name that could get pictures made.

Having played three precocious teenagers and a showgirl involved in murder, I was taken by Splendid's vulnerability. She was the only character I'd played that was so scared of sex. It was endearing because then so many young girls were depicted as sexually confident. I found her awkwardness appealing.

Once I signed up for the project David persuaded Faye Dunaway, Denholm Eilliot and James Earl Jones to appear and Leland Crooke reprised the role of Splendid's father that he had performed on stage. Jennifer Tilly and James Wilder were also signed up.

The budget was below $5 million so we were all asked to work for less than our usual salaries. That didn't concern me. I'd been lucky enough to have been well paid for *Cookie* and *In Country* and I liked the challenge of working on a production with a smaller budget. David struck me as very much an actor's director. After I'd expressed an interest we met to discuss the part and I felt he would give me a chance to do justice to the character. I hoped he would be as hands on and nurturing as David Leland was.

But for all the interest the project awoke in me I was coming to the production from a dark place. Looking back, I don't think I'd fully recovered from the exhaustion I'd felt on *Chicago Joe* and issues from my past remained unresolved. Voices continued to plague my mind, preying on my self-doubt. Constantly I heard an internal monologue. 'You don't deserve this success, this fame, you're not worthy of it'.

I hoped being back at work in different surroundings with less pressure would alleviate some of the anxiety. For a while it did.

Filming took place in the Bayou Teche, in the Mississippi Delta. The location was beautiful and entrancing and a world away from the bustle of Los Angeles. The shoot was lasting for only a month, but I arrived a couple of days before to immerse myself in the culture.

After tackling Brooklynese and a Kentucky drawl, my biggest challenge was mastering a slightly modified Louisiana Cajun for *Scorchers*. There was no budget for a dialect coach so I had to put my mimicking talents to use once more. Once I met the rest of the cast I discovered Leland had the accent down perfectly and tried to feed off him.

One of the key traits I remember picking up was pronouncing 'think' as 'tink', as in one of Splendid's lines: 'Daddy I don't tink I can do dis.'

The cast was a good ensemble – collaborative rather than competitive – but some egos were still on show.

Faye Dunaway was obviously the actor with the biggest reputation. The star of *Chinatown* and *Bonnie and Clyde* might have waived half her fee for the role but she still arrived believing normal Hollywood rules applied. She spent five hours in make-up and I think the majority of that time was spent on her lip-liner. She had demanded a specific light to enhance her features. The budget didn't stretch that far but the crew made her believe they had one to her specifications. They called it the 'Faye light' and it had to be in place whenever she was shooting a scene.

Denholm Elliott was a gent on set and I discovered he knew my grandmother through his wife.

James Wilder, a television actor who then was breaking into movies, played my on-screen husband and, ironically, given our predicament in front of the camera, we grew close off set. He was handsome, considerate and had a raging ego but it was nice to have some male attention.

Once filming got underway I found the director, David, was an eccentric and garrulous but in a nice way. He frequently wanted me to be more effusive. I spent nearly the whole film running around in my bare feet trying to escape the clutches of my husband. One of the things David did to get a reaction from me was get down on his hands and knees and suck my toes. I didn't see Faye Dunaway have to put up with that kind of close direction.

Leland, or Lee, Crooke also took a shine to me and represented a father figure on set. He insisted on buying me cuddly toys. I was used to fellow actors commenting on my childlike qualities but that was taking things too far. One of the toys I appreciated though was a cuddly alligator. It reminded me of a beautiful boat ride I took with Jennifer Tilly down the Bayou during a break in filming. The melancholic movement of the river, the sultry swamp cloaked by overhanging trees and the surreptitious alligators, slyly giving furtive glances as we glided past, will stay with me forever.

Once the shoot was over, I headed back to Los Angeles. The fleeting romance with James never blossomed into anything tangible. He would go off to find love with *Cheers* star Kirstie Alley, who was 17 years his senior.

Scorchers was a pleasurable experience, but I should have suspected by then that happiness might be just a fleeting episode in my general drama of pain.

I was in so much torment and still combating the voices that told me I was worthless.

Sometimes, when I was alone with only my thoughts for company I yearned for someone to have a gun so I could put it to my head and pull the trigger. I didn't want to die. I just wanted to end the pain inside my head, kill the person inside there that was making my life a misery.

I returned to the UK for a break after filming, vulnerable and fragile. The last thing on my mind was that I might fall in love. But fall hard I did.

CHAPTER THIRTEEN

We got chatting and Amy then revealed more to me about the
man she was keen on. Suddenly it occurred to me that it
was the same guy. It was Gavin.

When I allowed myself to dream of the moment I might fall in
love I imagined the full fairytale. My knowledge of fairy
stories by that stage should have warned me that most likely it meant
there would be a heavy dose of misery before any happy ending
materialised.

That didn't stop me wading right in, however.

I was at my Dad's one night when my friend Sacha Putnam, the
son of film producer David, arrived to take me out. He brought a
musician friend of his called Gavin Rossdale. Sacha might have had
designs on me – I don't know, he never said – but with Gavin and I
there seemed an instant connection. We hung out together and then
Gavin asked me out a couple of times on his own. Around this time
I became friends with Amy Fleetwood, the daughter of Mick, the
founder of Fleetwood Mac.

We were in the Hippodrome nightclub one night when Amy

started telling me about someone she'd met, a musician she was falling for. She never mentioned his name but I was happy she had found someone she cared about.

Meanwhile Gavin and I were growing closer. I became quite fond of him. This was in the days before he formed his band Bush. He had a group that played small clubs but he had yet to hit the big time. We were in a nightclub and he hinted he had feelings for me. Thinking Sacha might be offended, I said: 'It might be a can of worms.'

'I don't think it will be,' Gavin replied.

We had our first kiss. I could sense the fairytale beginning.

A few days later I was out with Amy and I told her I had met someone I liked. We got chatting and Amy then revealed more to me about the man she was keen on. Suddenly it occurred to me that it was the same guy. It was Gavin.

Suddenly that can of worms was turning putrid.

When I saw Gavin next I conveyed my awareness of the situation. He responded that, yes, he was involved with Amy but that the relationship was new and that he had developed strong feelings for me and didn't know what to do. Neither did I.

Amy returned to Los Angeles and had dreams of moving back to live with Gavin, who had a flat in Regent's Park. Yet he kept reiterating it was me he had feelings for.

If I had been any kind of friend I should have walked away. I hadn't known Amy that long but it's hard when your heart is telling you one thing and your head something else. Given my state of mind after my misery on *Chicago Joe* I probably wasn't best placed to make judgements on any situation.

While our 'relationship' was still in its infancy we probably had a chance to pull away before anyone got hurt. Hindsight is a wonderful thing, however. I felt a connection with Gavin, combined with my physical attraction and growing love for him, and the inevitable happened. It was the first time for me.

He announced the next morning: 'Oh, by the way, Amy is arriving from America today.'

That left me stunned.

Again, I should have extricated myself from the situation. But I was smitten. Even after Amy arrived, we continued to see each other. I'm not making excuses or condoning the fact but neither of us could help it.

I remember going with Amy to see Gavin in concert at a small venue, where there weren't that many people, and he was flirting with me from the stage. Amy was standing right next to me and I was feeling really uncomfortable thinking, 'why am I in this situation?'

We went away to Norfolk one weekend and Amy found out. It wasn't pleasant. She went to pieces and so did his grandfather's crockery. She had a right to be furious.

It's funny what you remember but I recall Gavin had a Puli dog called Winston who presided over every aspect of his life. In retrospect it was Winston who took precedence over Amy and I.

I was never his girlfriend but Gavin made it clear he wasn't going to give Amy up. I wanted to end it, to end the deceit and sneaking around.

At the same time, though, I was desperately searching for answers. I have always been interested in astrology and I was curious how well Gavin and I were suited to each other. He was a Scorpio, I was Libran. I had a reading done at a place in Covent Garden. The signs were good. I left with a healthy degree of optimism. Maybe our love affair was written in the stars.

I hadn't walked more than a few yards from the astrologer's when

I looked up and there was Gavin, walking towards me but far enough away so that he hadn't seen me. By his side, her arm linked through his, was Amy.

I felt cheated – not by Gavin or Amy, but by fate. Most people I knew seemed to enjoy being in love, for a while, at least. They were caught up in the blissfulness of new love. My first experience of love was a new form of mental torture.

Just a few months earlier I'd finally managed to release some of the pressure I'd been feeling from carrying the burden of my abuse. Now, I could barely believe the agony I was feeling. I think Gavin had an underlying conflict regarding me and Amy but he ended up hurting us both.

For a fleeting few months, the feeling of being wanted had blocked out my other pain. But then my relationship with Gavin became painful in itself. I didn't know who to turn to. I felt wrongful and wronged. I didn't want to repeat what happened on *Chicago Joe* but I could feel my mood spiralling downwards again.

My family was understandably concerned. I tried my best to reassure them it was a temporary relapse, a continuation of the stress I suffered on *Chicago Joe*.

Once again my hectic public life was completely at odds with my chaotic private life.

CHAPTER
FOURTEEN

*You had to make your own amusement because laughter was a
rarity. I used to modify songs to fit with the location. One of my
favourites was Annie Lennox's 'Walking on Broken Glass'
but changed to 'Bouncing off concrete walls'.*

The face staring back from the mirror certainly looked like me but
it didn't matter how hard I squinted I still couldn't get used to
this image.

For as long as I could remember blonde curls always framed my face.
Now they were gone. In their place thick were thick waves of black.

I was obviously used to transforming my character for a new role
but this was an altogether different performance. The black wig
was a disguise. I was in the Priory Hospital, the famous rest and
rehabilitation centre for many worn-out and washed-up celebrities,
and I was trying to escape without being noticed.

How had it come to this?

After all that happened recently I was exhausted. I desperately
needed a break. I returned to the UK to spend Christmas at my
Mum's but my energy levels had dropped drastically. I constantly felt

like I was giving blood. I realised if I didn't slow down I would make myself very ill. A friend recommended the Priory for a rest. And so in January 1991 I checked into the private clinic in Roehampton, in south west London. I would have several stays in hospitals like this and as such my recollection of the specific treatment is hazy but I'll never forget the atmosphere in there.

Some of the patients were sectioned with severe mental health issues. Although the private rooms were comfortable, it was not designed to be a holiday resort.

The patients were allowed out into the grounds and there was nothing technically stopping us from leaving but it still felt like a prison – a prison with pastel coloured walls and perfumed soap.

Mostly I appreciated the rest. Being in there meant I didn't have to rush half way around the world for an audition or a meeting. It meant respite from the constant demands I felt were being put on me.

During my time there I found refuge in reading *The Bell Jar*, Sylvia Plath's only novel. The semi-autobiographical account of Esther Greenwood's descent into depression while living in New York was something to which I could relate. I took comfort from the story that I wasn't alone in experiencing the darkness of depression and related the characters in the book to the other patients I met.

So there was Buddy, a chatty patient who was two years younger than me, with mousy brown hair, who took a real shine to me and seemed particularly fascinated with my hair. He asked to wash it on a daily basis from the moment I arrived. He was devastated when he saw me in the black wig as I was leaving. He didn't believe I was only wearing it temporarily.

Doreen was also about the same age as me. She was spindly with straight, dark hair. She was a lovely but intense young woman who repeated a sinister-sounding mantra every day: 'The devil is doubt, the devil is doubt, the devil is doubt.'

What she didn't realise is that I would probably need two week's therapy just to get the mantra out of my head. To this day I can still remember her voice.

Often you had to make your own amusement because laughter was a rarity. I used to modify songs to fit with the location. One of my favourites was Annie Lennox's *Walking on Broken Glass* but changed to 'Bouncing off concrete walls'.

My moods fluctuated dramatically. One minute I felt a brief burst of energy and was able to function, the next I was down and it took every effort to slope around in my baggy sweatshirt and tracksuit trousers.

I tried to strike up conversations with the other patients. Some were being treated for breakdowns, alcoholism, drug addiction and eating disorders.

I'd been in there for a couple of weeks when the *News of the World* got wind of it. The paper has since closed down because of its intrusion into people's lives. Even then it had no scruples about whom to victimise, even though then it didn't have the benefit of being able to intercept people's voicemail messages as it had latterly. Nowadays health matters are private affairs and someone seeking treatment would be protected from intrusive reporting. Not so in 1991. Then it was open season on anyone in the public eye. Confirmation that I was in the Priory could mean sensational headlines. People might even speculate that the reason I was in there was for drug abuse or alcohol addiction.

In fact throughout my life there's been speculation that my troubles have been down to drug addiction, but although I have dabbled in some substances over the years I've never been a slave to any of them. My difficulties have been largely down to managing the effects of the legal drugs that were prescribed to me over the years.

So from the minute the press started making inquiries, my agents and lawyers suggested my family do their best to deflect attention. They insisted I wasn't in the clinic and that it must be an imposter posing as me. The strategy was implausible but, although it seemed to scare them off, we knew it was only a matter of time before something ran. I had checked in under my own name without thinking of the repercussions.

In the meantime the torments in my mind escalated and the medication I was prescribed offered no relief. I wanted to leave there.

The doctors didn't agree. They wanted me to stay longer and said that ultimately, if I wanted to get back to work, I would have to stay for more treatment. With £2,000-a-night fees, it was hard not to think that the only reason the psychiatrists wanted me to get back to work was to pay the ever-mounting bills.

So I decided to escape.

It was Mum's idea to bring the wig. She thought it would make the perfect disguise and I had to agree. On the day I decided to leave we even heard that a photographer had been seen in the grounds. This was going to be harder than we anticipated. I decided to sneak out of the window and meet Mum in a cab outside.

When I was sorted with the wig and was about to leave I popped back into the corridor where a number of patients had gathered, surrounding Mum who, to my surprise, was handing out bottles of beer she had smuggled in.

I should have known Mum would have tried to make the best of a bizarre situation. She could always be relied on to find the fun when on the surface it didn't seem there could be any. In fairness she felt sorry for the other patients' plight and thought it would cheer them up. Never mind that she probably set any recovering alcoholic's 12-step programme back six months in the process.

'Oh Emily, don't look so serious,' Mum said. 'They all looked as though they were gasping for a drink. We're having a little soiree for you.'

Everyone looked at me expectantly, as if I was supposed to give some sort of speech. Some of them looked like they were genuinely sorry to see me go.

I tried to shake off the melancholic mood by breaking into my best Vera Lynn impression.

'We'll meet again, don't know where, don't know when…'

They seemed to appreciate my attempts to lighten the mood.

'Ok, then Mum,' I said. 'Shall we?'

I went back into the room, picked up my bag, came out and handed it to Mum.

I smiled at my little farewell committee, gave a wave and went back into my room. As I closed the door I saw Mum giving theatrical waves to them and even after I'd shut the door of my room I could hear her warm laughter echoing along the corridor. It's a good job that discretion wasn't important on this secret undercover mission.

I checked in the small en-suite that I had everything and made sure there weren't any little toiletries I could take as a memory. Then I climbed onto the window ledge and jumped down to the shrubs below.

It was only then that I realised that nothing was more likely to raise suspicion than someone climbing out of a window, black wig or no black wig. If a photographer had been snooping around in the bushes I would have been discovered for sure.

As it was I managed to get to the front of the building undetected. Mum was waiting for me in a mini cab.

We'd made it. We managed to leave the Priory without any confirmation that I'd been there. Mission accomplished. My only problem was that the health difficulties that had taken me there were still not resolved.

Alone with my anxieties, with no work to focus my mind I only had dark thoughts for company. The wig was long gone but it seemed that my head was enveloped in a black veil. The experience with Gavin had affected me more deeply than I had first realised. That, coupled with the repercussions of finally disclosing details about the abuse, made me feel worthless.

I couldn't work out why I felt this way. Speaking about the trauma of my childhood was supposed to make me feel better about myself. I felt that was always the issue stopping me from enjoying intimacy and falling in love. Then, to have waited for so long for the love of a man and to then be rejected was almost worse. I wished I could go back to the way things were. Now I was living with the worry and guilt of encumbering my family because of the decline in my mental health. I was also feeling that, regarding Amy, I had broken my principles.

Gavin had been in touch before I went into the Priory to check on my wellbeing. After I came out we met up again. I knew it was wrong but it was impossible to put my feelings to one side and it seemed he felt the same way.

One evening while I was waiting for Gavin at his flat a desperate state of despair overwhelmed me. I can't say now if I genuinely had suicidal thoughts but, in the death-throes of our short-lived and never-to-be relationship I searched the bathroom cabinet and found razor blades and aspirin.

After taking the tablets I slashed my wrists and arms. I don't know where the specific idea came from. Does anyone who self-harms? I had once fallen in New York and cut my arms on broken glass so severely I had stitches but it wasn't like I was overcome with some morbid fascination with blood. I wasn't trying to slit my wrists. I think I just wanted some form of release from the misery and to have some control over the pain I felt. Control, though, was the last thing I had.

If the last occasion had been a cry for help this was a scream.

The last memory I had was watching the colour red seeping forth and a sense of relief.

It was Gavin's friend that found me. My family found a private clinic where I could be assessed. The Charter Nightingale hospital in London would be my home for the next six weeks. In there psychiatrist after psychiatrist probed me with their constant questioning. They gave me medication to calm me, help me sleep and control my moods.

I'm sure they were trying to help but I felt like I was being experimented on. Maybe I didn't help matters but I was reluctant to go into the reasons behind my self-harming. I needed to feel trust before I could communicate and for the most part in there I didn't. The only specialist I connected with was a psychiatrist called Nadia. She seemed particularly considerate but I was still reluctant to divulge too much.

Not wishing to make the same mistake as I had with the Priory, I was admitted under the false name Jessica Blue and in all spent six weeks in a first floor room. No chance of jumping out of that window.

I took part in therapy sessions with names like Feelings and Problems. I was upset and bemused when I was included in an addictions group because I didn't feel like I belonged there. However I did find that talking with other patients made me realise that everyone has their traumas and dilemmas in life, whether you work in a shoe shop or star in movies.

A doctor encouraged me to keep a diary of thoughts and offered me sleeping tablets to help me rest at night. But, compared to the Charter clinic, the Priory now seemed like a five-star resort. My increasingly darkened mood might have been a major contributing factor but I did not enjoy my time in there. Towards the end of my stay I was allowed out for shopping trips with other patients but on one occasion I was so desperate for some sort of release from the pain I asked a nurse to take me to a chemist. Surprisingly, given my state and track record, she did. I pretended to buy something else but secretly bought some razor blades and smuggled them back in with me.

Alone in a toilet, I drew the blades across my skin and the relief was instant. When the doctors found I'd been self-harming again they increased my meds. When Mum came to visit me the following day I could see the look of horror on her face. In place of the bubbly and garrulous Emily was a husk of a human being, devoid of emotion.

Mum has since said it was as if I'd been lobotomised, I was so morose and uncommunicative. The only words I managed to say were: 'Get me out of here.'

She spoke to the doctor in charge and impressed upon him the importance of getting me somewhere more conducive to my condition. That conversation I do recall. Mum was wearing a rather eye-catching skirt and the doctor took quite a shine to her.

He seemed to be more interested in her legs than finding me the right hospital.

I was keen to get back to the United States where I was convinced there would be a better place for me. The doctor recommended one in Arizona. It sounded perfect. I could go there for treatment and then, if my health improved, return to Los Angeles where hopefully I could return to work.

Mum took the details for the clinic and arranged for me to have a consultation. Part of the conditions for my discharge was to arrange to visit the place we had been recommended, plus it was agreed that I could keep in touch with Nadia, the psychiatrist I liked.

As soon as I left Charter my mood seemed to improve. Maybe the bleak reality of that clinic had shaken me out of my black depression or the idea that I was going somewhere that might get to the bottom of my malaise but, whatever it was, by the time Mum and I set off, I felt better.

We flew to Arizona and seemed to be travelling for days before we found the right place. But as soon as we arrived we felt there had been some mistake. The hospital was dark and foreboding, more like a high security prison than a hospital. It rose out of the dust like a desert Alcatraz. I could only imagine what went on inside. We walked around the grounds but I was too nervous to go in. Mum stood expectantly outside waiting for me to make a decision.

'I can't do this,' I said. 'Whatever's wrong with me, I'm not ready for this.'

We went back to our hotel but before we packed our bags for LA we inquired with the clinic in London whether there was anywhere else we could try while we were in Arizona, in case they'd made a mistake with the hospital they recommended. They suggested a second clinic, which we visited. I waited outside while Mum went inside to ask if they treated people with my symptoms. They asked her if I'd ever had suicidal tendencies. Mum told them about the self-harming. They refused to take me.

'They won't take you, darling, because of your self-harm history,' Mum said.

'Where now?' she asked.

'I don't know,' I replied. 'How about the Chateau Marmont?'

Mum looked at me as though I'd named another private clinic. In a way I had. The Marmont was an historic hotel on Sunset Boulevard beloved over the years by some of Hollywood's greatest talents – generally during their most troubled days. Jim Morrison of the Doors nearly died there trying to climb into a window and Elizabeth Taylor chose the hotel for Montgomery Cliff's recuperation after he was badly hurt in a near-fatal car accident. It was also the place where actor John Belushi died of a drug overdose in 1980.

I didn't have a home in Los Angeles at the time because I'd given up the house in Benedict Canyon before I'd returned to the UK, so the hotel seemed as good a place as any. As soon as we checked in the hotel's opulent surroundings seemed to lift my spirits. I felt calmer and able to reconnect with the girl who four years earlier had arrived there with big dreams.

After a week, Nicole came to visit me to find out if I was well enough to work again. I told her I was. She sent over a script for a movie Robert Redford was directing based on Norman Maclean's novel *A River Runs Through It*. Set in 1920s Montana, during prohibition, it told the story of two brothers growing up, their love of fly fishing and how their lives changed when they went off to seek their fortunes. The part Nicole thought might have suited me was that of the love interest of one of the brothers. It was a cameo role but I felt it was perfect. There was no pressure on me to carry the movie and a smaller part could ease me back into filmmaking after my recent problems.

With Mum's help, I went shopping on Rodeo Drive and picked out a blue chiffon dress and straw boater for the audition. The thought of meeting Robert Redford sparked nerves I hadn't felt since I'd auditioned for David Leland at 15. He had seamlessly made the transition from actor to director, winning an Oscar for his first movie behind the camera, *Ordinary People*.

I needn't have been nervous. Redford, or Bob as he asked me to call him, was the most charming, divine person you could hope to meet. He talked to me about the movie choices I'd made and seemed genuinely concerned that I made the rights ones in the future. Two days after meeting him I got the part.

Filming was to begin in the idyllic setting of Missoula, Montana, in June, in two months' time. I dared to dream that this could be a chance for me to put my troubles behind me and pick up my career where it had left off.

CHAPTER
FIFTEEN

When Coppola took a shine to my pronounced canine teeth I thought
I was in with a chance. 'Nice fangs,' he said. Unfortunately it
wasn't a part I could get my teeth into.

'I'm tellin' ya. I've asked you out two times.'

'Believe me,' I said, looking into the ridiculously handsome actor's piercing blue eyes. 'If you'd asked me out I'm sure I would have remembered it.'

So began one of my earliest introductions to Brad Pitt on the set of *A River Runs Through It*. He took great delight in telling me I'd spurned his advances, not once but twice!

Although I denied it I could remember one time he expressed an interest. Years earlier George Michael had thrown a party at his house in London. While I was there Sinitta told me an actor called Brad Pitt was desperate to meet me. When I heard the name Brad I imagined some cowboy type guy and assumed the next few hours would be lost as he droned about ranches and horses. Charlotte was with me. She was crying and wanted to go home. She didn't feel well and was stressed about exams – as usual! I went home without speaking to him. About a week later I watched *Thelma and Louise* for the first time and there was the same Brad Pitt in all his glory with his top off. Charlotte was appalled I could be so careless. Hmm... who made me leave?

I kicked myself for weeks as I'd let one of the hottest men on the planet slip through my fingers. He insisted I'd also rejected him at another party later on. Brad also never missed an opportunity to tell me how much he was into his current love Juliette Lewis. He'd bought her a Palomino horse, he told me. How wonderful for her, I thought.

Aside from his playful digs, Brad was charming on set. With his distinctive features and soft blond hair, he was a dead ringer for a younger Robert Redford and, just like the screen legend, he had the capacity to be warm and friendly but dedicated and intense when the cameras were rolling.

A lot of factors made working on *A River Runs Through It* an enjoyable experience – and a complete contrast to the nightmare I'd suffered on *Chicago Joe*. At one point in the build-up to filming, however, it seemed I might never make it to Montana.

Redford had not been aware of my malaise when I auditioned for the part of Jessie Burns. I felt confident enough in myself to read well for the part, sounding convincing with my accent and my ability to accurately portray a 1920s Montana girl.

With filming about to start in a few weeks, I moved out of the Chateau Marmont and into a house in Venice Beach. I always loved the vibe down there, while close enough to the action it also felt a world away from the shallowness of Hollywood. I had a house that backed onto a canal, just a stone's throw from the beach. It had a beautiful stained glass window and a wooden patio with an outdoor Jacuzzi where I could sit and watch the ducks swim past in the morning. I could walk to the shops and restaurants and there was a tangible sense of community.

I started hanging out with some new friends and for the first time in a long time felt a creativity growing in me again. Gwyneth Paltrow, then a relatively unknown actress, became a close friend. She would come over and we would sit up writing poems together and sharing stories. I began seeing a surfer called Sacha, who was quite a character. He was American and used to wear a trilby hat everywhere. With his friend Adam, they modelled themselves on the Rat Pack and used to crack us up with their imitations of Captain Kirk. Actually before I started seeing Sacha, it looked like I might end up with Adam. After he got together with Gwyneth he confessed to me: 'There was a moment when I wanted to kiss you and then Gwyneth walked into the room.'

My old friend Johnny, Malcolm's boyfriend who had been my assistant on *In Country*, came out to stay with me. My Mum had gone back by this time but my Aunt and my cousin Ben, who was now 13, were staying in Los Angeles too. I wish I could identify the trigger that set me off again. But that's one of the many frustrations with a mental illness. You don't know when or how it is going to cripple you.

Something was festering inside me. The voices in my head were rampant and something from my past haunted me. Whatever it was, I felt the urge to self-harm again. In the absence of razors, I reached for a knife in the kitchen.

Soon after Johnny returned to the house. The sight of me with a knife, with blood coming out of my arm, understandably freaked him out. He, perhaps too hastily, called the police. He also called my business manager Marco.

Fearing a very public incident, I was jolted out of my state of mind and tried to reassure everyone I was okay. Marco insisted on taking me to a hospital. I steadfastly refused. Faced with an unpleasant interview with LA's finest, who were on their way, or a stay in hospital, I had no choice but to opt for the latter.

On the way there, however, I had an urge to take control of the situation and, as Marco slowed at some lights, I jumped out of the car. He went berserk, stopped the car and chased me. These days the incident would probably appear on Hollywood's version of *Police! Camera! Action!* Thankfully people then didn't walk around with phones, let alone ones with video cameras attached.

As Marco pushed me back into the car, he hissed: 'You fucking con artist.'

I didn't know what to say. I was clinically depressed, I see that now, but at the time I was battling against it and trying to convince people I was fine. I desperately needed help but sometimes the people who need it most are the last ones to ask.

Marco took me to the UCLA hospital in Beverly Hills where I was admitted. In America the universities are massive, industrial-sized corporations, with their own sports teams, science labs and, in the case of UCLA, a hospital with a psychiatric ward, where I was now housed.

It was like entering a prison where the wardens, instead of brute force, used Valium and psychological assessment to rule over inmates. When the police called at the house they were unhappy that I'd left but caught up with me at the hospital. By the time my Aunt and Ben arrived to visit me there was a police guard outside the hospital door. It was completely over the top. And, because the police had been involved, legally I was sectioned while doctors analysed me. I was cursing the seriousness of it all, but maybe on a deeper level it was another cry for help.

A warden accompanied Ben and Janice into my room. To everyone I appeared dazed and confused. My Aunt was able to convince the warden to leave us in peace. As soon as we were alone, I sparked into life and demanded they help me escape.

I was allowed to walk them to the gates – wearing sunglasses the nurses had provided to prevent me from hurting my eyes by staring into the sun. I watched them leave, not knowing when I'd be able to taste freedom myself.

At some point during this period I was prescribed Prozac, a trade name for the anti-depressant fluoxetine. The treatment of depression seemed, in my opinion, to be more advanced in the US than back home and doctors appeared to recognise the symptoms more readily. I'm not sure if I began taking Prozac directly as a result of that self-harm incident, but at that time I was grateful for anything that might calm the gremlins in my head. The drug had only been approved for use in 1987 but in two years had the reputation of a wonder drug worth $350 million a year. Only in later years would controversy rage that it was addictive and linked to violence. I knew nothing of those claims. All I knew was that it boasted a track record of achieving results, at least in the short term.

When I was in the grip of my malaise I seemed to regress without warning, but in the same way was able to mask it just as swiftly. This was one of those times. Once I had been assessed for a couple of days I made it clear I was much improved, not suicidal and I needed to be discharged. I didn't want anything to harm my chances of doing the film, which was about to start shooting in just a few weeks. I rang my Mum from a payphone in the ward and explained the situation. She had been distraught after hearing a report from her sister of the situation but was reassured when I rang insisting I felt strong enough to work.

Despite my appeals, for four days I was assessed in the hospital but eventually was able to call Nicole and ask for her help in getting me out. I raised the subject of slipping out with a wig on. Well, it had worked before. Nicole duly arrived with a change of clothes and a dark wig. We left unnoticed and drove away in Nicole's car. I got back to the house but realised it might not be safe so stayed away until I could be sure the coast was clear. As I expected two khaki-uniformed officers called at the house looking for me. They were not LAPD, but UCLA police. They were looking for a Miss Lloyd who had violated her patient rights. It seemed more like a Stalinist regime than the United States.

Eventually they left and I felt it was safe to return to the house.

Legally, if you have been sectioned for even one night, you have to notify an employer, so I felt I had no option but to let Robert and the film company know what had happened. Filming had already started near Missoula in western Montana by the time I was due to arrive.

When I got there the first thing I did was report to Robert's office. I feared a repeat of my hasty exit from *Mermaids* but I had no option but to tell him.

'I just want to let you know. I've been in hospital, I was sectioned for one night, but I'm fine now,' I said softly, steeling myself for the response.

He looked at me.

'That's ok,' he said. 'Thanks for letting me know.'

That was it. No tantrums. No recriminations. After that Redford and the company could not have been more supportive. They asked me if I wanted someone with me on set and I called Nadia, the psychiatrist I'd bonded with in London. She flew out and it was comforting to know she was there but it was amusing too. She seemed to be more of a white witch than a conventional psychiatrist, with unorthodox methods and a sackful of issues of her own. She also appeared to be more excited about seeing Robert Redford than she was interested in my well-being.

When it came to acting I somehow managed to overcome whatever the symptoms were. I used the truth of the character to propel me to play the part. Portraying Jessie allowed me to forget, momentarily, about my own pain.

Maclean's acclaimed book was a semi-autobiographical, lyrical love story about fly-fishing, religion, a stoic preacher and his two sons. One is handsome, self-destructive and doomed to a life of whisky and women (Paul played by Brad Pitt). The other brother Norman, loosely based on Maclean, is sober, sensible and academic (played by Craig Sheffer).

On set, I bonded with Stephen Shellen who played my on-screen brother and Elizabeth Leustig, the casting director. I knew Craig Sheffer – or Sheff as he was nicknamed – because he had been in a relationship with Gaby Anwar back in London when they were both filming there. Sheff was playing the book's author and fiancé to my character Jessie.

One of the most challenging tasks I had was driving a 1920s car over a bridge for one of the scenes. I had learned to drive a year or so earlier in Los Angeles but always questioned my suitability as a driver – especially after the instructor agreed to pass me in return for a signed photograph!

I didn't drive that often in LA but had bought myself a gold Audi convertible to run around in. But as soon as I got behind the wheel of the classic motor I began to regret being handed a short cut to my licence. It was impossible to control even before I began to think about acting. For *Cookie*, I'd been filmed driving a car but that was movie trickery and a truck with a mounted camera had towed the vehicle. This time I was all on my own.

Sacha, who had come to visit me on set for a couple of days, was watching as I approached the bridge. Part of the scene involved me turning to speak to Sheff in the car but as I moved my head my hands instinctively went the same way, pulling the wheel and the car perilously close to the edge. Sacha said he had to avert his eyes, so convinced was he that I would crash. Luckily I remembered to look in front at the vital moment and reacted quickly enough to avert disaster.

There was an element of stress as in every film but Redford seemed laid back. It was an enjoyable experience; although I was still battling my malaise the Prozac seemed to help stabilise me.

Away from the set, we had time to relax and enjoy the stunningly beautiful surroundings. Sacha and I went fly fishing, a central theme of the film, while on another occasion, Brad, Sheff, some of the rest of the cast and crew and I hired ponies and went for a long trek in the Montana countryside. We also took in a baseball game.

I managed to hold things together and produce a credible performance. When I had been on form I liked to think the bigger the challenge the better the work I produced, but in this case I was grateful for the support of the people on set. It benefited me not having to hide my problems and having a sympathetic director helped immensely. For the emotional scenes I had the ability to understand the character and tap into her sensibility.

During filming I got word from my business manager that Orion had settled over the *Mermaids* debacle. My lawyers had asked for the fee I lost, plus interest and damages. The film company agreed to pay $290,000, not the full amount we were asking, but a substantial award and one that showed I had been fully vindicated.

I was delighted. I had been worried it might have been a risky strategy and I could have been isolated. Fearing what the outcome might be hadn't helped my state of mind.

Even though it was a victory, the reaction was harsh. Agents speculated that while I'd won the battle the movie industry might win the war. The award was unprecedented. Only one star had sued the movie studios before and that was Sean Connery. Bette Davis also took on the movie moguls but people said they were big stars at the time with fearsome reputations. Despite this, I still had a lot to prove, apparently.

Back home, the headlines were negative. Rather than heralding a significant victory against the odds by a British actress in Hollywood, the newspapers lined up to speculate on what it would do to my career.

Again so-called experts were wheeled out to prophesise how I'd suffer for breaking an unwritten rule that you don't bite the hands that feeds you.

'Emily will be branded a snotty star,' one said, 'she may not get decent work for years.'

'These guys have memories like elephants,' other sources said. I felt I couldn't win. I was damned if I did and damned if I didn't.

The criticism knocked me and I feared another relapse.

I finished filming *A River Runs Through It* in August 1991. Almost immediately I was to fly out to a film festival in France to promote *Scorchers*, which was on the verge of being released. A couple of years earlier I would have been straight on the plane, the dutiful lapdog doing what everyone else wanted. This time though I knew I was in danger of draining all the positive feelings I'd had since I'd been working again. I pulled out citing exhaustion.

I returned to Los Angeles trying to remain positive about the future, but on a relationship level my life was still in a state of flux. Although I'd had fun with Sacha in Montana we both knew it wasn't going to last and we cooled things on my return.

At the back of my mind, since I'd last left the UK, I'd wondered if there was still the slightest chance of a future for Gavin and I. We had been in contact before I began filming and I had allowed him to stay at my house in Venice Beach while I was away. Any thoughts of a future, however, were dismissed after Mum informed me that she'd walked into my home to find Gavin staying there – along with three other friends, all female. They included the socialite Tamara Beckwith, then famous for her ability to grace the pages of newspapers and glossy magazines. In a manner not too dissimilar from the way Mackie used to chase children from our front step, Mum had ejected the unwelcome visitors from my house.

Any last modicum of respect between Gavin and I had been lost.

For a short time I grew close to Tim Roth, the British actor who later found fame in Quentin Tarantino's groundbreaking *Reservoir Dogs*, but who then was trying to make it in Hollywood and was also represented by Ilene. Tim had earned a reputation playing challenging parts in home-produced movies like *Made in Britain* and *The Cook, The Thief, His Wife and Her Lover* and since moving to LA had been part of what the media called The Brit Pack, a group of young stars threatening to take Hollywood by storm.

Tim was serious and intense and dedicated to progressing his career. We weren't really suited at that moment because part of me wanted to take stock while I worked out my next movie choice. Although I'd made it through my last film I was conscious of still feeling fragile.

In the immediate aftermath of the court ruling there didn't appear to be any sign of studios turning against me. At least the invitations to auditions kept coming. It felt good to be in demand, but I felt I needed to be cautious and not rush into things. I was selective in the parts to which I responded.

Francis Ford Coppola was in the process of assembling a cast for his adaptation of Bram Stoker's *Dracula*. I was summoned to a meeting with the legendary director at his office in San Francisco. To say I was nervous was an understatement. Coppola had recently completed his Godfather trilogy and was responsible for two iconic films of my childhood – *The Outsiders* and *Rumblefish*. The part he had in mind for me was that of Lucy Westenra, the friend of the object of the count's affections and a woman Dracula eventually turns into a vampire.

My mother and I travelled for four hours from Los Angeles to San Francisco. I really wasn't well and we both had reservations about whether I should meet him.

The meeting was cordial, however, and when he took a shine to my pronounced canine teeth I thought I was in with a chance.

'Nice fangs,' he said.

Unfortunately it wasn't a part I could get my teeth into – it eventually went to Sadie Frost.

Not long afterwards Nicole rang with an offer it seemed impossible to refuse – the chance to work with one of the most enigmatic filmmakers of all time. It seemed like an offer too good to be true.

CHAPTER SIXTEEN

I managed to overcome my malady on most of my films but this time
I wasn't able to. I am often frustrated that I wasn't able to give
the performance Woody Allen's direction deserved.

You might think that after working in movies for five years the audition process might get a little easier. Probably it should, but there was something about being back in Manhattan, the demands of the role I was going for – not to mention the director I was trying to impress – that set my compulsions off.

At the audition, bubbling with so much nervous energy, I couldn't stop talking. The words were gushing out of me. Eventually I paused for breath.

Then came the unmistakeable voice.

'Well, great! I feel like I know more about you than I do me.'

The offer to audition for Woody Allen's latest film was impossible to resist. So Mum kept telling me anyway.

'A wonderful opportunity to work with a uniquely talented director,' she said.

I knew she was right but at the same time I knew my own head and the wiring wasn't quite right. I was worried I wouldn't give a good account of myself. I feared the timing wasn't right. But if I passed up this opportunity would I get another?

The film was *Husbands and Wives*. I was reading for the part of Rain, a pseudo-intellectual young muse to Woody Allen's writer character Gabe, who is going through a marriage split with wife Judy, played by his real-life partner and long-time collaborator Mia Farrow.

I don't know whether I felt added pressure performing in front of a movie great like Woody or whether I was worried I might suffer another episode but I was sure I was blowing my chance. There were a lot of people there for the audition, including Farrow's adopted daughter Soon-Yi. At the time I thought nothing of the fact that she was hanging around but Mia was not.

Somehow I got through the reading and surprised myself with my performance, but I was still so flustered that when I busily said goodbye I walked into a door.

I remember going back to my hotel room afterwards. My Mum was there and I said to her: 'I can't do this. Even if I get it I'm not well enough to manage it.'

'You should do it,' she insisted. She was pushing me but I can't blame her. She believed in my acting ability and thought that working on another movie would help me focus.

I never imagined I'd get it though. Some of the hottest female talent in America was vying for it, including Gwyneth. Her mother Blythe Danner had been cast in the movie as Rain's mother so she thought she stood a good chance of appearing alongside her.

A week later I got the part.

I was elated. Woody Allen wanted me in his movie. Quickly that initial joy evaporated, however, and I began to worry whether I could do myself justice.

An internal conflict raged inside my mind. Instinct told me this opportunity had come too soon. But then, I counselled myself that anxiety can produce good art.

Shooting was to begin in New York in October. I was preoccupied with organising my birthday party. After working on *In Country* over my 18th, this was the first chance I'd had to have a proper celebration to mark my coming of age. A friend hosted the party. Mum was back in London and Charlotte was too busy to come as she was studying for her GCSEs. I'm not sure what hopes I had for the party. On the surface it looked a big success. Dozens of people came. I think Leonardo DiCaprio, who was creating a buzz in *What's Eating Gilbert Grape*, might even have been there. Everyone seemed to enjoy it – on the outside even me. Inside though I felt flat and empty. It looked like I was popular but the truth was many of the people there were hangers on who'd turn up at any bash. I wanted to be surrounded by people I cared about, not people trying to network.

Tim had joined me for the party, but we were on a different page artistically and emotionally and it was best to let it peter out before we got too involved.

With filming about to begin on *Husbands and Wives*, it was perhaps just as well I had few distractions as I travelled to Manhattan. Nadia, the psychiatrist who had accompanied me on the set of *A River Runs Through It,* arrived in New York, more on standby than anything else. I hoped her presence would reassure me but she wasn't allowed on set.

Woody Allen was enjoying a creative high point in his career when production started on his fifth movie in three years. He was hoping *Husbands and Wives* would follow the widely acclaimed *Crimes and Misdemeanours* and *Alice*, both of which had earned him

Academy Award nominations. It was also the 13th movie that he and Mia had made together.

The story centred upon two couples and their marital strife. Jack and Sally are friends with Gabe and Judy and over the course of the movie both couples split up. A sub-plot involves Gabe and a young student Rain who he strikes up a close friendship with. Woody had assembled an impressive cast. Mia would once again play Gabe's on-screen wife Judy, while Judy Davis and Sydney Pollack played Sally and Jack. Also appearing were Liam Neeson and a fellow English actress Lysette Anthony.

I relished the idea of playing the character. She was an opinionated WASP, a white Anglo-Saxon protestant, and the dialogue jumped off the page.

But when my scenes began we didn't get off to the best start. Just as we were about to begin rolling, a union guy stormed on to the set to protest that Woody Allen didn't use black actors in his films, a charge he has had to defend for years. The man was hustled away but it was unsettling and I couldn't focus properly on the script.

In one scene, Rain and Gabe are discussing *Triumph of the Will*, a Nazi propaganda movie by Leni Riefenstahl, Hitler's favourite film director. Rain had to say: '*Triumph of the Will* is a great movie but you despise the ideas behind it.'

It was a prime example of the dynamics between the characters. Rain believed herself to be an intellectual, her comments sounded profound but in effect what she was saying was really shallow.

For the first time in my career I started to have doubts I could pull this off. Normally I've relied on instinct and I've felt imbued by the character's emotions but this time I couldn't feel her inhabit me, as my anxiety and the voices in my head took over.

It didn't help that, for the scenes he didn't appear in, Woody would bark directions through a Tannoy loudspeaker system. Compared to the closeness of the direction I'd enjoyed with Leland, Jewison and Redford, this was remote and unnerving.

I spent a week filming and the longer it went on the less confident I became that I would last the distance.

Woody was on my back. He thought I spent too long on the set-ups, whereas he worked quickly and wanted scenes shot rapidly with an air of spontaneity. He also criticised me for spending too long in the trailer. What he didn't know was that I was making myself sick. I could feel dark thoughts returning and it was the only thing I could do to wrestle some control over my emotions. I knew I was on borrowed time. One morning in hair and make-up I said to the girl assisting me: 'I think I'm going to get fired.'

She said: 'Don't be silly, you look too much like Dylan.' She was referring to his adopted daughter with Mia Farrow. It was a curious response and one that did nothing to calm my fears.

As an example of my neurosis, on one occasion he introduced a banana to a scene and said: 'Eat this.'

I panicked and took it that he was adding a prop because I was inadequate in some way. Someone had warned me beforehand that Woody had a reputation for not speaking to his actors and many had found that uncomfortable but it was hard not to take it personally.

I was staying at the Paramount Hotel and when I returned one night there was a Post-it note waiting for me with a message to call my agent Nicole. The producer had rung her to say I wouldn't be needed the following day. I'd been fired.

That was it. There was no explanation, no right of appeal. I didn't even have a conversation with my agent about what happened. In some ways it was a relief. It wasn't working out, I knew that. But although I was devastated I became resigned to the situation and tried to adopt the philosophy that shit happens. I didn't want to talk to anyone, save perhaps my Mum, so I could say: 'I told you so.'

I knew it would become public knowledge very soon. It's tough when anyone loses a job but when you are fired from a Woody Allen film it becomes headlines all over the world and especially around the Hollywood village. The official reason given was that we'd parted company by 'mutual agreement' and Woody's spokesperson said the director still wanted to work with me in the future but once the news broke that I was off the set the speculation spread that it was because I couldn't master an American accent. That seemed odd given how well my accent had been received in *Cookie* and *In Country*. Nicole did her best to refute the allegations but once they're out there the damage is done.

I wasn't the first actor to be fired or replaced and I wouldn't be the last. Woody Allen had a reputation for making drastic changes to his cast, and on one occasion reshot an entire movie because he wasn't happy with the performances. But it still hurt.

Looking back now, I can see that I managed to overcome my malaise on most of my films but this time I wasn't able to. I am often frustrated that I wasn't able to give the performance Woody Allen's direction deserved.

Juliette Lewis, Brad Pitt's girlfriend, was hired to replace me. From what I've seen of the finished film she did a very good job. I understand she had her own issues to deal with. Her battles with depression are well documented, but apparently when she told Woody she had been a manic depressive, he allegedly said: 'Can we have less of the depressive and more of the manic?'

The only positive thing I could take from the time I spent in Manhattan was that I met someone who would become my boyfriend. I'd been in a hotel bar when a man introduced himself as

Bryan Kestner. I was immediately taken by how handsome he was. He was tall – it was no surprise when he revealed later that he was a basketball player – with chiselled good looks. He was close to making it as a professional but also held dreams of making it as an actor. He'd had a taste of the movie industry with small roles in Arnold Schwarzenegger's futuristic thriller *The Running Man* and he'd narrowly missed out on a part in *White Men Can't Jump*, a role that eventually went to Woody Harrelson.

He had an identical twin brother called Boyd, who was also an actor, and sometimes it was impossible to tell them apart, a fact I'm sure they used to their advantage when it suited them.

Raised in Virginia, Bryan was four years older than me and we hit it off instantly. He seemed calmer and less excitable than some of the other men I had dated.

He was keen to explore other opportunities and while we were in New York, Hollywood's finest gathered for the grand opening of Planet Hollywood, a restaurant venture fronted by Bruce Willis, Sylvester Stallone and Schwarzenegger. Bryan claimed to have had the idea for the movie-themed eaterie first and was once close to Keith Barish, the financier.

He had an apartment in Manhattan and I stayed there after *Husbands and Wives*. He offered some stability at a time when I was least expecting it. He'd also had his shares of ups and down, and when I slowly opened up to him about my health problems he was able to recommend people he knew who might be able to help. It's a feature of life in America that everyone either knows or has a therapist or shrink. People pass on numbers and recommendations and it's not unusual to have three or maybe more specialists on the go at any one time. Bryan put me in touch with a psychiatrist called Davina who had counselled a number of people in the movie business. I hadn't told Bryan everything about my past. I was not ready to be that open yet, certainly with a man, but he understood I'd battled depression and was sympathetic to the problems I'd suffered on set.

Davina charged $400 a session but I found it beneficial to have someone to talk to about my malaise. She was an eccentric. She told me she kept cats called Prozac and Valium. I told her about the black thoughts I often had. She gave me a rubber band, told me to wear it all the time and said if I ever had a bad thought I was to ping it, giving me the possibility of some very red wrists. I tried it for a bit but it didn't stop the barrage of destructive thoughts.

I went with good intentions but I needed to trust the specialist I was seeing. Like Nadia had been, I couldn't help but feel Davina loved the celebrity aspect of her client base. She was intrigued by Hollywood and movies and once asked me to read Chekhov. I wasn't sure how this was supposed to help me.

Therapy is such big business in the States. There is supposed to be client confidentiality, but everyone lets slip little nuggets of gossip. One therapist I saw told me about a well-known French actress who was complaining about her boyfriend's antics. In a moment of high Gallic emotion, she declared: 'I want to kill him.'

She had no intention to carry out the threat, she was just expressing her anger. However, the psychiatrist picked up the telephone and said: 'I'm sorry but legally I have to report this.'

Things progressed smoothly with Bryan, although we survived an early test that might have spooked a less-understanding girlfriend. We had been to see *JFK*, Oliver Stone's controversial movie about the assassination of President Kennedy. Bryan had some strongly held views and we'd had a heated discussion over the theories raised in the film about who was behind it.

I had been aware that Bryan sometimes talked in his sleep but I was to discover that occasionally he could get quite animated. That night the injustice of Kennedy's death must have been still going around his head because in the middle of the night he became very agitated. When I tried to calm him down he tried to strangle me and shouted: 'You fucking communist.'

At least I think he was still sleeping.

In early 1992 *Scorchers* was released to a lukewarm response. The movie had had its premiere at the Seattle International Film Festival the previous May but received its limited widespread release in February. The consensus seemed to be that, while the film boasted an impressive cast list and the performances were enjoyable, the script hadn't quite made the transition from theatre to big screen. Critics seemed to appreciate my accent, which was the one reassuring thing I took from it. The scripts I was reading weren't exactly exciting me. Many wanted me to reprise roles I'd previously played, but at least they were arriving on my agent's desk. In the early 1990s it seemed the British film industry was in a state of decline and was desperately in need of funding. If I was going to keep working I had no choice but to continue to look at American productions. Playing convincing US parts was my meal ticket and at that time I was settled in LA.

I was dividing my time between New York and Los Angeles and planning my next career move when something happened to turn my world upside down. I'd been feeling queasy for a while but put it down to a stomach bug.

Little did I know that, at 21, with no real career plan, in a serious but still short-term relationship, I was pregnant.

CHAPTER
SEVENTEEN

I kept saying to the head of security: 'I'm Emily Lloyd, I'm here to
open the film festival, I'm starring in a film by Robert Redford.'
The Hitler lookalike just replied: 'Who is Robert Redford?'

I had no idea how it happened. Well, I knew the basics obviously, but we'd been taking precautions because a baby was the last thing either of us wanted. I still had unresolved issues of my own to sort out. The idea of bringing a child into the world and the responsibility that brings was almost too much to think about, and think about it I had to. The shock of the unplanned pregnancy knocked me sideways and for a good while I didn't know what to do.

I have to admit a part of me wondered about the consequences of having a child. The odds were stacked against me but would it be the end of the world? I knew at some stage in the future I wanted to have children but what if you don't get to plan these things? What if this was the only chance I had to give life to another? Financially I was comfortable and although I worked in a fickle industry there was no reason why it had to be the end of my career. Plenty of young women had taken breaks from movies to have children. But then the reality set in. I was 21. I could barely take care of myself, my parents kept telling me. I was living in rented accommodation, I had no permanent roots anywhere and no support network. Would this mean I would have to move back to the UK? If so it would be practically impossible to resurrect a Hollywood career from there with a baby in tow.

How would this affect my relationship? Did I want it to be defined by a baby? I had been with Bryan for over six months – the longest I'd ever been in a relationship but I wasn't thinking about marriage and I didn't even know if I was in love. I used to dream about the kind of man I wanted to father my children. I wanted him to have a sense of humour, be open-minded, loving and accepting. I wasn't convinced Bryan possessed any of those qualities.

Then there were my mental health problems. Was it fair to bring a child into the world when I was uncertain if I could be a good mother? Would a baby calm me down though, give me some focus and emotional stability? I was completely torn. My heart wanted to believe there was a chance to make this work. My head told me a termination was my only option. I hadn't been well, I needed to be sure what I wanted to do with my life. I had too many unresolved issues.

Bryan seemed to shut off when I told him. It was clear whatever decision I made I would be dealing with the consequences on my own.

I didn't have a long time to think about it. I was several weeks pregnant and had to make a decision while I still had the option of a termination. Eventually I knew it was the only decision I could make in my current situation. A friend took me to a private clinic.

The procedure was clinical and over quickly. I emerged into the sunlight feeling bereft.

Gwyneth Paltrow came to visit me and tried, in her own way, to be supportive.

Two days later though, I was in crippling pain and doubled up in agony. I went back to hospital and to my horror they told me that the clinic had failed to spot that I had actually been pregnant with twins. Given Bryan was a twin – and there was a history of them on my mother's side – the doctors really should have checked. I'd put my faith in the experts.

Only one embryo had been removed. I had to go through the procedure again and was left exhausted, emotionally bereft and confused. I had already been grieving for the lost life. Now I felt doubly distraught.

I told Mum what had happened and needed her support, asking her to come to LA. My sister was going for an interview at this time for Cambridge University (for which she was accepted) and had wanted Mum to go with her. Mum felt however that, in this instance, my situation was more important. She got on the next plane out, gave me support and sympathy and commended me on my stoicism.

There was nothing for me to do but get on with life. I couldn't afford to sit and feel sorry for myself. I felt like I was on my own. I was to find that in Hollywood your friends couldn't be relied upon in a crisis. I confided in some of them what I'd been through but their reaction was unsympathetic to say the least. Some didn't want to know while one leading actress sent me a card while I was recuperating that read: 'It's a boy.'

To this day I cannot fathom the reasoning behind it. Was it an attempt at humour, suggesting I'd had a lucky escape? I don't know.

She has children of her own now and might be mortified if reminded of her heartless gesture but it confused and upset me.

My relationship with Bryan never recovered from the episode. Things were strained between us anyway and this just added to the uncomfortable atmosphere. I was discovering that it's only after the first flush of romance, when relationships settle down, that you discover the little annoying traits of a partner. Actors are habitually vain creatures but he spent more time in the bathroom than me. I also don't know if it was a Virginia thing but he seemed to have out dated ideas of domesticity and gender roles. He expected me to look after the house and cook meals and seemed dismayed at how untidy and disorganised I was.

Being a twin I wasn't surprised to learn he was competitive with Boyd, but as his brother began landing more TV roles, he became increasingly desperate to be more successful.

I also started to resent the influence he was having on my life. When we were in the loved-up period of our relationship I thought nothing of bending to his will and bowing to his superior knowledge on certain subjects. He professed to know a lot about the art world and convinced me to buy works by actor-turned-artist Duncan Regehr. I bought three – one called *Flowers on the Table* was about an abortion – but after what had happened to me they lost their appeal. Bryan was convinced I would be able to sell them for a profit but I doubted that. To this day I've never been able to shift them. I heard Olivia Newton-John owned some. I'm not sure if she's had any luck selling hers. Regehr made his name as the original Zorro on television. Maybe they'd be worth more if they had a 'Z' slashed through them.

The final insult, however, was when I listened to our answering machine and heard a message from an actress that suggested she and

Bryan were more than just friends. She was the star of an erotic movie sequel. I caught up with Bryan at Barney's Beanery, a famous pool hall and diner in West Hollywood. I confronted him there and a threw a drink over him. I didn't even want to hear his explanation. By then I wasn't devastated. I knew our relationship was over. My pride was hurt and I felt bruised that after all I'd been through he could be getting close to someone else.

I was entering a period of change. So much happened in such a short space of time it's hard to remember the exact chronology. In a matter of months I moved house again, parted company with Ilene, my agent of over four years, and split from my partner.

I moved into an apartment in Crescent Heights, West Hollywood. Although I would miss the community feel of Venice Beach and the pleasure of being able to walk to places I had an urge to move into the heart of it all again.

One day I was perusing the array of pets in the Beverly Hills mall pet shop when a coil of marvellous marbled markings caught my attention. I had always been fascinated by snakes and couldn't resist buying this six month old precocious python, whom I named Pyramus, after the ill-fated character from Roman mythology immortalised by Shakespeare. He caused a few dramas at my flat. On one occasion I received a hysterical call from my flat mate saying while she was on the loo she had felt a tickle on her left buttock. Pyramus had coiled himself under the toilet seat!

After the break-up with Bryan, I wasn't ready to jump into another relationship quickly. I was linked to Nick Savalas, the son of Kojak star Telly Savalas and the half-brother of actress Nicollette Sheridan. He accompanied me to the premiere of the British animated movie *Freddie as F.R.O.7* but he was never my boyfriend. I was gradually becoming reacquainted with the party scene and once more living out of a suitcase as I travelled between New York and Los Angeles. While on the east coast I joined fellow exiled Brits John Taylor, of Duran Duran, and his partner Amanda de Cadenet at the premiere of *In the Soup*, an independent comedy poking fun at the film industry.

Professionally, though, my career continued to be in a state of flux. Amid the proposed takeover of Triad by leading agency William Morris, Ilene decided to branch out on her own. She wanted me to go with her but I wasn't sure. Nicole was moving to William Morris and wanted to take her clients with her. It was a tough decision to leave Ilene. I was grateful for the help she had given me in the early days when she took me under her wing but I felt I might have more opportunities to do the type of movies I wanted to with Nicole.

By 1992 I was feeling disillusioned with the quality of roles on offer. It seemed that studios and film companies were being driven by accountants only interested in the bottom dollar and not the creative qualities of the films they produced. I often felt they rated scripts by the number of explosions there were in the first 10 minutes. Finding complex, challenging female roles was becoming increasingly difficult. I felt that to appear in the kind of movies I admired I might have to move into smaller, independent productions.

Before any serious decisions had to be made, however, came the release of *A River Runs Through It* and the publicity merry-go-round that entailed. Its premiere was to be at the Toronto International Film Festival and I flew to join Redford and the rest of the cast. For the screening I wore a stylish purple dress and enjoyed the festivities, but when it came to meeting the press I wasn't in the mood. In the early stages of my career I had loved speaking to journalists and enjoyed the media element of promoting films. But after a few bruising encounters and being the victim of some unkind reporting my guard was up. It was harder to hide my contempt at some of the more inane questioning.

Robert Redford was kind in his appraisal of my performance, saying: 'I was looking for somebody with a great deal of spontaneity and rebelliousness. That was Emily. I am very pleased with the way it turned out.'

I'd given some interviews since being removed from *Husbands and Wives* but as this was my first time on the circuit since then, people wanted to ask about the circumstances behind my firing.

Coincidentally, *Husbands and Wives* was having its premiere at the same festival. The focus there though wasn't on me but on Woody. Only a month earlier he admitted having an affair with Soon-Yi Previn, his wife's adopted daughter, who at 21 was 35 years his junior. Only then did I realise why she had been hanging around the auditions and was a constant presence by his side. Given the subject matter of the film – featuring Woody and Mia as a couple whose marriage was breaking up – he had far tougher questions to answer than I did, I suspect.

The media were the least of my worries when I was asked to open the Cairo International Film festival where *A River Runs Through It* was being showcased.

It says everything about how security on international flights has tightened in recent years because when I boarded the flight in New York to Egypt I'd forgotten my passport. Yet again I had forgotten something. Without any form of photo identification on me, I had a brainwave and realised I was on the cover of the previous month's *Tatler*. I had a copy in my suitcase and flashed that as proof of who I was. I was waved through. Imagine that happening today!

When I landed the Egyptian authorities took a more serious line than their American counterparts. I was detained, taken downstairs and led to passport control that looked more like a prison cell. They detained me for an eternity while a guard in a white uniform with a Hitler moustache tried to establish the credentials of the crazy lady who landed waving a magazine.

Mum was arriving an hour behind me and as the minutes dragged into hours, I feared she would land and panic, not knowing what happened to me.

I kept saying to the head of security: 'I'm Emily Lloyd, I'm here to open the film festival, I'm starring in a film by Robert Redford.'

The Hitler lookalike just replied: 'Who is Robert Redford?'

Mum arrived to find me remonstrating quite belligerently with the head of security.

'What do you mean you've never heard of Robert Redford?' I said.

Mum was trying to calm me down. I think she thought we'd never get out of there if we made them more annoyed. She was whispering to me to be subservient and to change strategy. By the end we were on our knees begging: 'Please let us go. We're not worthy!'

It worked. After four hours they finally let us go. A car came to take me straight to the festival because I didn't have time to check in at the hotel. Mum was left behind with the luggage.

I made it to the festival, did my stint and finally relaxed. In a small world, I got chatting to screen legend Christopher Lee who was delighted to learn of my movie-making heritage. He was a friend of my grandfather. They had starred in Hammer horror films together.

It was an extraordinary week. I met Margot Hemingway, the director Elia Kazan and his wife. I belly-danced on stage with a crazy Polish actor with whom I made friends. I visited a Coptic Church with Mum, where we lit candles for loved ones that were in Elysium

Above left: Me, having my first lesson in pouting.

Above right: Mummy and Daddy doing their best Bonnie and Clyde impression on their wedding day.

Below: Mackie with her dog Billy. When I pointed out she was using the dog's brush on my hair, she said: 'Oh, he doesn't mind.'

Above: Mummy's night time treat… to me and sis.

Below left: My sister Charlie and me auditioning for a Colgate ad (actually it was just our primary school photo).

Below right: On the set of *Wish You Were Here*, about to strangle Charlotte, who played the eleven-year-old me. It's just acting sis, believe me!

Above: All smiles now, but moments later Charlie believed I wouldn't survive my first diving lesson with our inebriated teacher Faustaus.

Below: In Padducah with my best friend and assistant Johnny. He loved to laugh, have fun and steal my toiletries

Making waves
aged 16 as *Wish You
Were Here* has its official
screening at Cannes.
© *Rex Features*

Left: With my python Pyramus. When I wore him round my neck to parties I never knew if he was squeezing me out of affection or strangling me.

Right: I was fired from *Tank Girl* because I was accused of not shaving my head, yet the look I tried to promote seemed suspiciously close to the one eventually adopted by my replacement.

Left: My first appearance on screen.

Left: Setting tongues wagging with Kevin Anderson, my on-screen boyfriend during *In Country*.

Right: In character as Jessie Burns in *A River Runs Through It*, with co-star Craig Sheffer and director Robert Redford: 'Why is it that people who need the most help won't take it?'

CAST
CREW
ONLY
PLEASE

Left: In Montana on a lunch break with the golden boy Brad Pitt.

Above: Mummy, Danny and me at San Sebastian.

Below left: Good times, but not good timing, with Gavin Rossdale.

Below right: Danny Huston and me enjoying the Mexican sun on a private beach.

Doing my best Betty Grable impression in *Wish You Were Here*.

© *Rex Features*

and argued over which was the correct way to cross ourselves as we left the church. The sad part was that our guides, who were wonderful, took us to a club where they sold alcohol and for this they were fired.

After that adventure, I returned home for Christmas. It was wonderful being back with Mum, Charlie and Mackie. The things people take for granted, like being able to yell up the stairs, 'Mum have you seen my jeans?' and her telling me, 'Go and look for them!' All that stuff you miss so much when you leave home.

It was like being a child again, being back in the family. Charlotte and I reacquainted ourselves with our old tricks and games. Like old times we'd change the answering machine message to something outrageous and we'd dance around Mackie singing 'Winnie Mandela'.

Being back in London meant reacquainting myself with old friends. Jane, who had accompanied me on my early trip to Japan, was marrying Tony Adams, the captain of Arsenal. The couple had their fair share of problems. Tony had not long been released from prison for drink driving, while she had battled her own personal problems. Their wedding was a typically raucous affair. Tony later said he couldn't remember much about the wedding day. Details are similarly hazy for me, but I do recall many of the Arsenal players had the hots for me!

Mostly, however, being back home gave me time to reflect, take stock of where my career was going. Charlotte was busy studying for exams – qualifications I'd never sat. She had always harboured dreams of going to Oxford or Cambridge. Now those dreams were becoming a reality and I envied the student life she would soon be enjoying.

I spent time with my Dad and it felt good to be able to talk about things that mattered, like the war in the former Yugoslavia and the problems facing the miners. In Los Angeles all people talked about was the industry. It was so insular. I missed having meaningful conversations.

I decided I wanted to take time off to educate myself. Jodie Foster had managed it, by graduating from Yale University with a degree in literature. I was conscious of not being educated. I wanted to learn about writers, artists, countries and civilisations. People might have thought I was crazy to want to risk throwing everything away when I had the chance to make more money, perhaps win big roles and build on what I'd achieved, but I felt if I waited until I was 30 the passion might have dwindled. I felt I had to do something now.

As well as getting an education, I wanted to travel – and not for a movie premiere, or to sit in a hotel room being quizzed by a succession of journalists. I wanted to see the ceiling of the Sistine chapel, I wanted to go to Provence, to read Graham Greene and Chekhov and Shakespeare. I wanted to live.

I told Nicole that I didn't want to read scripts for a while. I wasn't disenchanted with acting, but if I was to continue in the industry I wanted to learn what went on behind the camera. I did a short film for a friend in Los Angeles and became fascinated with the camera, the lenses, the lighting and the writing of a screenplay.

If I couldn't go to university, perhaps I could go to film school. I wanted to explore my options.

Nicole wasn't happy. In Hollywood you are supposed to be working all the time or you don't exist. She seemed to be on the phone all the time: 'You've got to get back here. You're hot right now.'

I really felt though that it was the time to do something different, more fulfilling. I felt I could always pick up my career again. I wanted to do a course in English literature and to have the discipline of studying and assignments.

I'd long suspected this but the more I thought about it the more I realised that people in LA lived a surreal existence. They wrote movies about poverty but had no idea what the reality was. All they knew was an air-conditioned version of poverty. At parties some people were scared about having a glass of wine in case they were perceived as an alcoholic. If they went to the loo people thought they must have been going for a line of cocaine. They all professed to be holier than thou but the atmosphere could be poisonous.

I had the money and the means not to be a slave to the type of films I didn't feel were fulfilling. I had a feeling there was more to life than churning out formulaic movies, telling the same stories.

I was looking for answers. I had no idea if I would find them.

CHAPTER EIGHTEEN

Michael Madsen seemed quite taken with me. His eyebrows were doing the talking. This was confirmed when he suggested quite blatantly, in his Midwestern drawl, that we retreat to his hotel room. Politely I declined.

I was at my Mum's when the phone rang. It was Quentin Tarantino. 'Hey Emily, how you doing?' he said, his high-energy delivery unmistakeable. 'Wanna come to the film awards with me tonight?'

It was February 1993 and the night of the Evening Standard Film Awards, the event that signalled my arrival in the big league with my best actress award five years previously.

I accepted and was excited to meet him. Quentin was the golden boy of Hollywood at that time. After *Reservoir Dogs* everyone was waiting to see what he would do for his next trick.

Over dinner he regaled me with his tales of movie making, his wish list of films he'd love to make and actors he'd love to work with. He was wonderful company. I was wondering why he had asked me to accompany him. It occurred to me, fleetingly, that he might have me in mind for a role. But I dismissed the thought and focused on enjoying the evening. His trademark enthusiasm was infectious – firing out strong opinions on everything from the judges' preferences to the choice of dessert on the menu. All the time he gesticulated wildly with a childlike excitement.

It transpired he had an interesting proposition for me. He was working on a project that required a sophisticated performance from a leading female. It sounded an original and ambitious project following *Reservoir Dogs* and he wanted to assemble an eclectic cast with a few surprises. I was intrigued but sadly I wasn't in the right state of mind. Ironically when I was in demand I couldn't respond.

The movie was *Pulp Fiction* and the role went to Uma Thurman. As gangster's moll Mia Wallace, she became the poster girl for the movie, which grew into a worldwide smash, relaunching the careers of John Travolta and Bruce Willis, and forged a partnership with Tarantino that would see him later create the lavish *Kill Bill* movies especially for her.

Later that evening, I took Quentin to Tramp nightclub in St James, where I was a member, and, while we were on the dance floor, told him a very long joke that took ages to recount, which he seemed to enjoy. Interestingly, when I saw *Pulp Fiction* – and the scene where Uma Thurman's character makes a big deal of telling John Travolta a joke – I was reminded of our night. Quentin has a reputation for drawing inspiration from everything around him and I wondered if he had our evening in mind when it came to scripting that scene.

Not long after meeting Quentin, I was introduced to Michael Madsen, one of the stars of *Reservoir Dogs,* at a movie event in Hollywood. He seemed quite taken with me. His eyebrows were doing the talking. This was confirmed when he suggested quite blatantly, in his Midwestern drawl, that we retreat to his hotel room. Politely I declined.

Now I was back in LA, a gay friend, who was always throwing parties, made a point of making sure I came to a specific one he had planned.

'There's someone you have to meet,' he said. 'He's perfect for you.'

I'm always wary when friends try to set me up on a blind date or pair me off with someone so I took this invitation with an air of scepticism. And when I discovered that the man in question was someone who had rejected me for a movie a couple of years earlier, I was hesitant.

It was at an audition for a French period drama called *Becoming Colette* – which transpired to be a disaster (good body swerve on my part) – that I first met Danny Huston. Apparently he was part of a renowned moviemaking dynasty. He was the son of legendary director John Huston, the man responsible for a host of classics like *The Maltese Falcon*, *The African Queen* and *Annie*, amongst others. Danny was also the half-brother of Anjelica, the Oscar-winning actress of *Prizzi's Honour*, which John also directed.

I'd worn a straw hat with flowers for the casting but we didn't click (needless to say I didn't get the part). And so, when two years later, my friend told me this was the man who wanted to meet me I was wholly indifferent. This time we connected. Danny was handsome in a blue Armani suit and, away from the pressures of directing his own movie, was charming, confident and engaging. Conversation was easy between us and we had a laugh together.

I must have made an impression on him because the following morning he called and asked me to join him for a coffee and a croissant. Danny lived just five minutes' walk away from my new apartment in Crescent Heights so I popped out to meet him. He was in touch constantly that week and I could feel a frisson of attraction. A week after we'd first properly met I stayed the night at his house. Part of me worried that it was all happening too soon. He had not long separated from the actress Virginia Madsen, but I told myself if it feels right, it must be right.

After two weeks, he asked me to marry him. It wasn't a formal proposal as such. We were lying in bed discussing our plans for the future when he said: 'I know, we should get married.'

I don't even know if I said yes. It was so impulsive and crazy but I just went along with it. We were having so much fun together there was a sense of anticipation.

Meanwhile, Pyramus my snake was growing into quite a handful. He went missing one day and I couldn't find him anywhere. Danny's friend was coming to take my car to the garage but soon I got a call from a very excitable Mexican guy at the garage. He'd found a python curled under the seat. I used to like taking Pyramus out to parties. He was quite the showstopper. As he got bigger he started to constrict my neck to the point where he came close to choking me. I wasn't sure if he was being affectionate or trying to kill me.

I wasn't actively looking for scripts during this period, but it was still a hectic time. In July I travelled back to England for a visit that coincided with the opening of Andrew Lloyd Webber's new musical *Sunset Boulevard*. Kevin Anderson was starring in the lead role of Joe Gillis, a character from the original 1950s film he had updated for the musical. He invited Charlotte, Mum and me along to the premiere at the Adelphi Theatre. It was a wonderful show and I was delighted to see Kevin at the top of his game in a production where he had star billing.

Following the show, I joined him and the rest of the cast at the aftershow party.

I was wearing a long skirt with slits up both sides and a crocheted top and felt confident. He looked like a true star and exuded sex appeal. That night we looked a great match and, given our romantic history, were at ease with each other. The romantic chemistry was re-sparked. We were completely in our own world together. We moved on to Annabel's club but then we slipped off to the toilet for a private chat. It sparked amusing 'Loo-dunnit' headlines in the tabloids, speculating that we were either taking drugs or up to no good. I was explaining to Kevin that I'd met Danny and it was going well.

He later remarked to my Mum that we'd seemed cursed by cruel timing and he had wanted to be with me. We'd been close for years but whenever either of us had been single the other was in a relationship. I was very fond of Kevin, but for the time being I couldn't commit to anything more than friendship.

Aside from the turmoil of relationships, while I was back home a girlfriend who was house-sitting for me back in LA, phoned in a panic about Pyramus. She couldn't get any live mice from the pet shop to feed him.

'So I got a hamster instead,' she said.

'A hamster? But they're so cute,' I said. 'They're practically human.'

'It was dying anyway,' she said.

Oh well, that's ok then.

I returned to Los Angeles, but in a few weeks even mice were no longer satisfying him. He needed rats. Not for the first time I was beginning to think I'd taken on more than I could handle.

Snake issues aside, I was enjoying something of a sabbatical. Danny and I spent most days together and had fun doing the simple things like hanging out and relaxing.

Danny was a friend of Alix Goldsmith, daughter of the billionaire Sir James Goldsmith. Sir James had retired to Mexico and it was to his palatial villa that Alix invited us to for a week. It was like nothing I had ever seen before. A beautiful, luxury estate, it was surrounded by avocado trees with gazelles and zebras grazing in the grounds. Three chefs cooked an array of mouth-watering dishes for us for the duration of our stay. We bathed in the sumptuous private pool and went riding on horses from the stables. That wasn't without incident. My horse was rather more exuberant than the others. It took off and I held on for dear life, as the others galloped after me. Thankfully, he calmed down before unseating me and an emergency was averted.

I felt comfortable and secure enough with Danny to start revealing to him the nature of my malaise. I told him I was on Prozac and I was reassured to see how concerned and interested he was. He had strong opinions about depression and its treatment (later when Elizabeth Wurtzel's groundbreaking novel *Prozac Nation* was published he was keen to read it). His interest meant a lot to me. He encouraged me to come off the anti-depressants. Previously I'd been wary of stopping the treatment because I was worried about withdrawal symptoms, but being in a loving relationship gave me the confidence to try it. Plus, I was aware the drugs levelled off my emotions so that I viewed happiness and sorrow with the same impassiveness and I wanted to feel normal again.

Mercifully, my fears of any withdrawal symptoms were unfounded and I managed to come off the drug without too many problems. I felt settled and secure and happy for the first time in a long time.

At least I wasn't alone in LA and my relationship with Danny seemed to be growing stronger. But, as often happened with me, just when I thought things were going smoothly, a little storm cloud appeared on the horizon.

Gradually I'd been feeling confident enough with Danny to open up more about the issues behind my health problems. It was the first time I'd ever told a boyfriend about what had happened to me. From his attitude to depression I thought he would be caring and understanding. Instead he was glib and made a callous comment about the abuse, which I'm sure he would be horrified about if reminded now how insensitive he'd been. The damage was done though. His reaction took me aback. Maybe he wasn't ready for that kind of admission, but his insensitivity made me regret telling him. For the first time doubts about our long-term future crept into my mind.

In September we flew with Mum to northern Spain for the annual San Sebastian Film Festival where I was to present the coveted Donostia Prize, for services to the industry, to Robert Mitchum. During dinner Robert regaled me with tales from his illustrious career, but one revelation will live with me forever.

'I can't drink too much coffee,' he confided to me. 'It makes me fart.'

Danny and I finished the year by spending Christmas at the ranch home of Anjelica Huston, who had invited a host of friends and family to stay with her. Nearly a year after his mock proposal, Danny hadn't followed it up. He had tried during one visit to London to pluck up the courage to ask my Dad for my hand but, despite them going for a drink to Black's private members club, he cowardly backed out.

But at his sister's house, without warning, he produced a ring. There was no fanfare, he just sort of handed it to me. I looked at it. This sounds brattish but I was distinctly underwhelmed. It looked like something he'd picked up from a sweetshop. If there was a diamond there you would have needed a magnifying glass to see it.

I couldn't have been able to mask my disappointment because he reacted angrily and an argument ensued. I burst out of the room in tears straight in to Anjelica. She took one look at my crimson face and dishevelled state and said tight-lipped: 'Don't show him your seams.'

I was upset but it wasn't that I was being ungrateful. I think my reaction was a reflection of a deeper feeling. If Danny had been the right man for me I wouldn't have cared had he proposed with a ring-pull. My mood wasn't helped on Christmas morning when we gathered in Anjelica's huge living room for the gift exchange. I handed over my presents. Anjelica was surrounded by piles of boxes and extravagant packages.

Anjelica gave me a present, and because I was surrounded by all this incredible wealth, given the context, I was rather surprised to receive a basic candle, but I appreciated the gesture nevertheless.

It was Mum who called with the news. I can't recall where I was or what I was doing but I'll never forget the feeling of emptiness. Johnny had died. He had been battling AIDS for years, but the inevitability of his fate didn't lessen the impact. I called Danny.

'I need to get some air,' I said. 'Can you take me to the coast?'

Danny picked me up and as we set off *The Rose* by Bette Midler came on the radio. It was Johnny's favourite song. I couldn't stop the tears. Astonishingly, what followed it was *Guilty* by Barbra Streisand – another favourite of his. I felt he was there with us somehow. Danny drove me to the cliffs to the west of Los Angeles and I watched the waves crash against the rocks and remembered the good times I'd shared with my friend.

Johnny's free spirited attitude to life had, for the most part, lifted me from my darkest moods. One of the last occasions I'd seen him was at a private screening of *A River Runs Through It* in London and he'd looked a shell of his former self, emaciated and skeletal, but his sparky personality was still there until the end. He had known what was coming for years and had faced death with his trademark dry humour. Not long before he died he had asked God for half a kilo of cocaine and a bag of marijuana to await him – announcing that he would party in heaven as hard as he had on earth.

He talked openly about his funeral and had said that when he died he wanted us all to wear black hats with veils.

I flew back to London for the funeral. It was held in an imposing church near Sloane Square and was packed with mourners. Nearly everyone adhered to his wishes. Malcolm hadn't been his partner for some time but he was there, complete with hat. It wouldn't be long until he suffered the same fate; another victim to a disease that ravaged the gay community during the 1990s before better treatment and an understanding of the risks was discovered.

I read an excerpt on death from *The Prophet* by Lebanese poet Kahlil Gibran. I hoped Johnny's many friends would find solace in the mournful, yet uplifting words:

Only when you drink from the river of silence shall you indeed sing.
And when you have reached the mountain top, then you shall begin to climb.
And when the earth shall claim your limbs, then shall you truly dance.

Not long after Johnny's death I received the news that David Jaeger, our former mentor at Dance Works, had also died. He'd moved to Australia but had succumbed to the same disease that robbed the world of Johnny. I recalled the fun Charlotte and I had enjoyed at Dance Works, with David excitedly putting us through our paces. I owed so much to him. Without his early nurturing, it's unlikely I would have grown into the actress I became.

It was just a short while later that Malcolm also died from AIDS – and a broken heart – following Johnny's death.

In losing three people who'd been such influences on my life I felt a piece of me had also died.

Danny had given me space following Johnny's death. After the problems we'd had at Christmas, we had managed to put our disagreements behind us – to a point. I still wasn't sure of our status at all. I wore the ring but wasn't sure if we were officially engaged. He might not have swept me off my feet with his proposal but, I convinced myself, he could be kind and considerate in other ways.

After a lengthy hiatus, I wanted to get back to work. I was on the lookout for interesting scripts when a quick and straightforward project presented itself. Showtime, an American cable television channel, had launched a series where well-known Hollywood actors could try their hand behind the camera. Danny Glover, best known for roles in *The Color Purple* and as the retirement-denied detective in the incredibly successful *Lethal Weapon* series, was directing a short film for the series called *Override*, based on the award-winning science-fiction novel *Over the Long Haul* by Martha Soukup. I only had a small part and was required on set for just three days. Danny joined me on set and it was an enjoyable but brief shoot. I've never seen the end result but it was a 30-minute short film aimed at showcasing untried directing talent.

The role was swiftly followed by an offer to appear as an extra in an ambitious but offbeat project. *Les Cent et Une Nuits de Simone*

Cinema (*101 Nights of Simon Cinema*) was a low-budget movie about a 100-year-old man who asks a young girl to tell him about all the movies ever made. What made the film especially interesting was that it featured walk-on appearances, most uncredited, from some of Hollywood's leading names. Clint Eastwood, Robert De Niro and Martin Sheen were among those taking part. I received a call from my agent asking if I wanted to appear as an extra. I had to go down to the set the following day. When I arrived Leonardo DiCaprio and Harrison Ford were among those filming.

I completed my scene and the following day I received flowers, accompanied by a card saying only 'From Leo'. Could they have been sent by the young Mr DiCaprio? Could be, but then I also remembered that the third AD, a Frenchman, was also called Leo. To this day, however, I'm not sure.

Working again, I felt energised and ready to go for more ambitious parts. Nicole thought she had the perfect one for me. United Artists, one of the most famous names in cinema, had been dormant after a takeover fiasco that could be traced back to the colossal flop *Heaven's Gate* in 1980. Given a new lease of life by MGM studios, it was returning with a big budget adaptation of the English comic book heroine *Tank Girl*.

Set in post-apocalyptic Australia in 2033, the cult action character drove and lived in a tank and was prone to random acts of sex and violence. Given the recent revival of comic book characters, the studio felt the time was right to unleash one of their own – this time with a female twist.

It seemed an ideal opportunity for me. For years I'd spoken out about the paucity of strong female lead roles and now here was one that espoused all the qualities I wanted to see – strength of will, impulsive, yet flawed. *Tank Girl* was like a female *Mad Max*, playing by her own rules. It was a role coveted by a number of strong female actors, and Madonna.

Despite this – and my recent setbacks – I felt confident I could recapture the spark that won me parts in *Cookie* and *In Country* and make the role mine. It was time to kick-start my career.

CHAPTER
NINETEEN

I managed to find Faustaus, a random and possibly drunk so-called
instructor, who agreed to take me diving with a minimum of training.
He taught me thumbs up for 'everything's okay', thumbs down for
'can't breathe', 'oh shit' for anything else.

I could scarcely believe it when Nicole told me *Tank Girl* was mine.
After the setbacks and false starts of the last few years, I was
optimistic my career was back on track.

Reading for the part, the confidence had flowed. I hoped that
I had impressed. Even when I'd heard that 700 other actresses
wanted the role unusually I still felt I had a chance. What sometimes surprises people is that throughout my turmoil I have tried
not to doubt my own ability, but my nerves and anxiety have been
debilitating. I've always known that when my head has been in the
right place I'm capable of producing a stellar performance. There
might have been questions regarding the movie choices I made
but there was always informed reasoning behind them. They
always seemed right at the time and, although the finished product

might not have met everyone's expectations, I gave my best to every role.

This was another project that on paper looked like a perfect fit for me. *Tank Girl* was one tough cookie – equipped with a killer line in wisecracks, bags of sex appeal and a dark sense of humour. Fighting for survival after a cataclysmic ecological event has made water the Earth's most precious and viciously fought-for resource, she has to use whatever means possible to stop an evil villain controlling the supply.

Rachel Talalay, director of *Freddy's Dead* – originally billed as the final movie in the *Nightmare on Elm Street* series – was at the helm. Producing were Richard Lewis, Pen Desham and John Watson, the team responsible for successes like *Robin Hood: Prince of Thieves* and *Backdraft*.

Filming was to begin in May and I had four months of training to get in shape to play the all-action heroine. I met with Rachel and we seemed to click. She was open to ideas and I was overflowing with them. As *Tank Girl* was originally a punky character, I wanted her to be like Sid Vicious – the former Sex Pistols' bassist who embodied punk attitude. I imagined his version of Sinatra's *My Way* as her theme song.

United Artists hired me a personal trainer and I worked hard to look the part. The fitter I became, the more energised I felt and before filming started I began looking for other projects to line up. My renewed enthusiasm for working coincided with a period of inactivity for Danny. I wanted to use my rediscovered clout to see if we could find a project we could do together.

It had been a long held dream of mine to play Eliza Doolittle. I'd been sounded out a few years previously about the prospect of playing her on Broadway in a new production of *My Fair Lady* but the timing hadn't been right. I made inquiries about the rights to *Pygmalion*, George Bernard Shaw's 1912 play on which the movie was based. I thought Danny could direct it. Danny and I had a meeting with United Artists, who seemed keen on the project. I liaised from Los Angeles with Roma Woodnutt, of the Society of Authors in London and the Shaw Society who owned the rights to Shaw's plays. Everything seemed to be falling into place.

Shortly before filming was due to start on *Tank Girl*, Charlotte came to visit. She had taken a year out before starting her degree at Cambridge and this was her last chance to let her hair down before the intensely hard work began. It was nice to introduce her to all the hottest celebrity hangouts. In the Viper Room, the nightclub partly owned by Johnny Depp, she met the *Edward Scissorhands* star – and then promptly ruined the moment by rushing off to be sick in the toilet (she'd drunk too much beforehand at Judd Nelson's Hollywood party).

Later, Charlotte and I went for a holiday down to Cabo San Lucas, the bustling resort on the southernmost tip of the Baja California peninsula. Cabo is famous for its scuba diving and I was desperate to try it. Normally it's recommended you have a few lessons before strapping on the oxygen tank but I managed to find Faustaus, a random and possibly drunk so-called instructor, who agreed to take me out with a minimum of training. I say minimum. He couldn't speak a word of English. He taught me three things – thumbs up for 'everything's okay', thumbs down for 'can't breathe', 'oh shit' for pretty much anything else.

Charlotte's expression told me she thought this was the most foolhardy thing I'd ever done. She came out on the raft, essentially just a piece of wood and a motor, that Faustaus used to take us to the ideal diving spot. It didn't look seaworthy. My poor sister tried to cram in some reading and was sitting there, scared witless, reading

Gustave Flaubert's *Madam Bovary*, in French, probably wondering if this was going to be the last time she saw me alive.

Faustaus and I dived into the water and, despite only having a two-minute lesson, I took to it like, well, a fish to water. It was wonderfully calming and liberating to be swimming, the fish darting around me. Yet while I was being mesmerised by the wonders of the deep, Charlotte was up above staring at the same patch of water where our bubbles had vanished from about half an hour earlier. Not much of *Madame Bovary* was being devoured. She was too anxious to concentrate. When we emerged the look of relief quickly turned to fury for putting her through the worry.

She soon forgave me though and in our hotel room we were in fits of laughter filming ourselves singing and dancing. My sister must share my ear for accents because she's a great mimic and actress when she puts her mind to it. We had a wonderful two weeks together. It felt like old times when we used to sing and dance in Milner Square as kids. I didn't want it to end and when the time came to wave her off at the airport I had to choke back the tears.

By coincidence, the scriptwriter on *Tank Girl*, Tedi Sarafian, was staying at the same hotel with his director brother Daran, whose works included *Terminal Velocity*. I don't know whether Rachel Talalay had a bit of thing for Tedi or whether the pressure was getting to her but when she found out we'd been at the same resort she became frosty with both of us. I'm not sure if she thought we were fooling around but there was nothing in our meeting in Mexico – her fears were completely unfounded.

But when I returned to begin working she suddenly said: 'You need to shave your head.'

When I was first offered the part, I asked Rachel if I'd have to shave my hair off. I didn't have that much against the idea, I just wanted to know. Now she was changing her stance. I questioned her demand and suggested whether it would not be better – given she was a punky character – to have some of her head shaved, but some spiked up, to look more outrageous, but also feminine to balance her masculine image.

I met with an artist and a photographer to demonstrate some looks. Using a latex bald head cap, I modelled some punk styles. Some just had a single braid out of the top of my head, others had more of a Mohican. I was delighted with the results and felt the images showed how much I wanted this character to work.

A meeting was then called between Rachel, my agent and me and executives from United Artists in a huge boardroom in the film company's offices. We thumbed through five issues of *Vogue* looking for the right style. In the end everyone agreed on one and we moved on. The following day I was to have my hair cut by a stylist who was coming to my house. The hairdresser arrived on time but then she said there was a dinner she wanted to go to. I told her not to worry, we could do it first thing in the morning. When Rachel found out she took it that I was being difficult over the whole shaving thing. She rang me and told me I was fired.

I couldn't believe it. I'd worked hard to get in shape for the role and had invested so much energy into making it work. To be sacked for nothing more than a personality clash was hard to take. Unlike *Mermaids*, I had no contractual claim on the decision, no right of appeal. I was out, plain and simple. My agent tried to sound sympathetic but I could detect she was thinking I must have been responsible. Once again I was going to have to face a very public humiliation but I felt aggrieved that this was not my fault.

The images from that time show how far I was prepared to go.

Danny tried to offer support but even with him I detected a sense that he felt I had been difficult. He said he hoped the movie would now bomb but also added: 'You can't mess around with a big studio.'

I felt numb though, unable to feel anything else other than hurt. I had been in great shape, spent months working with the personal trainer to get prepared for the role. I just couldn't believe it had been taken from me. I went over things again and again, focusing on every little thing to try and understand what had gone wrong. I couldn't get any closure.

I tried to refocus on work. Nicole had got me an audition for a Hugh Grant film called *The Englishman Who Went Up a Hill But Came Down a Mountain*. It was to be his first key role after the success of *Four Weddings and a Funeral*. I flew back home for the audition and was greeted by several paparazzi and reporters at Heathrow asking me about it. I just wanted to lock myself away from the world. I couldn't concentrate on the role at the audition and it was no surprise when I didn't get the part.

Lori Petty, a tomboyish actress seven years older than me, was cast in my place on *Tank Girl*. Best known as a female baseball player in *A League of their Own*, she was, perhaps unfairly, tagged as a mini-Madonna. It was difficult not to feel possessive to the role. I still saw it as mine but there was nothing I could do.

After months of inactivity, Danny was now working on a new project when I found myself unexpectedly unemployed. He was directing Burt Reynolds who was appearing as a psychopath in a tense thriller called *The Maddening*. Shooting was taking place in Florida in early autumn 1994. I flew down there to be with Danny, but he wasn't able to offer the support I needed. I desperately wanted him to be there for me but when he wasn't I took it as a sign that we were not meant to be. My mind kept returning to Christmas time and the row we'd had over the engagement ring and my suspicions that it had been the result of something more deep-seated. We'd had a lot of fun and he'd meant more to me than many men in my life but our relationship had run its course. There were no tears, no recriminations, just a sad inevitability.

To put it bluntly, I went to pieces after *Tank Girl*. Any new-found confidence was shot, I feared for my career and began to believe I was cursed. Being sacked from one movie could be deemed unlucky, but three times was definitely a habit. I worried I'd soon be more famous for the parts I didn't get or had won but let slip through my fingers than the ones I'd landed. The most galling aspect though was that this one – as with *Mermaids* – was not my fault.

Another issue at stake was the half a million-dollar paycheck I'd have collected – easily the biggest of my career. During my early years in Hollywood I'd earned enough not to worry about how I was spending it. My Mum was always a 'Spenderella' and insisted I was going the same way. Lately, however, as the bigger roles dried up and the gaps between large paydays had grown wider, I'd begun to worry how I could sustain my lifestyle. Running an expensive property in Los Angeles, cars and international flights were taking its toll. I never kept track of my cash but it seemed money was disappearing faster than ever.

Then I discovered why. My business manager Marco had been stealing from me. I probably would never have discovered it but his girlfriend – who had become quite a close friend of mine – came to tell me, over lunch, which I think I paid for! She said the man – who I'm not fully identifying because he's trying to get his life back in order – had a serious crack cocaine problem. He'd been stealing from me to fund his habit. When my accountants checked the information his girlfriend had given me they discovered he'd embezzled tens of thousands of dollars from my account.

Coming after the financial hit of missing out on *Tank Girl*, I once more felt like the fates were conspiring against me. It was a time in my life when I should have gone home and retreated into the bosom of my family. Past history told me I didn't react well to setbacks. Instead though I reeled from the misfortune I'd suffered. What was it about me that attracted this type of bad luck, I told myself. Was I being punished in some way?

If I couldn't trust those people hired to look after my best interests, who could I trust? Who else was stealing from me, or using me for their own gains? It was a horrible feeling. And crack cocaine? I'd heard of it, obviously, but it seemed like a problem confined to drug gangs and South Central LA, not Hollywood. So far I'd managed to steer clear of drugs. Now they were affecting my life, whether I liked it or not.

I'd known people that took cocaine, for some it was a regular habit, but I'd never seen the appeal. When I was first introduced to it I'd literally not known what to do. I'd been at a party when someone offered me a tiny silver spoon with a few grains of white powder on it. Without even thinking what it was I'd gone to swallow the spoon before the horrified reveller had wrenched it back in disgust. That had been my introduction to drugs. For years I believed I had enough problems without adding another. But they are impossible to avoid, especially in Hollywood, when everyone, it seemed was hiding a secret vice of some kind.

So drugs and I had been strangers to each other, but not for long. The despair of being rejected from a high-profile movie, splitting from a boyfriend of two years and the misery of finding out someone had been stealing from me meant my will was weak. When an acquaintance invited me to their apartment I was grateful for the company. When they revealed they had some opium and invited me to try some, I thought, 'What the hell?'

I wanted an escape, a release, anything to transport me from the state I'd found myself in. I would have run a mile from heroin, but opium conjured images of great artists and writers who seemed to have used it as a creative aid. The friend offered me a pipe and I tentatively took a few puffs. The buzz was like nothing I'd experienced before. Momentarily I was elated and I forgot about my recent troubles.

I sampled it maybe two or three times over the course of a couple of weeks but, while it offered temporary respite, I knew my career wasn't going to be helped by sitting around getting high. I needed to get back to work.

Not long after my business manager's embezzlement came to light, he was sacked. I could have demanded he face the full force of the law but he came to meet me full of contrition. His life was in ruins, but he vowed to pay me back and to get help for his addictions. I was very fond of him. It was sad to see someone you've worked with so closely for years end up that way and, while I still couldn't believe he had been ripping me off, I felt little would be served by involving the police.

More pressing to me was finding the right movie to do next. I needed something to get me back to work because I was worried about the consequences if I didn't. After signing up for *Tank Girl* I'd passed on a number of attractive propositions. One director wanted me to do a Polanski-style thriller that appealed because of its film noir element. It would have stretched me creatively. But that opportunity had since gone.

Stephen Baldwin had become something of a friend since I'd first met him on the Hollywood circuit and we'd always talked about making a movie together. He was working with director Jeff Celentano on a screwball comedy called *Under The Hula Moon* in the vein of the Coen brothers' *Raising Arizona*. It was about a trailer park couple, obsessed with all things Hawaiian, who dreamt of escaping their lowly surroundings.

It would be Celentano's first feature and the budget was miniscule but the project looked fun and something on which to focus my mind. Filming was in Arizona and it looked like being an enjoyable shoot. Also starring was Chris Penn, the brother of Sean, who I'd first met when he was still married to Madonna. Years later I'd met him when he'd been with his second wife Robin Wright. It was at an after-show party at the Bel Air hotel and Sean and I had got chatting. He has a serious and intense demeanour but within minutes I'd had him playing Knuckles and laughing uproariously. Robin glared at me with a 'keep away from my man' expression and was generally intimidating. I could see how they'd been attracted to each other.

On *Hula Moon*, we'd only been shooting for a few days when Chris approached me, a conspiratorial look on his face.

'My brother has a crush on you,' he said quietly.

'Is he not married?' I asked.

'Not at the moment,' Chris smiled.

Two days later, Sean arrived on set with his two children. We were reacquainted and we picked things up from where we'd left them at the Bel Air. He was relaxed and chatty and not at all like his public persona.

In the way teenagers do, we exchanged phone numbers.

I had the feeling more trouble was looming.

CHAPTER
TWENTY

I was at a party when a well-known actor asked me what I'd been up to.
I'd replied that I'd only recently returned from the funeral of a
close friend. 'Yeah,' he said, 'but are you working?'

'Where are you taking me?' I asked tentatively, trying not to appear nervous.

'Don't worry,' Sean replied, a glint in his eye. 'I told you,' he reiterated. 'It's a surprise.'

It was a few weeks after *Hula Moon* and Sean Penn had called me to ask me out. This wasn't a regular date, I knew that much. He said he was taking me to see a close friend of his.

He picked me up and we headed into the Hollywood Hills, which at night takes on a completely different atmosphere to the sun-kissed days. The drive resembled the car journeys in Hitchcock movies – long winding roads to the unknown. Eventually we arrived at a house shrouded in darkness. Sean banged on the door and when it finally opened Jack Nicholson was standing there. Am I going to dance with the devil in the pale moonlight, I thought to myself?

He invited us in. Despite its location on Mulholland Drive, Jack's house was not your typical Hollywood mansion. It was quite small, by LA standards, and had the feel of a grown up bachelor pad, which somehow lacked a woman's touch. Jack had lived in the same house for years and it was impossible not to think of the famous names that had partied here – Mama Cass, Jim Morrison, Warren Beatty, Joni Mitchell and Marlon Brando, who then still lived next door, amongst many others.

There was a joke that Nicholson was the only man in the world to whom the hellraising Rolling Stone Keith Richards would say: 'I have to go home now.'

I could see why. It was clear Jack still liked to have a good time but that night all he and Sean did was to drone on about their angst regarding women. After two hours or so of listening to them whinge about their past relationships, I became restless and said to Sean: 'This is boring. Why don't you take me dancing.'

Jack just laughed. On the way out Sean looked at me and said: 'I wish Robin was as much fun as you.'

It seemed hard for Sean to have fun, as if something was stopping him. It was a difficult time for him then. He and Robin were separated from each other. He was directing her in a film with Jack Nicholson called *The Crossing Guard*, but was having difficulties with the distributor Harvey Weinstein. After I'd met Sean on the set of *Hula Moon*, the location of the film moved to Hawaii to continue shooting there and he'd rung me there, mainly to offload about his problems.

Once back in LA, he'd invited me to his place. It made Jack's house look like a mansion. After splitting from Robin he'd moved into a trailer and it was there we hung out, chatting about many things. He was a close friend and admirer of Charles Bukowski, the poet once described as a 'laureate of lowlife', who died in March

1994. *The Crossing Guard* would ultimately carry a dedication to his friend. Sean also had a fascination with wolves and their pack mentality and was determined to share it with me.

He loved to talk about movies, the intricacies of filmmaking and the challenges of directing over acting. After a difficult few years in the wake of his high-profile marriage to Madonna – an experience that seemed to have left him scarred – he was gradually getting back into the limelight. When I met him, he'd not long completed *Carlito's Way* with Al Pacino. Sean played Carlito's bent lawyer (a performance for which he was nominated for a Golden Globe) and he told me when they were filming it took 30 takes to shoot one scene. It was a scene where Pacino wasn't even speaking – it was just his reaction they were trying to capture – and Pacino asked for 30 takes.

He was an interesting companion. We were never officially an item but we seemed to click. However, my friendship with him wasn't enough to dissuade me from a course of action I had been considering for a while.

I felt it was time to go home. Ultimately, it had been an easy decision to make. I'd had enough.

I'd enjoyed working on *Under the Hula Moon* but I still had restlessness in my soul. Although I had moved house, changed agencies, changed boyfriends even, if I was being honest the dream had faded a long time ago. I was losing faith in myself and what I had originally believed about Hollywood. Although it had given me a cornucopia of challenging experiences, these were becoming dissipated.

While I had been working on *Tank Girl* and been involved with Danny I'd had the impression everything was fine but I had just been delaying the inevitable. Now I had neither a movie nor a relationship. There was nothing to keep me there.

My family and friends were back in London. It's where I

belonged. I'd given Hollywood my best shot. There had been plenty of good times, but too many lows. LA was a hard enough place to survive in when things were going smoothly. If your star was on the wane, which I suspected mine was, it was an unforgiving place to be.

From the moment I'd set foot there I'd known people in the industry were superficial and it was a feeling confirmed to me on a regular basis. After Johnny's death, when I came back to LA, I was at a party when a well-known actor asked me what I'd been up to. I'd replied that I'd only recently returned from the funeral of a close friend.

'Yeah,' he said, 'but are you working?'

As Bernardo Bertolucci said when he collected his Oscar for *The Last Emperor* in 1987, 'If New York is the Big Apple, then LA is the big nipple. You go there to suck, suck, suck'. It's a town where people are obsessed with other people's business, if it has some beneficial impact on them. There was still much to recommend the place of course. Where else in the world could you experience the sea, the mountains and the desert within half an hour's drive of each other?

I travelled back to the UK and began house hunting. Jade Jagger was selling a place and I looked at it but it was beyond my budget. Eventually I found a found a flat in Notting Hill. I was in the privileged position of being able to put down a large deposit so the purchase went through quickly. By the time I was ready to leave it was quite rushed. I was pining for home.

I gave Pyramus away to a hairdresser friend. By then he needed live rabbits to fill him up, and I don't know about him, but that was something I wouldn't have been able to stomach.

I gave my car and a lot of other belongings to other friends and acquaintances. The rest I packed up and shipped back to London. From the moment I arrived back I felt a weight off my shoulders.

Although I'd travelled to and from London throughout my time in the States it felt good to be home, where people didn't take themselves too seriously.

I had only been back a few months when *Tank Girl* was released to a distinctly underwhelmed cinema audience. Expectations had been high from United Artists but reviews seemed to be unanimous that it didn't work. Some described it as a 'kitchen sink' movie, meaning all manner of special effects and devices were used to try and sustain interest. Despite a budget of $45 million it only went on to make $8 million. I didn't gloat over its failure, but let's say I wasn't crying over it either. I just mourned the missed opportunity, not just for me, but for the director. *Tank Girl* was a character with a cult following for a reason. Changing key characteristics, like her nationality, may have been an error of judgement. If the movie had been a success it could have heralded a new breed of female leads. As it was it probably put them back five years.

I did notice, though, that my suggestion of making Sid Vicious's version of *My Way* her signature tune made the final cut and, even more interestingly, Lori Petty sported a distinct crop of blonde hair.

There were still echoes of Hollywood in my London life. Sean was in town filming and we ended up being at the same party not far from my flat in Notting Hill. I can't remember the occasion, or who was hosting but Gwyneth Paltrow was there, as well as Carrie Fisher. I hadn't seen Gwyneth much since I'd had the termination but, interestingly, she was then with Brad Pitt. It's funny how things turn out. Anyway, Sean told me he'd promised Brad – who wasn't in London – that he'd look after Gwyneth and make sure she got to her hotel safely. But he gave me the name of his hotel and asked if I'd meet him there later. I duly did and we spent the night together.

He wanted me to audition for a film the Irish director Jim

Sheridan was making – his third he'd written about the IRA and his third collaboration with Daniel Day Lewis. Sean had put a word in for me and thought the part would be a good one for me. For some reason the schedule didn't fit and I wasn't able to take up his offer, but I was flattered.

I met him again while he was in town and we ended up in Tramp together. It was there I saw the short fuse that had famously got him into trouble in LA. Sean had sat down, but another guy felt he had a claim on the seat. He called Sean a 'midget'. Sean didn't take too kindly to the slur and confronted the man, who threw a punch. Sean held his own but, after seeing the guy off, had blood pouring from his nose. I took him into the ladies' toilet and patched him up.

A few days later he returned to LA but, although we remained in touch for a short while, the distance between us and the difficulty of the situation with his estranged wife meant it was impossible to keep up contact. I did find myself back there a few months later, but by then he had tried to patch things up with Robin and I was keen to move on.

One of the consequences of *Tank Girl* was that I had to turn down the chance of working with young director James Merindino. He was the director who had wanted to cast me for the Polanski-esque thriller he'd been directing but we remained in touch and he was keen for me to appear in his latest movie. *Livers Ain't Cheap* was the story of a crook who plans a £1 million nightclub heist to buy a new liver for his brother. Their problems really start though when a rival crook overhears the plot and plans the same robbery for himself. It all comes to a head on New Year's Eve. I was playing an English street girl who masterminds elements of the heist and spurs the crooks on.

I loved the role. My character, Lisa, was psychotic, violent and lived without morals. I got to beat the hell out of policemen and she was more than a match for the men she worked with. Normally it's only the men who get to lose it and the women have to make do with cowering in the corner, screaming.

For the part I went downtown to have my hair braided in a brunette Afro-style. The braids were heavy and I had difficulty sleeping with them but I loved the image.

The film also starred James Russo and I had the chance to work with Rod Steiger, who had a reputation for being difficult. I remember sitting with him in his trailer and he said: 'Brando was difficult, Montgomery Clift was difficult, James Dean was difficult. Now, if that's difficult, that's what I want to be.'

Around the same time I played a small cameo role in another American film. *Dead Girl* was the brainchild of writer-director Adam Coleman Howard and was a satirical look at the movie business. The dark comedy, about a struggling actor who kills the girl of his dreams when she rejects his advances but then continues to hang out with her dead body, featured a stellar cast for an independent film.

Val Kilmer nearly stole the show as the actor's shrink, but there were also appearances by Famke Jannsen and Teri Hatcher.

What appealed to me was that the script captured perfectly the lack of self-awareness and superficiality of Hollywood. It showed that every actor is prone to loneliness in a town rife with wannabes who will let nothing stand in the way of success. My involvement only lasted a couple of days but it was a nice little project that deserved a wider airing than it received. It didn't even get a release in America, showing that Hollywood isn't prone to self-examination.

I was in LA for a month and returned hungry for more work. I wanted to try and make some contribution to the British film industry. I started a production company with Fraser James, a friend who'd appeared in *Prime Suspect*, with the idea that we'd get English projects off the ground and tout them in LA and go to Hollywood to raise money to have films made over here.

It was to prove hard but I needed to be seen to be supporting homegrown productions. So when I was asked about *When Saturday Comes*, I thought it could be the perfect vehicle to resurrect my British film career. With a title from a famous football fanzine that had morphed into a nationally distributed magazine, the film told the story of a lowly factory worker's shot at soccer glory with Sheffield United.

The somewhat novice film director Maria Giese was making only her second movie, but she had devised the script based on the experiences of her then husband James Daly, who produced and co-wrote the film. The hero of the story was going to be played by Sean Bean. At the time he was best known as British soldier Richard Sharpe in the TV adaptations of Bernard Cornwell's novels, but had made telling contributions in movies like *Golden Eye* and *Patriot Games*.

At 37, he might have been considered too old as he was at the age most footballers are hanging up their boots rather than starting out, but as a mad Sheffield United fan (he has 100% Blade in reference to the club tattooed on his shoulder) he was deemed perfect.

We didn't get off to the best start. When we first met I told him I was a big Arsenal fan. I don't know if he couldn't take a wind-up or whether he had a hang-up because I'd worked in Hollywood, but there was a distinct frostiness from him towards me.

Filming took place in and around Sheffield and when I sat down with Maria I had ideas on how we could develop my character to elevate her from just the usual cliché of a love interest. She was Irish and studying literature so I wanted her to show this, perhaps by quoting WB Yeats, but Maria wasn't interested. If I needed reminding I wasn't in Hollywood any more, there was no budget for a dialect coach so I had to master an Irish accent as best I could – which wasn't easy to do in Yorkshire.

I dyed my hair auburn for the movie. It wasn't really a conscious decision but it was more fitting for an Irish girl and I felt if I was appearing in a British movie again it wouldn't do any harm to signal a fresh start without my trademark blonde curls.

At least when shooting began Sean had forgotten the Arsenal comment. He certainly didn't mention it but, then again, he didn't say much to me. We had a love scene to negotiate, which can be tricky at the best of times. They're awkward scenes to shoot, with the crew there staring, but usually it's ok, if you like the person you're pretending to be intimate with. I think Sean was a bit nervous, which seemed strange given his past history in *Lady Chatterley's Lover* but we managed to get through it.

In keeping with the football theme, there was camaraderie on set, particularly among the male cast. They went out on the town one night and ended up in a strip club. I don't know if Sean was worried about whether I'd let slip to his wife Melanie, because when she came down to the set he made a big deal about the fact that she was talking to me. He came over and said, in an ever-so-slightly threatening tone: 'Why are you talking to her?'

By the time the film was released I could tell it was falling short of its promise. Football films are notoriously hard to pull off. The action never looks as good as *Match of the Day* but there were some basic factual errors that were immediately picked up. It followed too predictable a storyline and there was too little depth to the characters.

I did my best to promote the film, agreeing to quite a few interviews, even though by then I'd grown weary of the press. It didn't seem to matter what I said, they always seemed to focus on the same things – the movies I'd been dropped from, *Wish You Were Here* and whether or not I'd fulfilled my potential. At least this time I gave them something else to talk about – and it was completely unintentional.

I agreed to a photo shoot with *GQ* magazine. I'd done shoots with them before and had no reason to suspect anything could go wrong. For the shoot the female photographer seemed keen to make it as racy as possible. I didn't have a problem with that as long as it was tasteful. The more layers that came off the more worried I became about how it would look. One top was so see-through I was convinced readers would be able to see even the faintest of birthmarks.

Around the same time I had an appointment with the renowned Scottish photographer Rankin who was shooting me for *Time Out*. We were toying with some ideas for the shoot when I suggested taking my top off but protecting my modesty with two footballs. Janet Jackson had done a similar thing on the front cover of *Rolling Stone* magazine, with the hands of her husband covering her breasts.

Rankin was all for it and we finished the shoot. I thought it was quite playful. What I wasn't expecting was the fuss generated from the *GQ* shoot. When the magazine hit the stands you could clearly see my nipple. For some reason, a section of the Press jumped on it as an indication that I was sexing up my image. When the *Time Out* piece followed swiftly afterwards, it merely confirmed the press's suspicions that I was going for a raunchier image.

I was 26, for goodness sake, but some people refused to let me move on. Would I ever be anything other than the precocious teenager in *Wish You Were Here*?

CHAPTER
TWENTY-ONE

*I ended up getting involved with one of the cast. He was older and
made a big play for me. It was only afterwards, he said, quite
casually: 'By the way, did I mention I'm married?'*

Do we ever learn from our mistakes? From my experience the
perception that many actors are neurotic and actresses are
insecure may hold truth. Nevertheless, on occasions I was unable
to resist the charm and personality of certain actors I met. Working
on a film shoot you were removed from reality and the security of
a familiar environment. Due to the intimacy of an enclosed setting
you are transported into a different world, and attractions and
flirtations inevitably materialise between the cast and also the
crew. Sometimes these liaisons are reminiscent of a holiday fling or
on occasions more serious, leading to the break-up of marriage
and relationships.

My protective radar failed me and I became involved with an
actor on my next shoot. For a start, the location and subject matter
of the film that was being made was not exactly conducive for
romance. We were in Bosnia and Herzegovina, not long after the

bitter and bloody war that ravaged the country, and focusing on the plight of thousands of children neglected by NATO and the United Nations during that conflict.

Michael Winterbottom's decision to film in Sarajevo just a few months after the ceasefire had ended a four year siege was a brave one. I didn't have to be asked twice. Michael was a young director but the output in his short career was both prolific and impressive. His first, *Butterfly Kiss* – about a lesbian serial killer and her impressionable young lover – won praise for its originality, while his third, an adaptation of Thomas Hardy's *Jude The Obscure*, starring Kate Winslet, released not long after we finished filming, would bring him international attention.

But his goal in 1996 was to shine a light onto Bosnia, a conflict largely ignored by the rest of the world for years before its conclusion. Basing his film on the true story of ITN reporter Michael Nicholson and his 1993 book, *Natasha's Story*, *Welcome to Sarajevo* concentrated on the frantic, desperate journey of a veteran British TV war correspondent who smuggles out a nine-year-old orphan girl because he is frustrated that neither NATO nor the United Nations will do anything to stop the fighting or rescue the children.

A key message in the film was that that nobody in the West was paying attention to the horrors happening in Bosnia. Even at the height of the siege, when former Yugoslav forces hemmed in locals, the United Nations continued to list Sarajevo as only the 14th-worst place on earth. The reporter upon whom the film was based had his story on a massacre, that included the slaughter of children, displaced in the bulletin back home by the news that the Duke and Duchess of York were separating.

Michael also wanted the film to be a cry for attention for the destroyed Bosnia and the unresolved conflict. Producers Graham Broadbent and Damian Jones originally wanted the film to come out while the war was still going on so that they could help get the West more involved.

They initially approached Nicholson about making a movie when his story broke in 1992, just as the ethnic civil war erupted in the former Yugoslavia. They waited for him to finish his book, then bought the rights. Frank Cottrell Boyce – who wrote *Butterfly Kiss* – wrote the screenplay while the fighting was still fierce, with the siege of Sarajevo at the centre of the conflict among Croats, Serbs and Muslims. Winterbottom's plans had to be put on hold because the logistics meant filming in a war zone would have been too dangerous. His goal had been to show the city but he couldn't do that with bullets flying. However, in the spring of 1996, just a few months after the ceasefire in February, he went to work.

He assembled an impressive cast, all keen to do their bit in raising awareness of a humanitarian issue. Playing Nicholson's character was Stephen Dillane, an actor best known as Horatio opposite Mel Gibson's Hamlet, and the film also starred American stars Woody Harrelson and Oscar winner Marisa Tomei, as well as the New Zealand actress Kerry Fox. I played hard-nosed journalist Annie McGee, loosely based on the award-winning Irish reporter Maggie O'Kane, whose dispatches for the *Guardian* were so crucial in highlighting the conflict.

When we arrived in Sarajevo there was destruction everywhere, but the city was trying desperately to return to normal as quickly as possible. We stayed in the Holiday Inn, a hotel that had taken a battering during the siege. The ceiling was falling in and if we had been in any doubt how the city had suffered, this was an instant reminder. By the time filming started much of the rubble had been cleared and the crew had to reposition some upturned cars and replace some debris to capture the scene as they'd first found it.

Michael used local workers where possible and I had the chance to sit in cafes and interview Bosnian soldiers about their feelings towards the conflict. One told me, simply: 'It was our destiny.'

The crew was of mixed ethnicity but, given the grounds on which the war had been fought, it was encouraging to see them want to be jointly described as citizens of Sarajevo. They had been attacked as one and they wanted to work to repair the city as one. The extras Michael used in certain shots had been victims of the war. During one scene depicting snipers, my character had to rescue a young boy who lost his arm. Between takes I lent this boy my Walkman which seemed to give him pleasure. Not thinking, I took it back. To this day I deeply regret not giving it to him and it still plays on my mind.

Like many of the cast, my part was secondary to the main story, but I wanted to go to Sarajevo and do something about the war. It was the subject matter that attracted me, plus the privileged opportunity to see for myself the destruction caused. It wasn't an easy shoot, however. The conditions were difficult and because of the erratic nature of the filming, I flew in and out when the script demanded.

It might have been the testing circumstances that pushed people together, but I ended up getting involved with one of the cast. He was older and made a big play for me. Initially I resisted his advances but, when I wasn't required on set and flew home, he'd send me little love notes. It was very flattering to be wanted. Eventually I succumbed and we slept together in the crumbling hotel.

It was only afterwards, he said, quite casually: 'By the way, did I mention I'm married?'

The look on my face must have told him, no, sorry, you neglected to mention that small detail.

'It's ok though,' he said, 'we have an open relationship. She knows I sleep around.'

Great, I thought, if I wasn't feeling exactly a million dollars a moment before I was certainly feeling tip top now. How reassuring. Thankfully, my time was nearly up on set and I returned to the UK for good a short while later.

The film was released at a crucial time, just as the United States was deciding how long it would keep its peacekeeping force in the region, and Michael and the producers did their best to ensure the film had an impact. He personally took the film to the White House for a screening, and there were screenings for other world leaders, plus distributor Miramax was pushing heavily for a buzz ahead of the Oscars. The gongs never materialised but the film was well received, crucially in Bosnia itself, and it played an important part in raising awareness. It was one of the movies with which I was most proud to be involved.

After 10 years as an actress I'd made 10 movies, but not all of them had turned out the way I'd hoped. But that's what happens in this industry and I defy any actor to be able to look back on their whole career with complete satisfaction. Almost every project you take on is a gamble. No one has a crystal ball to tell you which film will be a success.

Many actors begin performing in rep theatre. I hadn't had that experience but had always had an unfulfilled desire to work in theatre. Although I didn't feel the need to prove anything, well, perhaps, only to myself, the fact that my father and grandfather were both skilled stage actors encouraged me to try a new medium.

An opportunity to do just that almost literally landed on my doorstep. The Electric Cinema in Notting Hill was one of the first cinemas in the country when it opened in 1910. It has suffered a chequered history over the years, first being eclipsed by more modern picture houses and then being attacked during the second war amid suspicions it housed a Nazi-sympathiser. Sadly, in the early 1990s it shut its doors and fell into disrepair. But to mark 100 years of cinema, David Farr, of the neighbouring Gate Theatre, had the idea of merging both cinema and stage with a new production. Appropriately his play, *Max Klapper – A Life In Pictures*, was a story about cinema itself, with echoes of *Sunset Boulevard* and *Citizen Kane*. Max Klapper was a reclusive director, now living in Cheshire, who made his last Hollywood picture in 1947. A journalist tasked with discovering why his career was wrecked sought him out. It transpired that his final film, *The Beautiful People*, drove him mad in his quest to find the perfect heroine.

I was playing Bella Kooling, a part that, if I'm honest, had a ring of familiarity. She was an innocent girl who went to Hollywood, but that's where the creative similarity ended. She was manipulated by a Svengali-like director, whereas I sometimes had differences with directors.

I was excited at the prospect of acting on stage, but at the same time was nervous that I could do justice to the part. By coincidence my Dad was playing opposite Dawn French at the Savoy Theatre in *When We Are Married* at the same time. It meant he would be too busy to attend the opening night but he did help me with my lines and vowed to come to an alternative showing.

The transition to. stage was much harder than I'd anticipated. It was a baptism of fire. In rehearsals I was learning a lot. On the stage, however, I was excited by the interplay between myself and the audience and the immediacy of the performance.

The performances were on stage but the production skilfully blended film clips to show his search for a star and to show clips from his earlier movies.

Anthony Higgins, a veteran of theatre, film and television, played the manipulative Max and the production also featured Tracy Letts, an American actor and playwright who was also a member of the Steppenwolf Theatre Company.

The rehearsals were gruelling and as opening night loomed I was concerned about maintaining a high quality performance in an unfamiliar medium. In theatre I didn't have the luxury of second takes. I was being plagued by invasive thoughts and voices, which have been consistent throughout my life, and I really had to work on my concentration. I think my family were also worried whether I'd be able to cut it, but when the show opened their fears and mine were dispelled. The energy from the audience gave me a different kind of buzz. I can see how it can become addictive. Everything is immediate and when the show's over you can let off steam and congratulate everyone on a job well done, and then it's on to the next night.

On stage you have the chance to build the arc of the character, whereas in film you have to find the truth of the moment in short scenes. The stage relies strongly on language, so your verbal delivery has to be heard. There's a greater emphasis, too, on understanding the subtext of the script and portraying that subtly in the performance. Sometimes in film you have less rehearsal time to get into character and you are not always in control of the final performance, as the director has carte blanche in the editing room.

It was only a short run but I was pleased with my first foray into stage acting and now I had dipped my toe into the water I was eager for an opportunity to jump in.

At that moment in my career it seemed an alternative path to take other than movies. I felt I was approaching an age as a film actress where I was too old to play precocious teenagers but too young for the really strong heroines. I craved more absorbing roles, characters that had more of a voice but – and it might have been a reflection of the movies that were being made at the time – the parts just didn't seem to be there. I was fortunate that since I'd moved on from *When Saturday Comes* the interest in my private life had largely subsided. I could concentrate on working and it had been a relief to be part of a small theatre company. It was good to be an ensemble actor. I didn't have to worry about carrying an `Emily Lloyd' vehicle.

Reviews for *Max Klapper* were largely positive and I took heart from praise that said I'd lit up the stage. The play was well received and it was good to be part of something that breathed new life into the historic venue. The Electric Cinema was since taken over, refurbished and reopened, although, in 2012 was badly damaged by fire. I hope it can be restored to its former glory and continue to provide pleasure to people for years to come.

With my first theatre experience behind me I wanted to test myself with more, and my next opportunity seemed a dream come true.

Bill Kenwright was planning a new production of *Pygmalion*. Given my desire to play Eliza I jumped at the chance to be involved. The play was due to open at the Theatre Royal, Windsor, in July 1997 and then move to the Albery Theatre in the West End. Roy Marsden – known to millions of TV viewers as Detective Adam Dalgliesh in the PD James mysteries was going to play Professor Henry Higgins and Michael Elphick was Alfred Dolittle.

I was happy and in a good place health wise. It felt like things were falling into place. I'd recently taken up yoga and responded to the sense of calm it gave me. When it was time to start rehearsing for *Pygmalion*, I turned up with my yoga mat so I could relax properly between scenes. I think that immediately drew strange looks from the rest of the cast but I didn't see anything wrong with it.

Early on I could tell this was not going to be the dream role I hoped for. The director was the experienced Scot Giles Havergal, but we didn't see eye to eye. I greatly admired Bernard Shaw's writing. I was full of inspiration. Giles had previously directed a production of *Pygmalion* and had very set opinions which conflicted with my fresh approach.

He quit unexpectedly and Roy Marsden stepped in and offered to direct as well as star. Then the experienced stage and television actress Ann Mitchell was recruited, but by then I'd had enough. I didn't feel sure I could give my best performance and I wanted to leave. I was in conflict with what I thought to be, rightly or wrongly, a limited creative mentality towards a literary gem. I rang my Dad for advice. I was obviously aware of the stigma if I quit. I had a meeting with Bill Kenwright and explained the circumstances. He was nice to me and agreed with my decision.

Even after I left changes continued to be made. Ann stepped down and Ray Mooney, the playwright responsible for the hit *Run For Your Wife*, took over as director. My understudy Carli Norris, who had only officially left RADA the week I departed took over as Eliza. Some things happen for a reason and she took full advantage of her big break, did an excellent job and forged a successful acting career off the back of it. I'm pleased that some good came of it but, after longing to be Eliza for years, I had to realise that it wasn't meant to be.

My plan was to move on to the next project and try and put the setback behind me as quickly as possible. I didn't know then that it would be the start of a downward spiral that would take years to recover from.

CHAPTER
TWENTY-TWO

You're only supposed to give yourself once, but I became addicted.
Every week I went back I wanted to do it again and again and
threw myself at the stage. I think I was a bit too
fanatical, even for these zealots.

He was one of Hollywood's most enigmatic stars, with box office hits and memorable performances to his name, yet with a reputation for being difficult and demanding. More importantly, he was newly single. So when Val Kilmer rang me up and asked me out I was intrigued.

Who could forget him as Iceman in *Top Gun*? Then there was his turn in the fantasy epic *Willow* and of course his mesmerising performance as Jim Morrison in *The Doors*.

He was hot at the time. His stint as Batman had been a success and he was about to be seen in a big budget remake of *The Saint*, which had brought him to London. I had met him at a party also attended by Elisabeth Shue, his co-star in *The Saint*, but that night was notable for a long conversation I had with Laurence Fishburne. Larry was counselling me on the pitfalls of the movie industry. I'd first met him in LA, when I was living in Venice Beach and his career hadn't yet enjoyed the renaissance films like *Deep Cover* and *The Matrix* would provide. Among the words of advice he gave me, he said: 'I've had my share of problems, man, but I always kept my feet on the ground.'

I digress, however. Val and I hardly spoke that night. We'd actually appeared in *Dead Girl* together but I hadn't even met him during the filming. We had the same dialect coach in Tim and when my name came up Val asked him for my number.

I was aware he was about ten years older than me and recently separated from Joanne Whalley, the mother of his two children. There was a similarity to the situation with Sean Penn but I thought nothing of it.

'Do you wanna go to church?' he said, referring to the location for our first date.

Wow, I thought, I must really have made an impression. He wants to take me up the aisle already.

'Sure, why, not?' I said.

What he meant was not wedding bells but the Christian Science Church. There was one in Notting Hill not far from my flat. What's a girl to do on a first date? I didn't know anything about Christian Science but I thought it would be a normal church service with hymns. It wasn't quite what I expected. Followers of Christian Science believe there's two strands to the Bible, one spiritual, the other material, meaning that they believe that anything evil in the world doesn't actually exist and can be eliminated by the power of prayer.

There might not have been the traditional hymns I recognised, but the songs they sang were quite catchy and serene. There was none of the mumbling and mass miming you get at some church services.

Val explained that he had been raised a Christian Scientist and attended their school until the age of graduation. It was fascinating to witness a spiritual side to someone in the public eye and I could tell his faith must have helped keep him grounded when his fame escalated.

The whole experience was quite infectious. I grew quite interested in the movement and started reading the Bible constantly. I even attended services when Val wasn't there. When I'd lived in LA I'd often wondered if there was more to life than working and socialising. It seemed too self-centred, I craved for something more substantial. I liked the inner peace that yoga gave me but I wanted to be fulfilled. Perhaps a church could give me that. My friends were worried about it, though. They thought it seemed like a cult.

Val's family were very important to him and once I accompanied his kids and him to Madame Tussauds, and on another occasion he introduced me to his mother Gladys.

In all, I probably saw Val about five or six times. I have always been in love with the idea of love and on one occasion left a yellow rose for him at his hotel.

I enjoyed his company but, although we enjoyed a brief fling, we both knew it wouldn't last. He was an interesting guy but suffered from the same flaw that many actors do of droning on about themselves or their former wives. Just as I'd done with Sean, I was forced to listen to him talk endlessly about Joanne. Clearly the split was still raw. Val was also into his career, and although at first I was into listening to him talk about it, after a while it lost its appeal.

What I took from our time together was an interest in religion. I stopped going to the Christian Science but found a Methodist church that promoted the theory of being born again. On the first night I went I was amazed by the energy from the congregation.

New members were being reborn that night and it was spellbinding to see people who looked quite normal and reserved throwing themselves to the stage, symbolising the giving of themselves to God. The pastor encouraged me to give it a go. I was nervous at first but then I thought, what the hell, and threw myself forward. It was quite an unusual feeling but very uplifting. The rush you experienced from giving yourself to God was quite something.

You're only supposed to give yourself once, but I became addicted. Every week I went back I wanted to do it again and again and threw myself at the stage. I think I was a bit too fanatical, even for these zealots.

I found the gospel singing invigorating, but almost as quickly as it began I found a new obsession when my focus shifted to yoga. I had joined a class in Notting Hill around the same time but swiftly found myself being drawn deeper and deeper in to more intensive disciplines.

I suppose in a similar way to religion, yoga promotes spiritual wellbeing and nearly asks as much dedication of its practitioners. From the group in Notting Hill, I joined another class in Bayswater and became friendly with a yogic guru called Bhai Himmat Singh Khalsa. He was actually a New Yorker called Henry but he'd moved to Europe seeking followers to his way of life. He was 10 years older than me and I remember when I first met him he was wearing reflective sunglasses and I thought that was quite modern for a yoga guru. We became close but there was never anything sexual between us. On the contrary, he believed women should keep themselves pure. He taught me Kundalini meditation and mantras as a way of achieving ultimate peace. I'd tried Transcendental Meditation in Los Angeles but this seemed like the real deal.

I visited a yoga retreat in Lauche in France. It took a lot of getting used to. Everyone seemed to just sit around eating egg whites and mung beans. The devotees practised clean living and advised against having sex in order to keep your aura clean.

Kundalini is all about awakening a spiritual energy or life force located at the bottom of your spine. You needed a grounding in other yoga, otherwise you can become disconnected. We were staying in tents and meditating for several hours a day. It can get so intense you can slip into a trance. Other times you can almost feel high you are in such a state of enlightenment. At one point during the week I ended up in hospital because I was so out of it. I became convinced that a fellow yoga student, who had accompanied me to the hospital, had been a cruel mother in another life. I said I never wanted to see her again. I was in a bad state and hallucinating that my knickers were flying around the room.

It was quite intense but didn't take me long to calm down and snap out of it. I completed the week without any further mishap and, despite that rather extreme reaction, returned in a calm state of mind, with a fresh outlook on my health issues. I strongly believed drugs were anathema and that any underlying health problem could be treated either by prayer or by the power of positive thought.

A few months later I went with Bhai Himmat to meet Yogi Bhajan, the spiritual leader of Kundalini yoga and the man who introduced it to the United States at his ranch in New Mexico. There I met Courtney Love, who was irreverent towards most things and a free spirit. We sneaked a bottle of wine into our spartan tents.

When I returned from the yoga retreat my mother worried I was becoming obsessive again but she couldn't argue that physically I looked very healthy.

I should have known things were going a little too well.

I was not long back in London in the summer of 1997, when I

went to a party in Knightsbridge. It was in a big house and there were dozens of people there, all milling around. I was sitting on the floor chatting to a woman I knew called Davinia. She was an aspiring documentary filmmaker. She explained to me how she knew Uma Thurman's father who was a close friend of the Dalai Lama. This is true. Robert Thurman is a professor of Tibetan Buddhism who raised Uma in India not far from where his Holiness lived and the religious leader often visited their house.

Davinia was planning a trip out to India and asked if I wanted to join her to interview the Dalai Lama for the documentary. I thought it was a wonderful opportunity to do something different and meet one of the world's most inspirational beings. In the weeks that followed Davinia said she had spoken to Mr Thurman, who'd confirmed that I would be granted an audience with his Holiness in India.

We were leaving imminently and I didn't have long to get organised for the trip. As a precaution, because we were headed off the beaten track, I took a course of malaria tablets, which started before I left.

We flew economy to India, an interminable flight. As soon as we took off I knew something wasn't right. I felt queasy and light-headed and not altogether there. I began to wonder if I was having an adverse reaction to the malaria tablets.

We then travelled by car to Dharamshala, the remote home of the Dalai Lama. We were driving along when we passed a huge river, where people were bathing. Instinctively I thought it must be the River Ganges, the largest river in India and one fabled for its purifying properties. I said to the driver: 'You have to stop here.'

I don't know if it was the jet lag or the reaction I was having from the tablets but I jumped out of the car, ran down to the river and washed myself. When I got back to the car the driver said it wasn't the Ganges. There was nothing special about the water. It was just a very dirty river.

We eventually got to Dharamshala but no sooner had we reached our hotel than Davinia wanted to film a Tibetan dance ritual going on at a monastery nearby. I was outside when a black and white temple dog came up to me. There were lots of these mongrels around. They're looked after by the monks apparently. Anyway, I bent down to stroke this dog when it bit me quite hard on the knee, leaving a ring of teeth marks. I was shocked and hurried back to my hotel room.

The first thing I probably should have done was had a tetanus shot and possibly a rabies jab. Instead though, emboldened by my recent flirtations with religion, I decided to use this moment to test my power of prayer beliefs. I was holding my leg as blood was gushing out. I held the cut and said a prayer, hoping the wound would heal itself.

After a few minutes I realised the gash wasn't a figment of my imagination. It was very real and I realised I could be in real bother if the wound got infected. The hotel found a doctor who administered a tetanus shot but even after that I felt worse. In all it seemed like they gave me three tetanus injections. It wasn't very reassuring. I couldn't have had a worse start to the trip.

Only after I was patched up did Davinia reveal that she didn't actually have a definite yes to the interview. It had never been promised. She'd gone there more in hope than expectation. Before long it was clear the interview was not going to take place. The trip had been a waste of time.

We had no option but to kill time for the two weeks before our flight back to the UK. My health deteriorated alarmingly rapidly. I couldn't eat, was continually drenched in sweat and the weight dropped off me.

I remember going to a market place to try and sample some authentic Indian culture but it was horrible. The place was crowded with people and my Western looks attracted a lot of attention.

I tried to go for a walk, which wasn't advisable in the searing heat, but I ended up wandering for miles, it seemed, in bare feet until I came to another monastery. Looking back now, I can't believe I would have done something like that. I'm not sure if I had some sort of Christ complex back then, as if all of the setbacks were all trials to test my faith. I tried to get some rest at the monastery but there were no women allowed. Eventually one kindly monk took pity on me and let me go inside for a rest before I made the journey back.

When I made it back to the hotel there was a mix up concerning the rooms and I ended up being locked inside one by receptionists, supposedly be accident. It seemed anything that could go wrong was going wrong. I thought I had gone there to do something to help the Tibetan cause. I had gone out there thinking it was all set up. I wouldn't have gone otherwise.

Finally it was time to come home. Mum and Charlotte came to the airport to meet me but I only had to look at their faces to know how horrified they were by my appearance. Mum couldn't believe I was the same girl who'd left her looking happy and vibrant just two weeks earlier. I was dirty, visibly ill and distressed. I'd lost two stone in the time I'd been in India and was skeletally thin.

There was a surreal moment when Mum handed me a paper shortly after we went for a taxi.

Princess Diana had died.

CHAPTER
TWENTY-THREE

Instinctively, I lashed out and accidently knocked his turban. It didn't
fall off but sat, cocked, on his head. There was a moment of
silence when everyone looked at each other.

I could scarcely take in the news. The day I landed back was the Princess of Wales' funeral. In my head I felt like my systems were shutting down, yet outside the country had ground to a standstill.

There have been times throughout my malaise when it has been difficult to recall the precise emotions and sensations I've felt when my torment has been at its height, but this is a time I can remember all too well. My pain of the mind has manifested itself in many forms, but this time the mental torture was coupled with a new agony – physical hurt. My head throbbed constantly, my senses were numbed and it was as if I was enveloped in a thick fog.

I have vague memories of returning through London and trying to fathom the deserted streets. Mum tried to fill me in with what had been happening over the last few days – the horrifying news of the car crash in Paris, Diana's death confirmed, the spontaneous outpouring of grief, the universal fury at the Royal Family, assuaged only by the appearance of Her Majesty on television, desperately trying to reflect the mood of the nation's grief.

There was a feeling things were never going to be the same again. I'd been away for two weeks but had seemingly returned to find Britain a different country. My place in it seemed to have altered irrevocably too. I tried to make sense of my own pain and also take in what was happening around me. Things seemed strangely disconnected but then, the more I tried to think about things, a connection appeared. It's funny what associations flash into your mind but I recalled meeting Dodi Fayed – Diana's boyfriend who was also killed in the crash that took her life in Paris. I'd met him in Browns nightclub in London just a year before. He'd chatted me up and had given me his card.

It was too much to think about. Mum got me home to her house and she was in tears. I really was close to losing it. It was as if my senses were shutting down. Although I'd just made it back from a long-haul flight she didn't trust me to be on my own and insisted she look after me. I was in no mood to argue. After my ordeal in India, nourishment was all I craved.

I crashed out. My energy levels were at rock bottom. It transpired I should never have taken the anti-malarial drug Larium. As I had discovered to my cost, it had a reputation for side effects, which included insomnia, headaches, mood swings and psychosis. It was completely incompatible with anyone with a mental health issue. The more I researched into the drug, the more horrified I became. Some people had been known to jump out of windows after taking it. With my history I should never have been near it. The combination of the drug and being bitten by the dog unhinged me. In some ways, it was helpful to have an explanation for the pain I'd been suffering, but it was small consolation.

Although I'd had injections in India, the doctor gave me another tetanus shot and I had to go for a rabies inoculation as a precaution. After a few days I felt my strength returning and felt I was able to go home but Mum was insistent. She worried that I wouldn't be able to perform the basics on my own. I didn't put up much of a fight. There's no substitute for a mother's love and care and I was grateful for the chance to recuperate. She probably never expected to be a full-time Mum again but she didn't want to take the chance that I might suffer a relapse. She looked after me and gradually I showed signs of recovery, but it was a long process. The headaches, a constant presence since returning from India, slowly eased and the fog gradually lifted. It must have taken me about two months to get back on my feet, figuratively speaking, and even then I still felt pretty wiped out.

Bhai Himmat stayed in touch and came round with flowers to see how I was. Mum was suspicious of him – 'Henry the hermit' she called him – but his intentions were pure and I appreciated his concern. He was keen to get me back to yoga and I was desperate to try and pick my life up from where it had been before my disastrous trip. I was frustrated that after getting so healthy I'd suffered yet another episode. It seemed that no matter what I did to take two steps forward, something always knocked me three steps back.

I started practising yoga again and tried different disciplines like Ashtanga – a more physically demanding form of yoga I hoped would help build my strength up. Developed by K Pattabhi Jois, Ashtanga calls for practitioners to move through a series of flowing movement, jumping from one posture to another to build flexibility and stamina. It is normally only for the extremely dedicated but I'd say I fell into that category at the time. I attended a class in Bayswater

Road and gradually got my energy back. Practising yoga also improved my state of mind and calmed me down once more.

Despite my setbacks, I was still searching for some sort of higher purpose to life. I believed there had to be more than the materialistic existence we were all slaves to and put faith into Bhai Himmat's view of life. His presence may have caused consternation among friends and family, but he helped me refocus.

He still lived in Holland, so when it was time for him to go back home I travelled over there to visit him. His work took him to Germany and to Scotland where I joined him on a trip to Inverness. It was good to get out of the city and breathe some Highland air. We went to Loch Ness and travelled around, savouring the scenic beauty – although there was no sign of the monster!

Bhai Himmat never made his intentions for me clear, but I'm sure he envisioned a future where we'd be together. Our relationship never became physical but he continued to lecture me on the benefits of remaining pure. He advised me not to sleep with anyone else and told me it took seven years for a woman to cleanse herself if she did have sex with a man outside marriage.

I was happy to be led along. In many ways he was the teacher and I his pupil. When he was in London I took him to film premieres and showbiz parties. You can imagine the consternation that caused. When we arrived together for the premiere of the Robin Williams' movie *Good Will Hunting* I think the press saw it as further evidence that Emily Lloyd had flipped her lid. They had no idea who this mysterious Sikh character was and speculated that I was under the spell of this spiritualist guru.

Mum certainly worried that I was in a different world. Really though, I was simply seeking a greater fulfilment, and on one level Bhai Himmat appeared to offer that.

What he couldn't conjure up, however, was a decent paycheck, and because my illness had meant I hadn't been working for a while, my cash flow was something of a problem. As much as I loved my flat in Notting Hill it cost me a lot to keep. The money I'd earned in America had largely dwindled away and I was concerned about how I was going to keep up the mortgage payments. I was still living with Mum and increasingly the flat became an expensive luxury. Eventually I had little option but to put it on the market.

No sooner had I done so than I received an offer to appear in a British-based movie called *Woundings*. It was an intriguing concept. In a post-apocalyptic world, lonely soldiers had to keep the peace on a beautiful but dangerous island. To encourage colonisation the government sent in women, and the movie followed the fate of several of the characters thrown together in the remote location. First-time director Roberta Hanley wrote the script and she managed to assemble a credible cast. Guy Pearce, who rose to prominence in *Neighbours* but only the year before had cemented his reputation as an actor to watch with his performance in *LA Confidential*, played one of the soldiers, along with Charlie Creed-Miles and Jonathon Schaech. I was to play one of the English roses, with Sara Jane Potts and Sammi Davis, sent to keep them company. Ray Winstone played the domineering colonel and Twiggy was also appearing.

I initially had some reservations, but Roberta was very persuasive. She saw me as Kim, a hard nut from Bradford, who falls in love with one of the soldiers.

The longer I spent away from LA, the more the good roles dried up. Acting is such a fickle business. When you're hot the offers are flooding in but when you have been out of the limelight for a while you might as well be dead. I would love to have been considered for female leads at the time but the truth was I wasn't on the radar. It felt like I was scraping around for little independent productions like this one. I tried to maintain my standards, however, looking for the indication that might suggest a film could do well.

Woundings was one of the first European pictures from Los Angeles distributor Cinequanon and among the first to benefit from a new initiative to attract film investment to the Isle of Man. A £1 million government grant had helped establish a film commission on the island, prompting a spate of productions there involving Mickey Rourke and David Bowie.

Plus I needed to work.

The Notting Hill flat had not been on the market long when I received an offer for it. It was a generous one that would have cleared the mortgage and given me some to spare. Frustratingly, though, the offer came while I was on the Isle of Man and was too busy working to respond. By the time I was able to say I'd accept it the offer was withdrawn. It sat on the market for another few weeks before I was forced to drop the price and eventually accept a much-reduced offer.

From being able to afford a decent house in Venice Beach and having dollar bills spilling out of shoeboxes, I now had to accept I couldn't afford my own place in London. My name was down for housing association accommodation and I continued to live at Mum's until I moved up the waiting list. I had a tinge of regret that I hadn't been able to save more of my earnings in Hollywood, but when things are going well you never believe the big roles are going to dry up completely.

Like Mum, I knew I couldn't be trusted to look after the pennies. That's why I'd employed the services of business managers and accountants. Who'd have known they'd be the ones to rip you off?

My financial plight focused the mind, however, and when another script came my way for an independent film in LA I didn't want to turn it down. Roger Avary, a long-time friend and collaborator with Quentin Tarantino – they collected the Oscar for best screenplay for *Pulp Fiction* together – was the executive producer for a movie called *Boogie Boys*. Another friend of Tarantino, Craig Hamann was directing his own script about Jesse, an ex-con whose attempts to go straight are thwarted by a former cellmate. He gets sucked into one last drug job but is forced to go on the run with the money when the deal goes wrong. I was playing Hester, the wife of an hotelier who gives a room to Jesse but learns about the stolen cash. She's a slightly unhinged ex-stripper who finds the cash and hides it under the floorboards. It all comes to a head when the gang Jesse has ripped off tracks him down and there's a desperate fight for the cash.

Filming largely took place in the desert near Los Angeles and while it wasn't going to provide an instant solution to my financial woes it was an enjoyable shoot. I wasn't in LA for long but managed to squeeze in some yoga and felt my recovery from the Larium episode was continuing.

I came back to London, but all was not well with Bhai Himmat. He had helped me with my recovery but it was growing increasingly obvious we were not going to be compatible in the conventional sense. I'm not sure what I would have done if he had tried to proposition me. Thankfully perhaps, the situation never arose. I kissed him on the lips once and he said to my Mum, 'Oh my God, I couldn't believe it.'

I'm not sure if I offended him or excited him. I valued him as a spiritual friend but was growing weary of his unorthodox attitudes to women.

One night, while I was cooking dinner at Mum's for us all, he made a disparaging remark about my methods. It was the final straw. Instinctively, I lashed out and accidently knocked his turban. It didn't fall off but sat, cocked, on his head. There was a moment of silence when everyone looked at each other. The sideways slant of the turban matched my mother's sideward glance. Mum went into another room to stifle her laughter. Joining her, I had to bite my lip to stop a fit of giggles.

Silently, Bhai Himmat composed himself, righted his turban and climbed the stairs from the kitchen to the door upstairs. It was the last I saw of him. He did send me a letter a short while later but, just as he was in person, he was vague about what he expected from me and it was basically all about him.

Another reason things didn't work out between Bhai Himmat and myself was that I'd met someone. Matt was an advertising executive who was three years younger than me. Charlotte's then boyfriend, the son of the late Lord Robertson, had introduced me to him and as soon as we met I felt he could be a calming influence. I don't mean this to be disparaging but he was an uncomplicated guy from Malvern, the picturesque spa town in the beautiful Worcestershire hills. He was in advertising, loved rugby and having a beer and after the whole Bhai Himmat episode I found a sense of normalcy. He was also pleasing to the eye!

My family were relieved I was back in a conventional relationship and so was I. It had been fascinating having an alternative outlook on life, but it was equally important to have some fun. When I got word that a property had become available in Hackney I went to check it out. It was a generously-sized garden flat. I wasn't in a position to be choosy but the flat suited me perfectly. It wasn't long before I picked up the keys. I had a place of my own once again and seemed to be in a stable relationship. For the first time in my life, at age 29, I was on the verge of settling down. It couldn't last, could it?

CHAPTER
TWENTY-FOUR

Mel B – Scary Spice – invited me to her villa. She had a brand new white carpet but when I came in from the garden I trailed mud in after me. I was terrified she was going to erupt.

It was my first public appearance for three years and the audience was one of the smallest – literally – of my career. I was in Cornwall, reading to 150 schoolchildren to help launch a literacy campaign.

The event was held in the Camelot Castle Hotel in Tintagel and the brainchild of hotel owner John Mappin, the heir to the Mappin and Webb jewellery business, who with business partner Ted Stourton had plans to turn the place into a centre for story-telling. I knew John from Tramp but we'd had a strange encounter when I met him in Los Angeles while we were both living out there. He asked me to meet him for lunch one day and gave me an address. It was only when I had arrived at the location and was greeted by receptionists who welcomed me to the Scientology centre that I had a suspicion of being tricked into going there. There was no brainwashing or any attempt to get me to join the Scientologists, but it felt a little odd.

Anyway, I liked John and when he asked me to help out with his story-telling campaign I was delighted to. On the day I was there, in March 2000, supermodel Christina Estrada and boxer Chris Eubank were also doing their part by reading stories.

Once I was convinced about the merits of the campaign, I was eager to join in. Reading stories and having books read to me was such an important part of my childhood that I couldn't resist the chance to help pass that magic on.

Although I'd performed on stage before, the prospect of getting up in front of such a captive, but probably highly critical, audience was a bit nerve-racking. Children can tell when someone is genuine, though, and once I got going I found myself getting really into it.

I was reading the adventures of *Burglar Bill* and loved mimicking the characters of Bill and his wife Betty. The kids seemed to respond and it became great fun. Seeing the expressions on their faces as the story progressed was incredible. If only theatre audiences were so responsive! It was an enriching experience.

It was a small step back into the limelight. By having a little stability in my life, I felt confident enough to try and get back to work. I'd moved into the flat in Hackney and, not long after, Matt moved in. It was a little impulsive. We'd only known each other for a few weeks but it felt the right thing to do.

For the first time it felt like I was in a proper relationship – one not interrupted with either partner disappearing to film locations or parties. We hung out like normal boyfriends and girlfriends, did the shopping together and cooked meals. After years of living out of suitcases, I was discovering what domesticity was all about.

I might have been going through a quiet phase work-wise but I made an effort to raise my profile. I began to open up about the health problems I'd suffered. I wasn't looking for sympathy, just some understanding of the issues. Whenever my name was mentioned it prompted questions like: 'Whatever happened to her?' I felt it wouldn't do any harm to explain.

I spoke openly about the OCD I'd suffered and gave some explanation for my relative hiatus. There's always a worry when you reveal a part of yourself that it won't be received in the way you hope. I felt vulnerable and anxious that I wasn't shooting myself in the foot but, thankfully, the reaction was positive. It sparked articles looking at the triggers for the condition. At that time, even though as many as one in 60 people in Britain suffered some form of OCD, it wasn't common for those in the public eye to speak about it. A few years later several celebrities came out and said they too had compulsive behavioural traits – among them David Beckham. I doubt it was a link he paid much attention to, but funnily enough a couple of years after I made my public admission he and his wife Victoria invited me to their World Cup party in 2002.

It was a pleasant surprise to be invited and Matt accompanied me to the party. It was a glitzy occasion. The dress code was 'White Tie and Diamonds' but the theme of the party, held in marquees in the grounds of their Hertfordshire mansion, was Japanese garden. Guests were greeted by waitresses dressed as geisha girls who led them through to the dining area in the heart of the seven-acre tent village.

There was also a football theme throughout with surviving members of the 1966 England World Cup winning team invited, along with current players who would shortly be heading off to play in the tournament in South Korea and Japan.

The 350 guests was a *Who's Who* of British celebrity life. Sir Elton John and his partner, David Furnish, were there with Cilla Black, Sir David Frost, the DJ Goldie, Joan Collins, Jemma Kidd, Vivienne

Westwood, Sir Richard Branson, and the television chef Jamie Oliver, who was on our table.

Apparently feng shui experts had ensured positive energy flowed through the tent village and inside the huge banqueting hall, where we were all due to eat, there were dozens of lanterns.

Before dinner, everyone lined up to meet the hosts. I was surprised to see David was wearing make-up, almost as much as his wife. Victoria was charming. Although we only spoke briefly, she seemed warmer than people give her credit for and she praised my movies, saying she was a fan of my work.

I found it all very pleasant, but for some reason Matt didn't take a shine to Jamie Oliver and sat muttering about him throughout the meal. The food itself was exquisite – starters of asparagus, shiitake mushrooms and Thai salmon topped with seaweed followed by beef satay, chilled monkfish, stir-fried vegetables, jasmine rice, crispy duck and blackened cod. For pudding there was strawberries and cream.

There was music from tenor Russell Watson and soul singer Beverley Knight and an auction raised money for NSPCC. The party afterwards gave guests a chance to mingle, but I was slightly disconcerted to see the Australian actress Natalie Imbruglia flirting with my boyfriend. She was fluttering her Bambi-esque eyes at Matt and he wasn't doing a good enough job at putting her off for my liking.

Not by any grand design, my Spice-theme continued not long after the party when I met Melanie Brown and for a brief time hung out with her. She was great fun but could live up to her reputation as Scary Spice when she wanted to. Mel invited me to her villa in Buckinghamshire. She had a brand new white carpet but when I came in from the garden I trailed mud in after me. I was terrified she was going to erupt.

Not long after that, she came back to my house in Hackney after a late night in London. Matt was sleeping in bed. Mel thought it would be hilarious to shave off some of his eyebrows. Before I knew what was happening she duly had. Matt never stirred but in the morning he wasn't best pleased. It's not everyone who can say they've had their eyebrows shaved off by a Spice Girl though.

I switched agents around this time and employed the services of Lindy King, then of PFD, who looked after, among others, Ewan McGregor. She got me an audition with British movie company Filmhouse for a lead role in a thriller called *The Honeytrap*. Producer and director Michael Gunther had only a £1.4 million budget to shoot on location in London. I was to play Catherine, a woman who suspects her partner is cheating on her and enlists the help of a private detective agency to find it. A sultry young woman is put on the case and it leads Catherine into a dark voyage of discovery.

I liked the sound of it and the chance to appear in a British movie appealed to me. I got the part and enjoyed filming in London – a markedly different experience from the last occasion when I shot *Chicago Joe*. For a month it almost seemed like a regular job. I could travel to the set or the studio and go home at night. On some shoots I'd had to work hard to cover up my malaise but here I was stable. It helped a little that I had a friendly face on set as my hairdresser Sarah worked with me. It was fascinating to film around the city centre, using the iconic landmarks as the backdrop.

Despite some good moments and fine performances, sadly the movie was another that went straight to DVD, which was unfortunate because it was well received by those that saw it.

It felt reassuring to be working again, but I wasn't enjoying life. My relationship with Matt was stagnating. From what at first had seemed comforting domesticity had dwindled into monotony. Something had to give. I stuttered on for a few months longer than I should have. When you live with someone it's harder to call time on the relationship. Something nagging at the back of your head tells you to do something about it, but then another voice assures you things will improve. They didn't.

Eventually I asked Matt to move out. It was the only solution. I wanted my own space. He wasn't best pleased but he respected my decision and found a place to go. It was sad that it hadn't worked but I could feel the misery building in me and I was desperate not to be engulfed again.

I resolved to keep working and hoped that a part would come up that could define me once more. I didn't have the luxury of turning down roles and when Lindy said I'd been offered a part in a feature-length pilot for an American TV series I reluctantly said yes. It was a fantasy adventure called *Riverworld*, loosely based on *Alice's Adventures in Wonderland*. My character was a grown up Alice, who lived on a strange planet that existed as an afterlife populated by everyone who ever died on Earth. The trouble was that filming was taking place in New Zealand.

I'd never been to that part of the world before but I should have suspected that travelling that distance and working on a project that had no guarantee of being optioned might not have been the best idea. I felt I had no choice.

The flight was bearable but when I got to the location I realised it was quite remote, and near the sea. The shoot was to last three weeks but I spent most of my time in my hotel ordering room service. The only salvation was the fresh seafood served on a daily basis. I practically ate my own body weight in lobster.

Some of the other actors and crew went exploring the nearby

islands but I was content to stay where I was. If we'd been closer to civilisation I might have been able to sample what New Zealand had to offer but when my commitments were over it was time to fly home. I'd got through it and fulfilled my obligations but returned to the UK exhausted.

I wanted to keep working though and hoped that my next project could be something to inspire me. Luckily it did that and also enabled me to fulfil a lifetime ambition.

Robert J Williamson is a theatre director and actor who had earned a reputation for staging impressive retellings of Shakespeare's finest works in unusual venues. In 2003 he was planning a new touring production of *Hamlet*. The setting for this new performance would be outdoor venues in Brighton, Nottingham and London. In Brighton the mystical Royal Pavilion was chosen for the venue. I was approached to play Ophelia, daughter of Polonius and Hamlet's would-be lover.

It had always been a dream of mine to play Ophelia. A much-misunderstood character, I harboured a desire to waken her from the passive role she played in many portrayals.

Although the part is tragic I knew it would stretch me and, after my recent film roles, was something to energise me. It was a small production and at the Equity minimum pay rate I certainly wasn't doing it for the money, but I was relishing the opportunity to perform again. After I'd survived my *Max Klapper* experience unscathed I felt confident I could produce my best work.

Shortly before rehearsals began, however, my voice started to fade. I sounded hoarse and croaky, not the ideal preparation for an outdoor show. As I rested my voice, I started praying for a long, dry summer so I would last the pace. When I felt better my Dad helped me with some techniques on how to project my voice. As a veteran of the stage and of Shakespeare, his help was invaluable.

The character of Ophelia is often underplayed and during the first half of the play she acts as a mirror to Hamlet. She doesn't really do a lot but then the narrative is not about her. But the scene where she goes mad after the death of her father was where I hoped I could get really lost in that wonderful, beautiful, almost ephemeral picture. She is trying to explain her feelings. What I loved about it was that in life it seems we are all under pressure to communicate in a precise way. So to have the luxury of being emotional and getting carried away and being able to let someone know how you feel was liberating. If anything Ophelia was gentle, almost polite, in her madness. She was obviously in a great deal of pain and was trying to articulate that.

Often people think she was a victim of her circumstances, but I didn't see her that way. I don't think she cried out for pity, more to be understood, and that was something over the years I've been able to relate to.

If I'm being honest, perhaps those around me were worried about me taking on something so visible as *Hamlet*. There would be no hiding place if I messed it up. But I took heart from the desire that still burned in me to push myself. Just like I'd been at the start of my career I wasn't afraid to fall flat on my face. If that's what fate had in store for me so be it. I was sure though I would deliver. I enjoyed the preparations and the rehearsals. It felt natural again, what I should be doing. I embraced the creative journey that came with adopting a character.

Before the production I reflected on my career and came to realise that what I'd achieved at such a young age had been, in many ways, both an advantage and a disadvantage. *Wish You Were Here* had been such an opportunity but one I would be saddled with until the end of my days. Was that necessarily a bad thing? I wasn't sure. If I went to my local gym in Dalston, someone would say: 'Up yer bum!'

There was no escaping it. But then I had to remind myself that some people could spend their whole life searching for that one role that could define them, make them live forever in people's consciousness. The grass is always greener, as they say. I resolved just to try and enjoy myself and see what happened.

In any event, it was exciting to meet up with the rest of the cast and crew. It felt like I was entering a new arena. Robert was engaging and talented and completely focused on making the production a success.

He had his work cut out. Just before we were due to open in Brighton Tracy Shaw, the actress best known for her role in *Coronation Street,* pulled out, citing exhaustion.

Thankfully, I had no similar issues to deal with and once I got past the first performance felt I settled into it. It helped that I had an assistant on hand to make sure I didn't miss my cues and made the correct entrances. Given that I was by no means an accomplished stage actress and was relying largely on instinct to get me by, I felt the reviews were fairly encouraging. One said I was stilted but I was still feeling my way into the character at that point and in the main I was praised for my ability to capture Ophelia's descent into madness.

When my family came to see the play they teased me for failing to keep still during Ophelia's death scene but I'd challenge anyone to remain stock still when you're lying outside in the cool air!

Robert seemed pleased and praised me for not fluffing a single line. It was a short run but I was happy I got through it. After the difficulties with *Pygmalion* I had lingering doubts that I could do theatre again, but now I'd manage to dispel those.

Sadly, there were few other offers on the horizon. In the heady days of *Cookie* and *In Country* I could roll from one project to the next. Now the days stretched out in front of me. I hoped the phone would ring with a great offer but none came.

It would be too easy to say that being on my own again triggered what happened next. The brain is too complex a machine to be influenced by one single factor. More, it seemed like I experienced another build-up in emotions that gradually overwhelmed me.

Mum noticed the first stages. I started to zone out during conversations and lost my train of thought in mid-sentence. If I went over to the sink to pour a glass of water by the time I reached it I'd have forgotten why I was there.

Out of the blue I received an offer to appear in *Casualty*, the long-running BBC medical drama. It was only for one episode but if it went well there was a chance it might lead to more.

I should have let it go. I knew enough about my mental state to know when the darkness was descending but still I felt an innate urge to force myself to work. I knew the illness was hovering but I was determined to deliver the goods.

I've never told anyone this – I don't know why given the other setbacks I've suffered – but when I went to Bristol for filming it was hopeless. I was only there for a night. I turned up on set but it was clear from the off that something wasn't right. I simply couldn't engage – with the words, with the character, with the direction. A medic on set (that's the good thing about a hospital drama – there's always a doctor nearby) said: 'She's not well.'

That's about the only thing I have a clear recollection of. That and wandering around Bristol Zoo to pass the time before I had to get the train back. I felt completely lost. The director had no choice but to fire me. I didn't have the strength to argue. I remember wandering around the zoo empathising with the animals locked in their small enclosures. One greyback gorilla in particular looked miserable in his pen. He had a look of resignation on his face as if to say: 'What am I doing here?' I knew how he felt.

In the weeks following this latest setback my behaviour became even more erratic. I'm relying on the recollections of my family for this detail but I was prone to involuntary outbursts. It seemed like a form of Tourette's Syndrome but instead of the foul language that normally characterises the condition, I would say words like: 'Fairydust.'

I went to a specialist who diagnosed a mild form of Tourette's. I hadn't realised but the condition is related to OCD so perhaps there was a correlation there. I was given an anti-psychotic medication called Haloperidol to control the outbursts but suffered an extreme reaction to it.

We were at a restaurant celebrating my aunt Janice's birthday when in the middle of my meal my jaw locked and I could not shut my mouth. My body seized up, my hands formed into claws and my frame hunched like Quasimodo.

As I looked around the table it seemed the whole family had been struck by the same affliction. Everyone was staring open mouthed. They were only stunned by the spectacle before them. After a few moments they could at least close their jaws, whereas I was suspended in animation. Mum urged the restaurant to call me a taxi and she accompanied me to accident and emergency. All the time I looked like I'd been hit with a stun gun.

At the hospital, when told the medication I'd been taking, the doctors calmly told me I was suffering a side effect. They administered an antidote to loosen my muscles. After a few moments I had the wonderful sensation of being able to close my mouth again. It had all been remedied in an hour or so and Mum and I rejoined the others at the restaurant.

I was urged to continue with the Haloperidol but the doctors gave me an additional drug to stave off the side effects, while also giving me my own supply of the antidote should my face freeze up again. Thankfully it didn't.

Despite the medley of medication they expected me to take, my condition worsened. Trying to think back and piece together the events of those days is difficult, perhaps because years of insomnia and medication has muddled my mind, or perhaps because it is too painful for me to revisit. I don't know. Episodes flash into my mind like flickering images on a projector screen, but it's hard to place them in context or order.

I know the voices in my head returned – the same ones that plagued me in New York when I was 17. It's hard to describe them, but they filled my head with self-doubt and questioned everything I was doing.

My family were understandably worried that I was having another episode. I can sympathise with their situation. There seemed to be no rhyme or reason to when this malaise would heighten.

I saw more specialists. Sometimes these meetings were not unlike the auditions for stage school. They comprised of me, sitting answering questions in front of a panel of experts, each analysing and studying me. There was a neurologist, a cognitive therapist, the obligatory student I always seemed to have sitting in on my consultations.

After one such appointment I was prescribed a new drug – Sertraline, an anti-depressant also administered to treat obsessive compulsive disorder and anxiety.

I was willing to try anything. I can't remember if it stabilised me or not. My abiding memory is that one of the side effects was that it made you put on weight. For an anti-depressant that's not a great selling point. The last thing you want when you're feeling miserable is to see you're gaining pounds at will. Initially I tried to exercise to burn it off. I went swimming and went to the gym but nothing I tried seemed to work.

At another point in my career I might have been able to bounce back but this time I felt myself succumb to the depression. I had no work to focus and fall back on. Again the days just seemed to stretch out in front of me. When you've tasted the highs of being feted by the cream of Hollywood and having some of the most renowned names in the business keen to work with you it's hard to settle for mediocrity. Yet that was all I could see for myself now.

Perhaps I should have kept things going in moderation. The yoga I'd been so obsessive about just a few years earlier seemed an alien concept to me. It was as though a creeping blackness was enveloping me, a nothingness that blocked out all light.

After spending many years thinking drugs were anathema to me, now, when I mingled with people who used them regularly, they seemed an enticing alternative. I'd put my faith in conventional medicine but I felt that had failed me. I wasn't in the right frame of mind to be indulging myself, but the people I was socialising with weren't best equipped to deal with someone with such long-standing mental issues. I should have known better but when you hit rock bottom you'll do anything to come up.

I started dabbling in cocaine. The relief from my everyday misery might have been fleeting, but it was respite. Soon I began taking it on a weekly basis, my weekend treat. I was probably drinking too much during this time too. My judgement was skewed.

What began as a weekend buzz, something to lift me out of the doldrums, became a regular occurrence. I was mixing with a bad crowd but I felt so worthless I was grateful for anyone and anything that made me feel better, no matter how temporary the feeling was.

I thought I'd hit rock bottom, but I was wrong. There was lower to sink.

I'm not proud to admit this but in my lowest moments I have even resorted to crack cocaine. Certainly nothing else had quelled the ceaseless, raging battle in my mind. It was on offer. It will make you feel better, I was promised. Why not, I thought. I'm lucky that I was never addicted to drugs, but my brief and unfortunate experiment with crack cocaine was futile and unfulfilling. I sympathise with those who are its victims.

CHAPTER
TWENTY-FIVE

In my worst moments I felt like a commodity, a guinea pig,
another statistic on the conveyer belt. I didn't feel like I was the
architect of my own destiny any more.

The day had started innocuously enough. I had been round at
Mum's and, after enjoying what had seemed like another of our
informal catch-ups, had gone out to use the phone box. Why I went
and who I was intending to call I can't remember. All I know is that
when I came back the police were waiting to speak to me. I had no
idea why.

The mind can play tricks on you. If it doesn't want you to
remember certain details it won't. If it wants to protect you from
painful memories it will.

I think I had been so morbidly depressed, so despairingly desolate,
that I couldn't be trusted not to harm myself. In the preceding weeks
I had been prescribed new medication called Ritalin after a doctor
felt I displayed symptoms of attention deficit disorder. The drug has
become well known as a treatment for hyperactive children. It is
supposed to calm them, but is essentially a stimulant. Initially I felt a

positive reaction. I seemed able to connect the thoughts in my head and articulate them. I even cleaned my flat. My family felt I seemed a lot sharper.

Gradually though I felt wired and unable to express my emotions. After about two months the medication caused me to lose my voice. My frustration manifested itself in moments of erratic anger. It seemed ironic that a drug used to control tantrums in children might be causing them for me.

My family were on the receiving end of my outbursts. At the height of this, while at my Mum's, I threw a glass at the wall. Mum must have felt she had no choice but to call the police to make sure I was all right. On my return to the house I was shocked to see two police officers.

Did I even say something to someone on the phone that set alarm bells ringing? I cannot say. It must be frustrating to read an account riddled with so many holes. If that's the case, imagine what it must be like to live a life where your memory is filled with blank spaces.

I tried my best to appease them. Maybe the seriousness of the situation was a wake up call. Given my history of self-harming and stays in hospital Mum was rightly worried that I might take a knife to my arm again or seek solace in a bottle of pills. I was that close to the brink.

I needed help. I could see that. The police officers were reassured when I insisted I was fine and that I wasn't harbouring suicidal thoughts. It was a watershed moment however.

My GP referred me to Homerton Hospital in Hackney, an NHS facility I had been to before for assessments because it had a specialist psychiatric unit. This time however he was recommending an extensive assessment, which would mean a prolonged stay. I didn't know it then but it was to be the start of one of the bleakest six months of my life. The hospital didn't section me but wanted me to stay so they could assess my behaviour. I quickly found out, however, that, like the Hotel California, once you check in it's very hard to leave.

Admitted as an in-patient, a nurse led me into an all-female ward and to a small wooden bed. My personal space extended to a metre width from the bed and all that separated me from the willing or reluctant victim on either side was a thin plastic curtain. The locked ward door added to the feeling of being incarcerated.

The procedure, as it was explained to me, was that I'd be assessed on a regular basis so that doctors could get to the bottom of my malaise. The reality was somewhat different. Medication seemed to be the only answer. The treatment of mental health might have evolved considerably from the closed asylums of the Victorian age but, in some aspects, the old ways remained in evidence. Before any assessment was made of my mental state, I was sedated with strong anti-psychotic medicine.

When Mum first came in to see me she was shocked. She felt it was like I had been lobotomised. I was unrecognisable as the daughter she knew. I have no idea why the doctors thought it necessary to sedate me. Yes, there had been the incident with the police, but once inside the hospital I wasn't a danger to myself or anyone else.

Despite my incapacitated state, the doctors expected me to be responsive during ward meetings, which were supposed to be held on a regular basis but, as time wore on, took place only sporadically. During the first evaluation Mum attended she sat shocked as doctors fired questions at me. She says I sat motionless staring blankly ahead as I had lost my power of speech and had difficulty finishing sentences. Eventually she took me out of the meeting.

As the days progressed I became more responsive. I'm not sure if this was because they reduced my medication or if I just became more acclimatised to my surroundings. I found, under the circumstances I coped relatively well. It was a sink or swim scenario. I tried to settle into a routine. My life was the ward. There was a television and a ping-pong table, but in the first few weeks of my stay there was a distinct absence of mental stimulation.

I discovered the seven other people in my ward had a myriad of conditions. There were drug addicts, anorexics and people with other mental health issues.

One lady, two feet away from my bed, had a chronic grunting affliction that made me restless, bringing on an anxiety so I tried to remedy this by listening to audio tapes. One of them was *Memoirs of a Geisha,* Arthur Golden's novel about a hostess in Japan. I found solace by escaping into the world of Chiyo, the narrator. I imagined the nurses as the characters to pass the time. Like Chiyo, I longed to be free from my surroundings, yet my imagination was my only ticket to escaping the stark reality of the four walls I was soon, scarily, becoming too familiar with.

As my so-called assessment continued, I was assured my stay would be no more than three weeks, but when that time came and I asked to leave, I was told I couldn't. No reason was given, no explanation forthcoming as to how my treatment was going. I returned to my bed dispirited and defeated. I felt the purpose of in-patient care was to explore the root cause of my problems and try to treat it accordingly, but now I felt my identity was being erased. I was being left to rot. Containment seemed the solution. I felt about as free as a bird in a cage.

My condition resulted in an inability to communicate. The doctors said they would continue to monitor me on a weekly basis, but the following appointment time came and went with no meeting. It's hard to convey the feeling of nothingness that provokes. You feel like you don't exist, at best an afterthought.

The nurses, who came round frequently, might have been updating the doctors but it was impossible to gauge what progress, if any, I was making.

I tried to focus on small pleasures. When I first arrived in the hospital, patients were allowed tea whenever they wanted. After a few weeks, however, tea provision was rationed. The powers that be decreed you could only have one every five hours. When you are stuck in a small place like that having a cup of tea is a relief. I began to feel I had a supporting role in a real-life version of *One Flew Over the Cuckoo's Nest*. Like the rebellious McMurphy, in the classic for which I'd once failed to credit Milos Foreman, I seemed to come to life the more restrictions were placed on us. I didn't think I could last five hours without a cuppa. I started to become friendlier with the nurses, buttering them up to see how strictly they enforced the new laws. It worked. Soon I was able to get a cup of tea when I wanted. Other patients were grateful too. A sense of camaraderie was building with my fellow inmates. We were all in the same boat after all.

A long-lasting memory from my stay at the Homerton was of an Afro-Jamaican patient called Rachel who was deprived of her teeth and had a pronounced limp. While we were in the ward garden, one sunny afternoon, Rachel began to sing a sorrowful version of *Summertime*. Her voice was as haunting as Billy Holliday's. Moments of pleasure were few and fleeting, but when they came they crystallised in my mind.

Some other memories stick with me for other reasons, however.

On one occasion when Charlotte came to visit I was sitting down to lunch with a girl who was there being treated for anorexia. The girl was looking longingly at her roll, plucking up the courage to take a bite. I began to eye it enviously, living up to my childhood nickname of 'Gannet'.

To Charlotte's dismay, I asked the girl: 'Are you going to eat that?'

My sister says the girl looked like she might well have eaten it but, when faced with an option to give it away, felt compelled to do so.

'No,' she said. 'You can have it.'

'Thanks,' I said, swiping it off her plate before she changed her mind. The hospital portions were never enough. Charlotte was appalled but saw the humour in it.

Slowly I was beginning to wake from my slumber and engage more with my surroundings. I think I realised there was not going to be a quick solution to my predicament so I might as well try to make the most of it. I asked about activities that would provide some much-needed mental stimulation. It transpired art therapy and cookery classes were available. I wondered why this wasn't mentioned when I first entered the hospital.

I took part in the classes and found them fun – well, as much fun as it can be in a regimented environment.

After I'd been in there for several weeks, there was a family birthday party I was desperate to attend. I asked if I could have special dispensation to leave for the evening and to my surprise it was agreed. I was free, if only for a few hours.

It felt wonderful to be back home, albeit briefly, and engage in some normal conversation and catch up with news that didn't involve the standard of the food or the cleanliness of the ward. I returned dutifully to the ward after a couple of glasses of wine and was feeling merry. One of the patients I knew was looking depressed.

'Don't be a glum chum,' I said, attempting to lift him up. 'Don't be a sad cad.'

The next day in the ward round a nurse told me I was banned from any more day release. Apparently I'd come back too elated. My taste of freedom might have been sweet, but I had no idea when I'd sample it again.

The weeks stretched into months. I tried to remain upbeat but it was easy to get dispirited. Once again, there seemed to be no structure to my programme, no answers to my malaise. I received no word as to how long I might be in there. I felt helpless, lost and alone. I was sure that, rather than treat me according to my symptoms and experience, the doctors were trying to make me fit a particular character or ailment. They suggested a new anti-psychotic medication called Clozapine that was to be injected every month. I looked into it but discovered one of the side effects was that you blew up like a balloon. That, coupled with my discomfort at the thought of being injected every month, prompted me to decline the treatment.

I tried to engage once more in the activities and workshops, but I was only going through the motions. I was shutting down. Any spark left inside was fading. I longed to be back in the outside world, to be back with my family, but the longer I spent in there the less hopeful I was that I'd be reunited with them anytime soon.

Then, out of the blue, at a weekly meeting with the doctors – in itself a rare occurrence – I was told I was fit enough to go home. After six months I was being released.

I don't really know why, after all that time, they suddenly decided I was fit to get out. Perhaps my moroseness indicated I was calmer. By then I didn't care. I could go home. That was all that mattered. The frustrations that six months of medical care failed to properly analyse what was causing my malaise and how best it could be treated would surface in the coming months, but for now I wanted to breathe the fresh air again and feel the wind on my face.

Mum came to meet me, with flowers for the nurses, and collected my things. Home beckoned. My journey through the labyrinth of my mental illness had taken me to private hospitals, prison-like establishments in Arizona, a guarded-room in Los Angeles and an NHS institution in Hackney. In my experience there wasn't much difference between private and publicly funded health care. The professionals do their best in difficult circumstances, but often I felt too little information was communicated to me about my prognosis and treatment.

In my worst moments I had felt like a commodity, a guinea pig, another statistic on the conveyor belt. I didn't feel like I was the architect of my own destiny any more. Instead it felt like patients in psychiatric care were treated like a number – anaesthetised and alienated from the heartbeat of life. Maybe I had been trying to aspire to an idealised reality, maybe that was my problem. Perhaps this was a result of an avoidance of the environment I was accustomed to.

The pain in my mind that had enveloped me since I was a young child might still be present but, that day, as I left Homerton and stepped out into the sunlight, I had the fleeting impression it might be easing.

EPILOGUE

In the middle of the journey of our life
I found myself in a dark wood
For I had lost the right path
And so we came forth, and once again beheld the stars

Darkness Visible: A Memoir of Madness – William Styron

In his groundbreaking memoir into his depression and ultimate recovery, the American writer William Styron modified the opening and final lines of Dante's *Inferno* as a testament to his enduring spirit and his conquest over personal struggles and it's a passage that resonates with me still.

I am midway through the journey of my life and I have found myself in a dark forest when the straightforward pathway had been lost. At times I felt myself in new levels of despair, increasingly dictated to by the master I call my malaise, to which I wondered whether I would always be a slave.

Now, however, as I look to the future, it is with renewed optimism. I'm trying to see the wood for the trees and I believe I can once again, like Dante does in his epic poem, behold the stars. Or failing that I can sing *Twinkle Twinkle Little Star* backwards!

In the last nine years of my life I have spent periods in and out of the Homerton Hospital. That last six months there was the longest and worst stay. I would not liken it to a walk in the park.

For the last five years I have been prescribed Abilify, a brand name for a drug called aripiprazole, an anti-psychotic medication to treat mild schizophrenia and depression. I am on the lowest dose and it has helped provide an element of calmness but one of the side effects is insomnia. For that same period I have survived despite a chronic lack of sleep. I'm lucky if I get two hours in a night. It's like the medication is giving with one hand and taking away with another. I didn't appreciate how restorative sleep can be until I was deprived of it. In the first few months and years I couldn't handle the constant tiredness. I would lose my train of thought and zone out of conversations. It seemed a constant battleground.

Doctors were amazed that I could function at all on such little rest. At times I have tried countless remedies – the strongest sleeping pills, attending a sleep clinic, trying cognitive therapy and herbal treatments acupuncture, hypnotherapy and reflexology – with only limited success. I try exercise to tire my body out and have tried other medications to try and induce rest but these were only short-term fixes.

When you spend most of your hours awake it's sometimes hard to find the humour in your situation. But, as it has been in other testing times in my life, a laugh comes from the most unexpected places. Occasionally I've rented movies to while away the hours and on the way from my house to the DVD rental shop I often passed a homeless man who slept rough in the park. He was aware of my affliction.

One night he asked where I was off to. When I replied where I was headed, he quipped: 'Well, Emily, you know what film we're in don't you? *Eyes Wide Shut*!'

Over the years, however, my body seems to have adapted in some small way to this enforced restlessness. For the most part I can function on a daily basis now and have a life bordering on the normal, even though I am still dealing with intrusive thoughts.

Much of my energy in the last decade has been spent combating my illness. I haven't had the time or inclination to focus on acting. Although I have been out of the limelight for a while, I have been offered work that could propel me back into the public eye on reality TV series like *Strictly Come Dancing* and *I'm a Celebrity… Get Me Out of Here*. For a variety of reasons I have turned down the requests, primarily because I didn't want my recovery to be played out on the nation's TV screens.

During my acting hiatus I have tried to find other ways of fulfilment. I've worked in an Oxfam charity shop in Hackney, where I got my fingers stuck in the till. No, dear reader, I hadn't resorted to dipping into the charity's profits, I actually did get my hand stuck in the drawer!

I've also helped out at a residential old people's home, making cups of tea and playing games, such as 'What's the Time Mr Wolf?' Sadly, however, my squeaky shoes meant it was always dinnertime for me. They taught me a thing or two.

Volunteering with the Peter Bedford Housing Association, that assists people who have found themselves excluded from society due to homelessness or mental health issues, I helped with drama therapy, playing memory games – a tricky one, even for me (!) – and putting on a small production for Christmas. With some other helpers we donned wigs and dressed up for a rendition of *Dancing Queen*. It reminded me of the days Charlotte and I would entertain the local kids. Such work I've found extremely rewarding and it has given me confidence.

Sometimes my acting history seems like another life I've lived, but hopefully one day I can return to my career and do justice to it.

I would like to work again and am sure I will be strong enough to deliver a performance that does credit to my earlier work. Given my first-hand experience of the subject I'm convinced I could give a powerful portrayal of a character battling a mental illness. It's a subject that too often is overlooked by the film industry, or one it only pays lip service to.

Mental illness continues to challenge society's perceptions. If you have a broken leg you can fix it, but mending the mind is not so simple and sadly there is still a stigma attached to it. There have been times when I've viewed the reaction to my malaise that I have felt like a social leper. The longer I struggle with my condition, however, the more I have insight into its complexities.

In the process of writing this book, I've explored events in my past I would rather not revisit. It's been painful but I'm glad I did it. I've tried to analyse when, how and why things happened. I do believe we are architects of our destinies, but with me somewhere along the line something came loose.

I've found that with my condition my brain doesn't always recognise that it is lacking serotonin – the body's contributor to wellbeing and happiness – and dopamine – the chemical responsible for reward-driven learning – so there has been a disconnection between a pleasurable event and my reaction.

Who knows if I would have suffered the same health problems had I not been abused? My malaise has possibly been a combination of a chemical imbalance and the psychological effects of the trauma I suffered. Against all rationality, the abused feels responsible for what's happened, feels shame, guilt and is compelled to keep secret the terrible acts. You are loath to admit how you've suffered, even to yourself, because you feel guilty. That's the crippling and terrible effect it has. Victims take on that shame for themselves. Only now, as victims find the courage to speak out about abuse, do we realise that it is all too common a scenario.

What I've come to suspect is that on some level my illness didn't want to be cured. My behaviour was my way of relating to the world and perhaps I was scared of losing that. After my rituals were first examined by a psychiatrist when I was eight years old I changed them. The impulse to challenge the specialists came out of what they'd find behind it. It was a way of protecting myself, a form of defence. It made it difficult for everyone concerned to talk about what the best treatment was. Part of my emotional and mental make-up was to challenge doctors, refusing to let them into my inner self. It was part of the manifestation of my illness. So even in the medical profession it was not widely understood what might have been underneath these rituals.

For years I couldn't talk about what lay beneath. It's only recently that I have been able to articulate my feelings about what happened. But even that has led to conflicting opinions about how best to proceed. My Dad always had a keen interest in analysis. He thought it was helpful in understanding how you live that you understand how you were treated as a child and how you developed.

My Mum, on the other hand, is more sceptical of therapy and exploring the past. She's witnessed the pain of exploring the past and counsels a more cautious approach. I don't believe any approach is more beneficial than the other, but hope a combination of the two might unlock some answers to what happened to me and might, in a small way, help others find their way.

I hope that by showing how my illness manifested itself might shed some more light onto this much misunderstood and complex condition. I also hope my account of what it has been like to combat such an illness in the public eye challenges people's perception of what a condition like this means. I would simply urge people not to have a closed mind to what the potentials are of the misery coping with mental illness causes. And I ask that people do not close their mind to what sufferers can achieve – because the answer is limitless.

The most recent years have been calm and stable for me, apart from the agony of sleep deprivation. A combination of the medication and coming to terms with my condition have made this possible. I now look to the future and am excited about what lies ahead.

For cinema-goers that have seen the film, I will always be the teenager in the pink dress shouting 'up yer bum'. *Wish You Were Here* gave me so many opportunities that I will always be grateful for. I have no regrets, but I wish that on a few occasions I'd been able to enjoy the experiences fully. At times I've felt like a bystander, watching the light and shade of my life as if it was happening to someone else.

The cards my mental illness dealt me were the king of schizophrenia, the queen of compulsions, the jack of Tourette's and the ace of intrusive thoughts. I didn't realise the cards were stacked against me. I made people think I had a royal flush, but in my heart I was only bluffing.

I'm ready to reconnect now. I realise I may never once again soar so high as I did in the early part of my career. But that's okay. Maybe this time my wings might not get singed.

ADDENDUM

A TRIBUTE TO MY FATHER

On Wednesday, 15 January 2014, I took a phone call no child wants to receive.

It was my father's wife Jehanie urging me to come to their house because I might want to see him. At first the importance of her request didn't register. The last time I had spoken to my dad was two weeks previously. He had been suffering from pancreatic cancer but he had made light of his illness and said he had felt fine.

When I got to his bedside I immediately saw that his condition had taken a dramatic turn for the worse. The illness had taken its toll. I had braced myself to be strong but he was unrecognisable as the father I knew.

I didn't know how to react. I had never been in that situation before. Should I make light of the situation and smile to mask the utter pain and devastation inside, or should I say something profound?

Jehanie, together with two of his sons, Hartley and Louis, were around his bedside but, although there was a doctor and paramedics there, the room was quiet.

Someone suggested making a cup of tea and when sugar was mentioned I spontaneously sang the line 'Sugar for my honey', after which Hartley continued 'sweets for my sweet'. It was a brief attempt to make light of a sombre situation.

When my father had first been diagnosed with his illness in 2013, he approached it with such positivity. He listened to conventional doctors but wanted to take the holistic route as well, seeking out alternative treatments that might alleviate his symptoms. It was amazing to see how bravely he faced his mortality. He never once passed on any of his own anxieties or fears to his family. He continued to work until it was physically impossible and took an active part in the campaigns dear to his heart.

He took that positivity into his finals hours and it was a privilege that I was able to be by his side during those heartbreaking last moments. I tried to use those final minutes with him to reassure him that I would be okay. I held his hand and told him he didn't have to worry about me. I think it registered with him because he acknowledged what I was saying.

Finally, I blew him a kiss and said goodbye.

He passed away in the early hours of Thursday morning. Fittingly, for someone whose outlook on life was so positive, his last words were: 'I'm fine.'

In the immediate aftermath of his passing I felt numb, shock and unbearable sadness all at once. Grief did not overwhelm me, but came over me in waves. Rather than the actual enormity of the situation, it was little, inconsequential things that brought on my tears, like seeing his number in my phone and knowing I would never be able to call him again.

The following day I met with my family and we shared stories about Roger. Mummy recalled that time at my birth when she had to have him removed from the delivery room when he kept spinning around the room on a chair. My aunt Janice remembered when Roger had a small part in *Coriolanus* in 1969 in Stratford, while he and Mum were renting a wooden bungalow by the river. They threw a party but didn't think anyone would turn up as it was so remote. As it happened, the whole cast appeared, including Ian Richardson. One friend even turned up in a small rowing boat. It sounded quite a party. At one stage Mum jumped into the river along with several others.

On another occasion, Dad was appearing in Tony Richardson's *Hamlet* in the same year, with Nicol Williamson, Anthony Hopkins and Marianne Faithful, who was understudied by a very young Anjelica Huston. Dad had a small part as Reynaldo but had managed to get Janice a job as a dresser to all the female actors. Janice remembered exchanging amazing stories with Dad about the cast and crew during the production but, unfortunately, she vowed they would never be revealed!

Dad's death made the front page in some of the papers and led the news on the BBC website, which opened a forum for people to post their comments. Many renowned actors, including David Jason and several of his co-stars in *Only Fools and Horses*, released statements paying tribute to his talent and qualities. It was touching to see how many people held him in high regard. Obviously he was best-known for the part of Trigger, but it was gratifying to see him also remembered for his other roles, notably his Shakespearean parts, his performances as Owen Newitt in *The Vicar of Dibley* and as Barty

Crouch Senior in *Harry Potter and the Goblet of Fire*. I remembered seeing him in *One For The Road*, a Harold Pinter play about prisoners of war, with Alan Bates, and another, *Wild Honey* by Anton Chekhov, with Ian McKellen. I had always dreamt of him directing me in a play. Sadly that was now never to happen.

In the days after his death I recalled many memories from my childhood of our time together.

When I was seven I was obsessed with catching a wild rabbit and keeping it as a pet. Dad eventually conceded enough to build me a hutch – but the actual rabbit would remain elusive. Two years later, when I needed a winter coat at the age of nine, he suggested buying one to fit an eleven-year-old. He said I'd grow into it and would therefore get more use out of it. Mummy got angry and shoved him out of the flat. His bag broke and all his homeopathic pills spilled over the floor – he was really into homeopathy and alternative treatments. I remember getting a fit of the giggles even as I was picking them up.

We also used to play a game together when I was young called, simply, 'who can make the other laugh first'. We'd sit, staring at each other, trying to make the other crack. Much to my annoyance I always lost. We shared the same quirky sense of humour and would often find amusement in things other people did not.

Roger was always open to new ideas but he was also a strict disciplinarian. When I was 11 I was staying at my father's country cottage in Norfolk with a friend. We were feeling a little bit mischievous so we started a fire with some dry leaves. To our dismay, we couldn't put it out. The next thing I knew my father was strolling across like the great green giant. He grabbed our hair, wound it round his hands and banged our heads together. We didn't start any fires again.

I also remember going to his flat in Tufnell Park at the age of 13 and flicking through his record collection. He had eclectic tastes, liking anything from the Boomtown Rats and Bob Dylan to black gospel music and traditional folk. At that time I often walked around with something of a hunchback. 'Stand up straight,' he'd tell me. 'Be proud of your tits.' He always wanted me to carry myself properly and believe in myself.

Even though we didn't have a conventional father–daughter relationship, he still influenced me in many ways. For example, politically he was very left wing and a socialist. I asked him lots of questions about it over the years and, while he responded passionately on a range of issues, he never rammed his views down my throat. I recalled him taking me to a play about the miners' strike and how the communities were decimated by the pit closures. Stories that he told me about how one of the miners couldn't afford to buy his children's shoes, and of how the police horses charged through the miners' houses have stayed with me. He also campaigned on behalf of the Palestinians and continued campaigning for his political beliefs as late as last year. I even joined him on a march recently to prevent the closure of a hospital.

I remembered the times we spent on the film sets in New York and Kentucky. He hadn't been keen on me following him into the profession. He would have preferred it if I had continued with my education and gone to university, but I guess he never stopped trying to protect me. Even more recently, in 2007, Russell Brand asked him for my phone number during a radio interview. Dad, mindful of the comedian's reputation, refused!

Sometimes, when both of us were working, I wouldn't see him for up to six months. When we finally saw each other again it could take a little while for us to warm back up, but our sense of humour always helped us reconnect.

Dad had always encouraged me to undergo therapy. When my health deteriorated, he urged me to attend the Castle Clinic, renowned for its long-stay treatment. I was against it. Perhaps, in retrospect, I should have taken his advice but, then again, he respected the defiance in me.

In interviews he gave before his illness, he expressed his guilt over my problems, saying if he had not left my mother things might have turned out differently for me. I don't think he should have blamed himself although we never spoke about this together. Despite them splitting up I had a happy childhood. It was truly unnecessary for him to feel that way.

Although Mum and Dad hadn't always seen eye-to-eye, over the last three years they became friends. Mum also became friends with my step-mum, which I was very pleased about. Roger and Jehanie came over to a birthday party for me a couple of years ago at my mum's and watching them jive together put a smile on my face. When he and Jehanie had first got together I saw how supportive they were of each other's work and really admired their harmony.

When I came to write this book, he was supportive, he cooperated and he encouraged me to explore the events in my childhood that, for right and wrong, have shaped the person that I am today.

At the time of writing, his passing hasn't sunk in yet. I imagine it will hit me when I next need his advice and suddenly I realise he's not there. More and more, I have found I have been clinging on to those final words.

I really do hope 'he's fine'.